POEM, PURPOSE AND PLACE

For Liz

Poem, Purpose and Place

Shaping Identity in Contemporary Scottish Verse

COLIN NICHOLSON

Polygon
EDINBURGH

© Polygon 1992

First published by Polygon
22 George Square,
Edinburgh EH8 9LF

Typeset in Linotron Sabon
by Koinonia Limited, Bury
Printed and bound in Great Britain
by Redwood Press, Melksham, Wilts

British Library Cataloguing
in Publication Data
Nicholson, C.E.
Poem, Purpose and Place: Shaping Identity in
Contemporary Scottish Verse
I. Title
821.009

ISBN 07486 6138 7

The publisher acknowledges subsidy
from the Scottish Arts Council
towards the publication of this volume.

Contents

Series Preface

CAIRNS CRAIG

Scotland's history is often presented as punctuated by disasters which overwhelm the nation, break its continuity and produce a fragmented culture. Many felt that 1979, and the failure of the Devolution Referendum, represented such a disaster: that the energetic culture of the 1960s and 1970s would wither into the silence of a political waste land in which Scotland would be no more than a barely distinguishable province of the United Kingdom.

Instead, the 1980s proved to be one of the most productive and creative decades in Scotland this century – as though the energy that had failed to be harnessed by the politicians flowed into other channels. In literature, in thought, in history, creative and scholarly work went hand in hand to redraw the map of Scotland's past and realign the perspectives of its future.

In place of the few standard conceptions of Scotland's identity that had often been in the past the tokens of thought about the country's culture, a new and vigorous debate was opened up about the nature of Scottish experience, about the real social and economic structures of the nation, and about the ways in which the Scottish situation related to that of other similar cultures throughout the world.

It is from our determination to maintain a continuous forum for such debate that *Determinations* takes its title. The series will provide a context for sustained dialogue about culture and politics in Scotland, and about those international issues which directly affect Scottish experience.

Too often, in Scotland, a particular way of seeing our culture, of representing ourselves, has come to dominate our perceptions because it has gone unchallenged – worse, unexamined. The vitality of the culture should be measured by the intensity of debate which it generates rather than the security of ideas on which it rests. And should be measured by the extent to which creative, philosophical, theological, critical and political ideas confront each other.

If the determinations which shape our experience are to come from within rather than from without, they have to be explored and evaluated and acted upon. Each volume in this series will seek to be a contribution to that self-determination; and each volume, we trust, will require a response, contributing in turn to the on-going dynamic that is Scotland's culture.

Acknowledgements

It is a pleasure to record my gratitude to the writers who gave freely of their time, and doubly so to Norman MacCaig who overlooked my technical incompetence and agreed to a second run. I am grateful to the Scottish Poetry Library, without whose help and resources my task would have been considerably less easy. I thank Laureen Piddock for her assistance, and record my special thanks to Harold Best.

The Scottish Arts Council and the Arts Faculty at Edinburgh University provided financial support for the completion of this book.

Earlier versions of the chapters on Sorley MacLean and on Norman MacCaig appeared in *Studies in Scottish Literature*, vols xxii and xxiv respectively. An earlier version of the chapter on Edwin Morgan appeared in *Cencrastus*, no. 38, and shorter versions of the interviews with Liz Lochhead and with Ian Abbot appeared in *Inter-Arts*, nos 5 & 7. I am grateful to the editors for permission to reprint.

Introduction

There appears at first to be an unbridgeable gap between the
existential declaration of Norman MacCaig's 'Patriot':

> My only country
> is six feet high
> and whether I love it or not
> I'll die for its independence[1]

and the political parable produced in Derick Thomson's 'Rabbits',
after Scotland failed to deliver a convincing result in the 1979
referendum it had struggled to obtain:

> A rabbit
> in the car's headlight
> almost safely
> across the road
> when it sensed danger,
> when fear struck it.
> It turned back.[2]

But between the individually performative and self-sustaining confidence of the one, and the collective paralysis of the other we can
trace a significant moment in the evolution of Scottish perception
and process.

While few topics can be so notoriously difficult to grasp as the
idea of a popular culture, the poets I talk to and about in the pages
which follow, however, give depth and definition to specifically
Scottish contours of identity. And they express, too, an opening of
the field of possibility since Thomson recorded his disappointment
over a decade ago.

The evidence exists for a preliminary assessment of the distinctiveness achieved in recent Scottish writing, for which a question
already asked by Cairns Craig remains relevant: 'Why then should
Scottish literature have retained and indeed asserted its independence in a context where the Scottish people – unlike the Irish, for
example, – have seemed deeply resistant or apathetic about other
forms of independence?' For me, having lived in this country for
over twenty years, Craig's answer rings true, but provokes a series
of further questions: 'In part, it is that Scotland has, despite both
internal and external pressures, never been integrated into the
culture values of the British State. The texture of Scottish life, in its
religious, educational, legal, linguistic forms, remains distinct from
that of England to an extent which is little recognised in England, let
alone the outside world.'[3] But while the texture of Scottish experience as its poetry represents it adds to the country's cultural specifi-
cations, the lack of recognition to which Craig refers also entails a
denial and displacement which take effect in a variety of ways. Most
immediately, it leads to an assumption in favour of Scottish reference and local allusion, although Douglas Dunn's reminder that:
'Imaginatively, Scotland is as multiform or infinite as anywhere
else' is timely. The current diversity in Scottish poetry effectively
challenges comprehensive treatment, and I eschew any claim of that
kind. As a non-Scot, I have one eye on an English readership
perhaps unaware of what has been happening in the verse of a
northern neighbour, and some of this material may seem self-
evident to those familiar with the work of poets included here. Yet it
seemed worthwhile to bring together some of Scotland's senior
practitioners with some established contemporaries in order to
explore further Dunn's subsequent contention that '*any* poet has to
struggle with the historical and cultural constraints of the country
in which he or she lives'.[4] Scotland continues to experience, and
must perforce struggle with, the imperatives of a homogenising
culture emanating from London and the south-east of England, still
imperially powerful over the domestic territories of the British Isles.
Such metropolitan systems of culture marginalise whatever diver-
gencies happen to exist on so-called 'peripheries'. But for those who
live there these peripheries are centres.

Liz Lochhead remembers the ways in which prescribed language
values operated: 'Nothing in my education had ever led me to
believe that anything among my own real life ordinary things had

the right to be written down. What you wrote could not be the truth. It did not have the authority of the English things, the things in books.'[5] So it should not be too surprising that disaffections from anglocentric assumptions occur when self-identifying literary practice privileges a Scottish centre, itself multiple and diverse. 'You have a passport,' Edwin Morgan once wrote, 'which says you're UK or British, and you obviously have to acknowledge that in a purely official sense, but I don't feel British. I don't feel, certainly, English.'[6]

Most people aren't poets of course, but it might be worth while considering why 1979 produced the frozen rabbit's stance. After all, the ways in which MacDiarmid's and MacLean's poetics are differentiated by, for example, Edwin Morgan's radical libertarianism, ought to have encouraged an appropriately aware political commitment within a confidently Scottish provenance.

Perhaps the problem lies with poetry's audience, or more properly speaking, lack of audience. Contributory factors here might be Scotland's integration with the cultural and economic dominance of the South – and an earlier failure of the Scottish education system to promote and stimulate native versions of culture and society. Gaelic writers point to the difficulties they have had to face in recovering from the ethnocidal effects of the 1872 Education Act, which imposed English upon their culture by making attendance compulsory in schools, with no provision for instruction in the Gaelic tongue. But recognition in poetry is also self-recognition, and that is an authenticating process both personally and across a wider spectrum of perception and opinion. If contemporary Scottish writing is not a natural curriculum component in our schools and universities then critical enquiry into what might constitute either a nationhood or a personal identity is correspondingly impoverished. It is because literature is our way of speaking to each other, within and across time, that looking into it helps us to look into ourselves. In this respect, a widely sloganised remark by the Canadian writer Robert Kroetsch, himself addressing a diverse culture effectively penetrated by a dominating power to the south, becomes relevant to Scottish experience. What Kroetsch says about the self-defining aspects of novel-writing holds true for the patterning of poetry: 'The fiction makes us real.'

In Scotland it is beginning to be more widely recognised that as far as schools and universities are concerned, the historical construction of 'English Literature' by the metropolitan culture of another country was designed to 'promote class harmony in a divided society by offering a "national" identity to which all could subscribe, and to promote an ideal of English civilisation which the peoples of the Empire would accept as representing the highest values to which they could aspire.'[7] Also recognised more openly these days is Scotland's educational complicity in this process. When a Cambridge professor proclaims that 'it is our job to teach and uphold the canon of English Literature,'[8] his prescriptive writ (and the exclusions it implies) still finds ready adherents north of the border, adherents who should be aware (and perhaps are) that 'canon' originally defined the 'collection or list of books of the Bible accepted by the Christian Church as genuine and inspired' [OED]. We are no longer dealing with specifically Christian but with secular English definitions of what is canonically acceptable and appropriate. So it is all the more remarkable that after nigh on three hundred years of such attempted incorporation, Scottish imaginations continue to offer possibilities of escape from discursive dominance and subservience. One does not have to search for this in Scottish writing: it is presented in the poetry in unavoidable ways.

The need to respond to such cultural invasions may help to account for a note of wistfulness that appears at times in the English-language translations provided by Derick Thomson for his Gaelic originals. The experiences of Gaeldom frequently offer an intensifying blueprint for wider aspects of Scotland's story. The effects of a sustained attempt at ethno-cultural eradication, brutally manifest in the Clearances, are still apparent, giving rise to a 'Perplexity' at once ontological and historical:

> There's a child in my heart
> sleeping in the dark,
> who moves in nightmare
> seeking a place of protection. (CnC p. 21)

These fears, both personal and collective, and generated and sustained by what he terms 'internal imperialism' are traced in Iain Crichton Smith's essay 'Real People in a Real Place'. This document explores the compromised survival of the Gaelic community in ways which also connect with more generalised Scottish developments. Crichton Smith quotes Thomson's poem 'The Scarecrow':

> he took the goodness out of the music.
> But he did not leave us empty-handed:
> he gave us a new song,
> and tales from the Middle East,
> and fragments of the philosophy of Geneva,
> and he swept the fire from the centre of the floor
> and set a searing bonfire in our breasts   (CnC p. 141)

and sees a destructive doctrine in the Calvinist permutations of Christian ideology: 'When the fire was moved from the centre of the floor then the magic ring was broken.' Given his own Island orientations and departures, Crichton Smith is well-placed to testify to the success with which 'the fire became internalised as hell, which was once the fire, common and warm and storied, which nourished the island house'.[9]

It is a characteristic of Thomson's writing in its English-language versions that Highland and Island themes, imagery and vocabulary, are usually re-located by a modernising, psychologically perceptive consciousness. In Thomson's reconstructions of favoured Gaelic *topoi*, nostalgia for a lost past is a dangerous attraction to be resisted, and the poem 'Steel?' explicitly urges the rejection of 'soft words':

> When the tempered steel near the edge of the scythe-blade is worn
> throw away the whetstone;
> you have nothing left but soft iron
> unless your intellect has a steel edge that will cut clean.
> (CnC p. 99)

When Hugh MacDiarmid based *A Drunk Man Looks at the Thistle* (1926) on the narrative of 'Tam o' Shanter', he recovered a Burns tradition from the nostalgia to which it had fallen prone. Injecting into it a modern, West of Scotland vernacular articulation of metaphysics, as well as a host of other registers of feeling, he set in train a programme of poetic possibility whose agenda has not yet been exhausted. When Tom Leonard's acidic collocations, 'There is Nothing Like a Dame: The Examination System seen as Florence Nightingale', include lines from Edward Sapir's *Culture, Language and Personality*, he implicitly acknowledges MacDiarmid's pivotal position in the linguistic revitalisation of Scottish perception:

For the normal person every experience, real or potential, is
saturated with verbalism. This explains why so many lovers of
nature, for instance, do not feel that they are truly in touch
with it until they have mastered the names of a great many
flowers and trees, as though the primary world of reality were
a verbal one.[10]

Elsewhere, Leonard quotes Edwin Morgan's 'To Hugh
MacDiarmid': 'You took that hazard of naming', (IV p. 97) and in
an essay on voice in poetry published fifteen years before its inclu-
sion in his *Selected Works*, he draws attention to the Scottish
usefulness of the American William Carlos Williams. But Leonard's
caustic attention is firmly fixed on the prescriptive codes of English
grammar when he examines its intended erasure of native and
regional rhythms of speech: 'The tawdry little syllogism goes something like this':

1) In speaking of reality, there is a standard correct mode of
   pronunciation.
2) In writing of reality, there is a standard and correct mode of
   spelling and syntax.
∴ 3) In reality, correct spelling and correct syntax are synony-
   mous with correct pronunciation. (IV p. 95–6)

More recently, extending his argument for 'a democratic freedom of
encounter with Literature', Leonard's introduction to his anthology
of hitherto largely ignored verse, *Radical Renfrew* (1989), reminds
us that 'no caste has the right to possess, or even to imagine it has
the right to possess, bills of exchange on the dialogue between one
human being and another. And such a dialogue is all that Literature
is.'[11]

So it seems appropriate that Leonard's volume of selected work
from 1965 to 1983 should be called *Intimate Voices* and should
display on its front cover a poem that subjects its opening line, 'in
the beginning was the word', to a phonetic reconstruction in which
Glasgow accents glisten typographically on the page, before ending
'in the beginning was the sound'. Leonard's de-signing is a political
intervention on behalf of the local, and he will use an often subversive irony to trace personal and familial tensions in both the acqui-
sition and the definition of literacy. 'I remember', the poem 'Fathers

and Sons' opens, 'being ashamed of my father/ when he whispered the words out loud/ reading the newspaper', and then switches to:

"Don't you find
the use of phonetic urban dialect
rather restrictive?"
asks a member of the audience

before ending:

The poetry reading is over
I will go home to my children. (IV, p. 140)

Leonard takes us into the sound-world of Glasgow's working-class expressiveness in uncompromising ways. 'Noah's Green Izzam Cabbage Lukn' (IV p. 42) registers a desperate vitality *and* a recognition that entrapment within cliché remains entrapment no matter how strikingly it is rendered in 'phonetic urban' transcription. The same transcription exposes the sexual prejudices and repressions of 'The Hardmen' (IV p. 58) as well as the brute and mindless violence of 'No Light' (IV p. 59). Though he can often be hilarious, Leonard is clear-eyed about prevalent realities of life and language in his native city. He is concerned too to register the philosophical and social implications of his phonetic inventiveness. Poem's like 'Poetry' (IV p. 36) and 'The Qualification' (IV p. 50) explore the gaps and fissures between the cultural claims and procedures of traditional liberal-bourgeois humanism and the everyday voices of Scotland's industrial capital. As Leonard probes the power-relations of acceptance and expulsion in linguistic usage, a sequence of seven 'Unrelated Incidents' includes a warning against any casual approach to his poetry:

fyi stull
huvny
thoata lang-
wij izza
sound-system;
fyi huvny
hudda thingk
aboot thi dif-

> frince tween
> sound
> n object n
> symbol; well,
> ma innocent
> wee
> friend – iz
> god said ti
> adam:
>
> a doant kerr
> fyi caw it
> an apple
> ur
> an aippl –
> jist leeit
> alane! (IV p. 87)

Elsewhere, Leonard makes explicit the overlaps between language and validating systems of power:

> And their judges spoke with one dialect,
> but the condemned spoke with many voices.
>
> And the prisons were full of many voices,
> but never the dialect of the judges.
>
> And the judges said:
> "No-one is above the Law."[12]

If the mirroring and articulation of poetry help to compose our self-apprehensions, then a lack of recognition of Scottish distinctiveness might still jeopardise that process. Since the poem's last act is that of being read by others, a scripted sense of self-definition gains immeasurably from public acknowledgement. Yet Scottish writing is still generally excluded from the world-wide conference agendas and publications of what is still, though with increasing discomfiture, called Commonwealth Literature.

Given that the trope 'Great Britain' first inscribed itself in public consciousness with the 1707 Act of Union, it becomes symptomatic of this wider invisibility that when three Australians produce a book called *The Empire Writes Back: Theory and Practice in Post-Colonial Literatures* (1989) – (post-colonial in this usage signifying anything written after colonisation takes place) – Scotland does not appear in the index and no Scottish writer is mentioned:

> While it is possible to argue that [Irish, Welsh, and Scottish] societies were the first victims of English expansion, their subsequent complicity in the British imperial enterprise makes it difficult for colonised peoples outside Britain to accept their identity as post-colonial.[13]

For many Scots, too, it would appear. Yet much of what Ashcroft, Griffiths and Tiffin have to say finds articulation in Scottish literary practice. To read *The Empire Writes Back* with Scotland in mind is to experience a disconcerting but liberating re-location of how poetry signifies, and more particularly how Scottish poetry operates within the discursive varieties of English across the globe.

Scotland's participation in the processes of Empire and its subsequent embroilment with the forms and apparatus of English power is further problematised by the domestic availability of three languages, Gaelic, Scots, and English, for its self-identification: a complex psychological terrain. Which helps, perhaps, to explain why Scottish poetry is frequently constructed as neither a unitary nor rigidly bound totality, but as a heterogeneous, overlapping network of social and human interaction.

'Narratives,' says Jean François Lyotard, 'determine criteria of competence and/or illustrate how they are to be applied. They thus define what has the right to be said and done in the culture in question, and since they are themselves part of that culture, they are legitimised by the fact that they do what they do.'[14] It is tempting to accept this as sufficient validation of Scotland's self-defining narratives. The poetry is published and needs only to be read. But literature competes with many other kinds of representation and the varied stories that poets tell reach out to a shared sense of the past that helps forge a community's apprehension of its own present. So the forms of identity which this poetry elaborates are both assumed and indeterminate; accepted and still to be voiced. The engagement of poetry in an arena of competing discourses which led Frederic Jameson to suggest that it 'must be read as a symbolic meditation on

the destiny of community.'[15] leads also to particular effects when a
body of writing is self-evidently committed, as Scotland's is, to the
survival of distinct structures and relationships.

Instructive ironies proliferate. While theorists of the Adam Smith
Institute extol the atomising principles of consumer sovereignty,
Scottish poetry insists upon a nation's patterns of kinship and
networks of community in which consumerism is subordinated to
alternative priorities, and desires accorded very different codes, very
different intimations of what is possible. It is heartening but not
unexpected to be reminded, in the middle of an essay on Edwin
Morgan's Sonnets, of the relevance of Hölderlin's epigram
'Advocatus Diaboli':

> Deep in my heart I abhor the nexus of rulers and clerics,
> Yet more deeply I loathe genius in league with that gang.[16]

It should hardly need emphasising that many of the values
expressed and embodied in English poetry, at both formal and
thematic levels, become a natural sustenance for the writers we are
dealing with. A sense of differences among themselves, and their
shared sense of difference from some of contemporary England's
defining attitudes, suggested that the interview form incorporated
in the following chapters might be most appropriate. To explore the
literary construction of a Scottish subjectivity and intersubjectivity
without the active participation of the writers concerned seemed
something of a contradiction. And although the writers cannot be
held in any way responsible for what is said about their writing,
their involvement is additional evidence of the codes of value to
which the poetry testifies. What is often at issue in this verse seems
nothing less than a crisis of historical memory: or rather a poetic
confrontation with the extreme difficulty of recovering collective
memory, and from that recovery a reconstruction of collective
political responsibility. Aristotle's description of the human personality as *zoon politikon*, is resurrected not in its currently restricted
usage as 'political' but in its original meaning of 'social' being. Both
the difference, and the resurrection, are crucial. For there is then an
investigation of a diverse culture that both authenticates and tran-
scends its existing vernaculars.

In *Orientalism*, Edward Said showed us how we in the West have
constructed an area of human geography which then assumes for us

the dimensions of the real, with implicitly self-imposed limitations upon what might properly be said and thought about it. In Scotland's small corner of Europe, scripted space is being domestically re-possessed and redefined in ways that abolish both the parochial and the insular. We can substitute 'Scotland' and 'England' for the Orient and the Occident respectively – and add women too – to re-focus something Said says. The Orient is not, he is arguing, simply that which it is made out (by the Occident) to be:

> Just as the Occident itself is not just there either. We must take seriously Vico's great observation that men make their own history, that what they can know is what they have made, and extend it to geography: as both geographical and cultural entities – to say nothing of historical entities – such locales, regions, geographical sectors as 'Orient' and 'Occident' are man-made.[16]

If this book contributes in some way to that process, it will have served its purpose. In 1979, and using a different metaphor, Edwin Morgan outlined a reason for putting it together:

> The hope is that as the 'idea of Scotland' begins again to emerge, the parts and pieces of its literary production will be seen to belong to the same animal, and that this animal will be worth a bit of describing and investigating.[17]

Notes

1. Norman MacCaig, *Collected Poems: A New Edition* (London, 1990), p. 266.
2. Derick Thomson, *Creachadh Na Clarsaich (Plundering the Harp): Collected Poems 1940–1980* (Edinburgh, 1982). Subsequent citations are marked CnC and given parenthetically.
3. Cairns Craig, 'Twentieth Century Scottish Literature: An Introduction', in *The History of Scottish Literature, Volume 4, Twentieth Century* (Aberdeen, 1987), p. 2.
4. Douglas Dunn, '"As a Man Sees": On Norman MacCaig's Poetry', *Verse*, vol. 7, no. 2, p. 59.
5. Liz Lochhead, 'A Protestant Girlhood', in *Jock Tamson's Bairns: Essays on a Scots Childhood*, edited by Trevor Royle (London, 1977), p. 121.
6. Quoted in 'A declaration of Independence', by Robyn Marsack, *About Edwin Morgan* (Edinburgh, 1990), edited

by Robert Crawford & Hamish Whyte, p. 25.

7. Cairns Craig, op. cit., p. 3.
8. Christopher Ricks, quoted in *The Guardian*, 17/1/81, p. 26.
9. Iain Crichton Smith, *Towards The Human* (Edinburgh, 1986), p. 22.
10. Tom Leonard, *Intimate Voices: 1965–1983* (Newcastle, 1984), p. 63. Subsequent citations are marked IV and given parenthetically.
11. Tom Leonard, *Radical Renfrew: Poetry from the French Revolution to the First World War* (Edinburgh, 1990), p. xxxi.
12. Tom Leonard, *Situations Theoretical and Contemporary* (Newcastle, 1986).
13. Bill Ashcroft, Gareth Griffiths, Helen Tiffin, *The Empire Writes Back: Theory and Practice in Post-Colonial Literatures* (London, 1989), p. 33.
14. Jean François Lyotard, *The Postmodern Condition – A Report on Knowledge,* translated by Geoff Bennington and Brian Massumi (Manchester, 1979), p. 23.
15. Frederic Jameson, *The Political Unconscious: Narrative as a Socially Symbolic Act* (London, 1981), p. 70.
16. Edward Said, *Orientalism* (New York, 1978), p. 5.
17. Edwin Morgan, *Nothing Not Giving Messages* (Edinburgh, 1990), p. 202.

Against an Alien Eternity

SORLEY MACLEAN

> Another day this upon the mountains
> and great Scotland under the doom
> of beasts:
> her thousands of poor exploited,
> beguiled to a laughing stock,
> flattered, doctored and anointed
> by the nobles and godly bourgeois
> who make a bourgeois of Christ.[1]

'All Poetry', Sorley MacLean wrote in the 1930s, 'reflects social phenomena, and in the Highlands of the 19th century emigration of one kind or another was the phenomenon of phenomena'. He goes on to remark: 'The Highland Clearances constitute one of the saddest tragedies that has ever come upon a people, and one of the most astounding of all the successes of landlord capitalism in Western Europe, such a triumph over the workers and peasants of a country as has rarely been seen achieved with such ease, cruelty and cynicism.'[2] The rapid transformation of clan chieftains from quasi-feudal seigneurs to profit-motivated landlords entailed a shattering of hitherto assumed structures of kinship, and drawing upon memories of the Clearances, MacLean's verse explores traumatising experience of both personal and transnational kinds. The elegiac praise-poem for his native Skye, 'The Island', expresses remorse for generations of enforced migration:

Great lsland, Island of my desire,
Island of my heart and wound,
it is not likely that the strife
and suffering of Braes will be seen requited
...
there is no hope of your townships
rising high with gladness and laughter,
and your men are not expected
when America and France take them. (WR p. 59)

As part of this evocation of the historic depopulation of Gaelic
territories, the demise of Scotland itself as a national entity is
envisaged:

Pity the eye that sees on the ocean
the great dead bird of Scotland. (WR p. 59)

Referring in an essay to 'the great service of the Highland soldiers
to the Empire', which might have been expected to stand crofters in
good stead, MacLean quotes Alexander Mackenzie on the cynicism
of England's imperial manipulation of India, which exposed deceit
of another kind. 'At the very hour that Nana Sahib was being
crushed and Cawnpore taken by the 78th Regiment, the fathers,
mothers and children of the 78th were being evicted within a few
miles of Dunrobin Castle' (RB p. 50). It was a lesson in realism
which becomes a benchmark for many of MacLean's subsequent
reflections. The historical temper of MacLean's writing is one of its
distinguishing characteristics, as in the continuing confrontation
between personal passion and political commitment: It has been
rightly said that 'power that can overwhelm features strongly in
MacLean's poetry, as it does in Highland experience.'[3]
   As notions of familial and public duties collide with private
pressures and demands, a disruptive sense of betrayal and self-
betrayal infiltrates MacLean's poetry. Historic memories of resistance, felt on a genealogical pulse, connect with a continuing and
seemingly irresistible bleeding of a people and its language from its
islands of survival. The conjunction of time past and present tensions construct themes appropriate to MacLean's situation.
   But he is alert to difficulties involved in an historicising poetry.
'Nostalgia is the most common sentiment in nineteenth-century

Gaelic poetry, and there is a huge body of verse that says nothing explicitly about the Clearances, but that an emigrant's sadness pervades. ... It is a remarkable characteristic of the poetry of the clearances that it is mostly retrospective.' (RB pp. 64-5) There are times when it can seem to an outsider that Sorley MacLean single-handedly wrenched Gaelic poetry out of its nineteenth-century pre-occupations and into the maelstrom of modernity. For Iain Crichton Smith, who first translated a selection for English-speaking audi-ences, *Poems to Eimhir and Other Poems* (1943) remains the great achievement. 'An electrifying book', he has called it, which 'takes a new leap in consciousness, and a new Highlander emerges ... a Highlander who wasn't there before.'[4] Also writing from within Gaeldom, John MacInnes confirms it as a publication that marked a revolution in Gaelic poetry:

> The poetry was so essentially Gaelic and yet it expressed something which hitherto had not found a voice in Gaelic – certainly not in Gaelic poetry – and never in this particular form. It was not just a matter of paraphrasable content, of ideas, or of structure and organisation of themes: the newness was in the very movement and rhythm of the verse.[5]

MacLean's mastery of the full panoply of aural patterning in Gaelic versifying, his confident awareness of its traditional density of verbal texture, combines with the sensuous impact of his internal, cross- and end-rhyming, and with his alternating and contrastive rhythms to create distinctive effects. Although these things are impossible to reproduce in translation, they transformed the possi-bilities of his native tongue. Certainly *Poems to Eimhir* exposes Gaelic sensibility in new ways, bringing high Romantic passion under the scalpel of post-Freudian exploration. Personal distress and political conflagration fuse here in a manner markedly different from the verse produced by the English 'thought-world' of the 1930s.

For those who can only enjoy MacLean's verse in English, the sound of his Gaelic readings adds a considerable dimension. He has said himself that he 'could not be primarily a Gael without a very deep-rooted conviction that the auditory is the primary sensuous-ness of poetry', (RB p. 13) and George Campbell Hay has aptly characterised this aural impact: 'It is an impressive experience to

listen to Sorley MacLean as he performs. ... He is gifted with what
the Welsh call *Hwyl,* the power of elevated declamation, and his
declamation is full of feeling.'[6] Seamus Heaney first read MacLean
(in English) in the 1970s, and remembers that 'there was a feeling of
unspecifiable freedom and intensity. The voice in the poems was at
once unleashed and stricken.' Heaney was referring to the voice on
the page. When he first heard MacLean reading, 'in the deep lamenting
register of the Gaelic', it struck him with 'the force of revelation':

> The mesmeric, heightened tone; the weathered voice coming
> in close from a far place; the swarm of the vowels; the surren-
> der to the otherness of the poem; above all the sense of bardic
> dignity that was entirely without self-parade but was instead
> the effect of a proud self-abnegation, as much a submission as
> a claim to heritage. All this constituted a second discovery,
> this time of the true climate of his linguistic world.[7]

Born in 1911 on Raasay, a small island off the east coast of Skye,
MacLean now lives on Skye itself, a few miles south of Portree. Less
than a mile to the north, in 1882, began 'The Battle of the Braes,' an
unprecedented development in crofter resistance, being both well-
organised and the first offensive measure to be taken against efforts
to remove them.[7] In his garden MacLean points to hawthorn bushes
planted by a great grand-uncle, Angus Stewart. Stewart lived in the
house at the time when he was the first crofter to give evidence
before Lord Napier's Crofter's Commission in 1883.

More immediately, MacLean has recorded some of the domestic
influences upon his development. 'In my early teens ... I realised
that I was a traditional Gaelic singer manqué, for I was born into a
family of traditional singers and pipers on all sides, and that in a
Free Presbyterian community, of all the most inimical to such
"vanities".... I think that the first great "artistic" impact on me was
my father's mother singing some of the very greatest of Gaelic
songs, and all in her own traditional versions' (RB p. 6). MacLean
puts his inability to sing down to a 'defect in pitch', (RB p. 8) but
there is a wry pleasure to be gleaned from his reflection that 'even to
this day, I sometimes think that if I had been a singer I would have
written no verse.' (RB p. 9). Perhaps in reaction to this 'defect',
MacLean became, very early in life: 'obsessed with the lyric, first of

all because of my unusually rich Gaelic background; with the lyric in the Greek sense of a marriage of poetry and music, and then, because I was not a musician, with the lyric in the Shelleyan and Blakeian sense of a short or shortish poem suggesting song even if it could never be sung'.

An introductory remark in *Ris á Bhruthaich* recalls some of the wider pressures at work in this poetry. 'In 1938 the continuing existence of Gaelic as a spoken language seemed a forlorn hope and Europe itself appeared about to be delivered into the hands of Teutonic racist fascism.' (RB p. 3). The Spanish Civil War had awakened profound fears in MacLean about the course of European civilisation, and these circumstances help to contextualise a sometimes impatient note in essays he wrote at the time. 'The great poem is always in some way realistic in that, however transfigured it is by passion, emotion or fusion of emotion and intellectuality, it has its roots in reality, not in a dream world.' (RB p. 17). MacLean is writing from within an embattled position, and given the existential nature of his political awareness he could derive little comfort from what could only have struck him as the evident accuracy of Marx's sole reference to the Gaels:

> There is no country in Europe that does not possess, in some remote corner, at least one remnant people, left over from an earlier population, forced back and subjugated by the nation which later became the repository of historical development.[8]

MacLean's perception of cultural decline united in his poetry with the emotional stress of frustrated loves and a world at war. At the end of the nineteen-thirties, while fascism, democracy and communism contended for supremacy, Sorley MacLean's involvement with two women collapsed painfully amid complicated intensities, uncertainties and doubt. For a year or two in the early thirties, he loved a Lowland woman he had first met at the beginning of the decade. Then, in August 1937 he met an Irish woman to whom he was irresistibly drawn, but to whom he could never make any kind of advance.

[SM] *I had never really made any advances to her because I was under the mistaken impression that one of my greatest friends, who had been responsible for me meeting the woman in the first place, wanted to marry her himself. So I held off.*

In December 1937, MacLean left Skye for Mull. This was to be a doubly traumatic time for him, since evidence of the Clearances was much more pressingly felt there than on his native island, and MacLean is the best-known of all Mull names. 'I think', he has since recorded, 'Mull had much to do with my poetry: its physical beauty, so different from Skye's, with the terrible imprint of the Clearances everywhere on it, made it almost intolerable for a Gael.' (RB p. 12). He was already deeply affected by the Spanish Civil War which in one of its aspects appeared to him not unlike the Clearances. It took, after all, no great leap of the imagination to perceive in Franco and his landlord, big capitalist and Roman Catholic support, a Hispanic version of the landlords of the Clearances and the Church of Scotland at that earlier time. But that was not the only dilemma.

For economic and domestic reasons, MacLean could not volunteer to fight in Spain. Yet, says MacLean, those would not have been the only reasons which prevented him from joining up. In his poem 'Prayer', he writes how he would experience a 'death-like life' because '... I preferred a woman to crescent History.' (WR p. 19).

The question which haunts this poem, and which came to undermine many of MacLean's subsequent self-reflections, soon follows:

> When the spirit has been flayed,
> it will lose every shadow,
> it will lose every faintness.
> But who will call my white love
> surrender, faintness or shadow? (WR p. 21)

[SM] *It was not a case of an actual choice between the woman and Spain. I was prevented from going to Spain by family circumstances. But I realised that if it were a pure choice between the woman and Spain, I'm afraid I would have chosen the woman. I knew, I knew that would have been my choice.*

'The Turmoil', a poem written before the outbreak of civil war in Spain, had already expressed MacLean's sense of the claims and counter-claims of love and political commitment:

> And her beauty cast a cloud
> over poverty and a bitter wound
> and over the world of Lenin's intellect,
> over his patience and his anger. (WR p. 7)

That division also articulates 'Reason and Love', but with 'The Cry of Europe', a sharpening sense of opposing demands and a growing feeling of shame is evident:

> What would the kiss of your proud mouth be
> compared with each drop of the precious blood
> that fell on the cold frozen uplands
> of Spanish mountains from a column of steel? (WR p. 9)

Yet, again, in 'The Selling of a Soul', while MacLean's perception of the woman's faults remains there is still the evidence of unreasoning love:

> Therefore I will say again now,
> that I would sell my soul for your sake
> twice, once for your beauty
> and again for that grace
> that you would not take a sold and slavish spirit. (WR p. 15)

Worse was to come. When the Irish woman married in December 1939, it was not to MacLean's friend. It subsequently transpired that there had never been any question of that marriage taking place, a discovery which exacerbated feelings of humiliation:

> I did not take a cross's death
> in the hard extremity of Spain
> and how then should I expect
> the one new prize of fate? (WR p. 23)

There now began for MacLean a period of wretched melancholy. The emotional cataclysm which he experienced interrupted the writing of 'The Cuillin', the long poem on which he had been working; 'The Blue Rampart' charts aspects of this disturbance:

> But for you the Cuillin would be
> an exact and serrated blue rampart
> girdling with its march-wall
> all that is in my fierce heart. (WR p. 143)

In this poem, metaphors of landscape and displacement express psychic dislocation:

And the brown brindled moorland
and my reason would co-extend –
but you imposed on them an edict
above my own pain. (WR p. 143)

In 'Poems to Eimhir', MacLean created mythical allusions –
Eimhir was the loveliest of the heroes' women in the early Irish
sagas. An imagery of 'tearing' in the mind suggests a 'consciousness
disjunct',⁹ 'since time and root and top are plucked'. (WR p. 149).
Such verbal patterns form a leitmotif of division and self-division:

I do not feel kindly towards Nature,
which has given me the clear whole understanding,
the single brain and the split heart. (WR p. 21)

With Gaelic itself apparently in danger of disappearing from the
face of the earth, the imminent devastation of Europe projected the
death of the language onto a contemporary world-stage:

I do not see the sense of my toil
putting thoughts in a dying tongue
now when the whoredom of Europe
is murder erect and agony. (WR p. 157)

Imagery of personal helplessness is extended to register the impact of international events; MacLean pushes his language to the
edge of emotional tolerance just as Gaelic territory seemed destined
for narrower confines. Remorse and confusion of an intensely
personal nature find correlations in historical contexts. As the poet
strives to 'put the people's anguish/ in the steel of my lyric', (WR
p. 137) a personal distress complicates and confounds his
intentions: 'The knife of my brain made incision/ my dear, on the
stone of my love.' (WR p. 145). 'Glen Eyre' explores division
specifically in terms of an otherwise loved geography:

That evening on the ridge
I realised the unhappy thing:
that there was a wall between joy
and my harsh little croft,
a boundary that would not be changed

to set joy free:
...
that I would not get the thing I wanted,
with the gift of my environment and heredity
and with another gift, my talents;
that I could not stand on Blaven
and stay in the garden
where fruits were growing richly. (WR p. 41)

Conversely, 'The Woods of Raasay' brings landscape and emotion together in erotic imagery expressing 'the venom of the cry of
pain in the lovemaking':

The thrust came from the Cuillin,
from the mountains hardest
to climb to a pleasant summit:
the tender softness was stung by a monster. (WR p. 177)

In this poem subterranean disruption produces a metaphor which
pre-scribes the despair in poems to come:

It is that they rise
from the miserable torn depths
that puts their burden on mountains. (WR p. 181)

This was, then, as MacLean acknowledges, a period of creative
anguish:

[SM] *Quite a few of the poems were not published at all in 1943
because they would have been too explicit. There were some in
which I actually represented myself almost as a rejected lover,
which I wasn't by any manner of means – as far as I knew then. The
part of the* Selected Poems[10] *called 'The Haunted Ebb' was written
between December 1939 and late July or early August, 1941. 'The
Woods of Raasay' was written during the summer of 1940 before I
went away to the army. A lot of people think my very best stuff is
'The Woods of Raasay' – you know, everything else was accelerated
by going away to the war. Those poems which are grouped together
under the sub-headings 'The Grey Crop' and 'The Broken Image'
are a commentary on my state of mind between December 1939
and August 1941, and they were written after September 1941 and
before the end of 1943.*

What MacLean came later to call his 'rash folly' is transmuted in his poems into a self-lacerating imagery of constancy become obsessive and of resolution disfigured by a kind of delirium. Continental developments became, for him, a fitting environment of betrayal, deceit and strife through which to express his own sense of humiliation, loss and exposure. Isolated on the fringes of beleaguered Gaeldom, MacLean feared even more the life and death struggle for the defence of the West. At any rate, this is in some sense the measure of 'The Haunting'.

[SM] *You see, I knew from the beginning, I think, that Hitler would attack Russia, and I considered Russia then the only thing that really stood between us and even a thousand years of fascist domination of Europe. You must remember that America was not yet in the war. 'The Haunting' was written in July 1941. Hitler attacked Russia on the 22nd of June 1941 and his armies reached the Dneiper on the third of July; a hell of a rapid advance. I really thought the game was up. Good or bad, the behaviour of the Russian government, they saved us.*

'The Haunting' fuses meditations upon love for a woman with those of time and transience. Implicated in its structure is the survival of Gaelic itself. Characteristically, the syntax is persuasive and logically sequential in form, yet predetermined by a fatalistic certainty. At its ending, the poem becomes as much a lament for the misdirection of its creator's own 'newly-lit consciousness' as it is for the absent woman. A sense of personal and historical displacement emerges, as a duty to sing his people's fate comes into conflict with his heart's desire:

> Though the Red Army of humanity is
> in the death-struggle beside the Dnieper,
> it is not the deed of its heroism
> that is nearest my heart,
> but a face that is haunting me,
> following me day and night,
> the triumphant face of a girl
> that is always speaking. (WR p. 165)

The poem that was begun in 1939 and stopped by all this emotional turmoil, 'The Cuillin', ceased in late December, 1939. Any possibility that the poem might have been returned to at a later date was

effectively destroyed when, as MacLean puts it, 1944 disgusted him
with some of its politics: 'Especially when Sydney Goodsir Smith
convinced me that the behaviour of the Russian government at the
time of the Polish insurrection was far worse than Professor
Erickson's *Road to Berlin* now shows.' (WR p. xv). Written at a
time when MacLean felt closest to communism, its concern is to
connect the fate of Gaeldom both with oppression world-wide and
more particularly with resistance to it. Though incorporating different genres, its incantatory invocations in epic mode might now seem
out of key. As one otherwise admiring reader has suggested, the
register of the poem can, in its heroic moments, seem at times 'over-
rhetorical, praising heroism and denouncing the exploitation of the
poor with excessively simplistic fervour'.[11] But 'the Cuillin' also
presents a range of MacLean's feelings at that time. Its opening
hymn to Skye's landscape as the poet climbs to a suitable vantage
point both for view and reflection is a demonstration of MacLean's
ability to bring together the physical contours of place and the
marks of human history left upon them.

'The Cuillin' issues a cry for revolutionary transformation in
human relationships, and evokes an optimism directly related to the
pressing realities of the time:

> I heard that a breaking was seen
> and a startling on the horizon,
> that there was seen a fresh red rose
> over a bruised maimed world. (WR p. 97)

Unyielding perceptions of history which characterise poems written before and since 'The Cuillin', derive in part at least from
MacLean's immersion in one of the strictest Calvinist sects.

[SM] *Although our people were really rather lax Free Presbyterians, they hadn't the tremendous rigour of a lot of the others. But
still. ...*

Terence McCaughey has provided ample evidence for the position of Calvinist discourse in a poetry avowedly opposed to any
religious commitment.[12] MacLean's political radicalism constantly
secularises a vocabulary hitherto appropriated by Presbyterian
sects. But its assumed terms of reference are undermined when the
poetry opens up alternate possibilities:

No catechist or examiner is needed
to see that there is not in my prayer
Effectual Calling or sincerity,
and though I am clear-sighted in scripture
that my spirit is not one-fold. (WR p. 21)

MacLean provocatively turns back upon the self-righteous those
terms of reference by which they sought to maintain their own
dominance:

My eye is not on Calvary
nor on Bethlehem the Blessed,
·but on a foul-smelling backland in Glasgow,
where life rots as it grows (WR p. 35)

From his vantage point on 'The Cuillin', a wider view is taken:

Jupiter, the brutal coward, has failed,
and so has Jahweh the Jew,
but a time has never come
when rulers have not found a god
who hangs on pious mountains
the sacrificed bodies of surpassing men. (WR p. 121)

What is seen on Skye's earth is 'chiefs and tacksmen plundering,/
with the permission of divines shearing,/ clearing tenants and planting brutes', and the vision becomes a nightmare:

Multitude of springs and fewness of young men
today, yesterday and last night keeping me awake:
the miserable loss of our country's people,
clearing of tenants, exile, exploitation,
and the great Island is seen with its winding shores,
a hoodicrow squatting on each dun,
black soft squinting hoodicrows,
who think themselves all eagles. (WR p. 67)

It is not difficult to imagine the rancorous ruffling of feathers that such
imagery would cause among the hooded crows of island Calvinism.
And this critical vein, traced in poem after poem, frequently achieves

memorable effects. On one occasion, 'A Highland Woman', the poetry is explicit, sardonic, and directly addressed to Christ himself: 'Hast Thou seen her, great Jew,/ who art called the One Son of God?':

> And Thy gentle church has spoken
> about the lost state of her miserable soul,
> and the unremitting toil has lowered
> her body to a black peace in a grave.
>
> And her time has gone like a black sludge
> seeping through the thatch of a poor dwelling:
> the hard Black Labour was her inheritance;
> grey is her sleep tonight. (WR p. 29)

Signifying the spirit-crushing work required for survival, 'Black Labour' in this context condemns the economic arrangement which demanded work for a landlord in lieu of rent. '"Blackwork" in the sense of working for the landlord without wages had existed for at least three centuries.'[13] In several respects, Calvinist doctrine demanded the enclosure of minds while land was opened and cleared in the service of hitherto unknown economic priorities. With their faith locked into submission and their independence of judgement thus biblically expropriated, political quietism might be expected. Such contexts expose the radical nature of MacLean's political appropriation of religious terminology. Part III of 'The Cuillin' includes a symbolic presentation of the island's flora and fauna in terms of human, including specifically Christian, values: 'Every flower that grows has been seen,/ even the tortured wounded side'. Yet the union of values actively sought remains elusive:

> but in one there has never been seen
> the judgement of Lenin and the red side of Christ. (WR p. 91)

At any rate, such networks of meaning suggest that Douglas Sealy's response is accurate and to the point: 'Viewing the poetry as a whole, it would seem that the great burst of love-poetry found in *Dain do Eimhir* was an accidental deflection of the poet's talents and that the more enduring passion was the cause of justice and equality among men, nourished by his resentment of the waste of lives and land that is still to be seen in Scotland today.'[14]

But the issues and uncertainties which engendered that great burst of love-poetry were no nearer to resolution when MacLean left Britain for active service, during the early years of the Second World War.

[SM] *I was in the Libyan desert first, and the Western desert for most of 1942. And it wasn't a very pleasant place. Well, the point is, after such an experience, and the fact that the business was not really properly resolved. It wasn't so much a tragedy now, but a kind of perplexity; not knowing what was what. It was the business of having to go away to the Desert on top of all this; of having made a fool of myself, through what I can only describe as a kind of quixotic rashness. But then, I don't know in the circumstances what else I could have done except forgotten all about her.*

The desert may not have been a pleasant place, but it provided a healing-time for MacLean:

> I go westwards in the Desert
> with my shame on my shoulders,
> that I was made a laughing-stock
> since I was as my people were
> ...
> And be what was as it was,
> I am of the big men of Braes ... (WR pp. 206–7)

The poem 'Going South' records MacLean's first experience of battle.

[SM] *It was a strange business: it was the first day I was in action, and I was out at a forward observation post. Our truck was hit twice and I was slightly wounded, though I didn't become a casualty; and dammit we were nearly captured the first time.*

'An Autumn Day' brought MacLean into close contact with death – 'six men dead at my shoulder', and the religious inflection of his reaction is symptomatic:

> One Election took them
> and did not take me,
> without asking us
> which was better or worse:
> it seemed as devilishly indifferent
> as the shells. (WR p. 215)

The range of his compassion is evident in 'Heroes' which records
the death in battle of an unprepossessing but courageous English-
man:

> I saw a great warrior of England,
> a poor manikin on whom no eye would rest;
> no Alasdair of Glen Garry;
> and he took a little weeping to my eyes. (WR p. 211)

And it is as effective in 'Death Valley', (WR p. 211–12) an elegy for
a dead German youth.

Wounded in action in November 1942, MacLean was in various
military hospitals until late 1943.

[SM] *I was in a battery command post, and went up on a
landmine. The wheel of the command post was thrown about thirty
yards, and it was mostly my bones in my feet broken; metatarsals
and heelbones, by blast. I had superficial flesh wounds on my legs,
but it was my feet that took it. Mind you, I was hit twice before that
but didn't become a casualty. I got wounded with a bit o' shell
business in the thigh away back in May, '42. I was dressed for that.
The second time, Oh Christ I was lucky. I was hit there* [strikes his
chest above the heart] *by a bit of shell casing as big as that* [his fist].
*but it had ricocheted so much. … It would have torn me to bits.
That was during the big retreat, which started on 15th June, '42.*

It is difficult to read the last stanza of 'The Haunting', or a line like
'my thought comes on you when you were young' from 'Spring
Tide' (WR p. 193) without being put in mind of the preoccupations
of Thomas Hardy. There are moments when the rhythms and
intonations of, say, Hardy's 'At Castle Boterel' seem to speak
through MacLean's English versions:

> What was and what is now of us,
> though they would last forever,
> how would a tale of them come
> from distant shores. (WR p. 163)

Both poets are haunted by the absence of a loved woman and for all
their acknowledged differences, in their respective combinations of
elegiac historicism and passionate affection, there may well be

something of a common inspiration. Both MacLean and Hardy, moreover, pressed lyric into the service of a profound cultural pessimism, and though he is diffident about accepting the comparison, MacLean talks eloquently of the religious environment which helped to shape his own perceptions.

[SM] *I don't know whether some people are sanguine and some melancholy due to chemical reasons; I suppose there is something in that, but certainly upbringing is important. You see, I have a very great admiration for Hardy's poetry, and of course I have a very definite pessimism. I was brought up in an island where everybody was of a church which envisioned an eternity of physical and mental torture for practically everyone: where works did not matter unless you were Effectually Called, unless you saw the light and all that. Even the best people didn't necessarily see the light; and that included not only people of other creeds, but the great majority of the adherents of that church itself. So that was bound to cause a pessimism. In any given congregation of the Free Presbyterians, only about 5% of the adults took communion. The rest were just adherents. And although they didn't say that all the adherents were going to hell, the assumption was that the great bulk of them would – unless they saw the light, unless they were Effectually Called and so on.*

It isn't easy to determine the line between sincerity and mischief when MacLean adds with a twinkle in his eye: 'Mind you, the Church of Scotland has not believed that for a hell of a long time.'

[SM] *The Free Presbyterians and the Free Church talked about the filthy rags of human righteousness. How it didn't signify, unless, unless.... And they still believe that. D'you know, the most remarkable description of the Free Presbyterian hell I have ever read is the sermon in James Joyce's* A Portrait of the Artist as a Young Man. *Oh God that is a powerful thing! But still, although human righteousness may be filthy rags, they are by-products of a Saving Grace, and their non-existence is a very serious thing. The Roman Catholics had a safety-valve in purgatory, and also the fact that they did not throw the responsibility so much onto the individual. If you were alright in the eyes of the Church, there was at least some comfort in that. It was effectually milder, at least. But there was nothing like that Mass business in the strict Calvinist churches.*

MacLean's perusal of the history which his early lifetime spans suggests its formative influence upon his own sense of time.

[SM] *Having been born just before the Great War, I remember being terribly affected by the miners' strike in 1926, although I'd only be fourteen then. And y'see, actually, though Edinburgh hadn't as many slums as Glasgow, it had some of the worst in Europe. It was 1929 when I came to Edinburgh University, and that's when the Wall Street Crash was, and the Great Depression was at its height in 1931. And of course, there came in this hellish National Government.*

The interview came to an end with a question which a cultural historian capable of such precise recall has every right to ask: 'What is the time now, because I've got this damned watch which keeps stopping?'

Notes

1. Sorley MacLean, *From Wood to Ridge: Collected Poems in Gaelic and English* (Manchester, 1989), p. 83. Subsequent citations are marked WR and given parenthetically.
2. *Ris á Bruthaich: The Criticism and Prose Writings of Sorley MacLean* (Stornoway, 1975), edited by William Gillies, p. 48. Subsequent citations are marked RB and given parenthetically.
3. Robert Calder, 'Celebration of a tension', in *Sorley MacLean: Critical Essays* (Edinburgh, 1986), edited by Raymond Ross and Joy Hendry, p. 157.
4. Ian Crichton Smith, 'Poetry, Passion and Political Consciousness', *Scottish International* (1970), 10, p. 10.
5. John MacInnes, Review of *From Wood to Ridge*, *Lines Review* (1990), 112, p. 40.
6. George Campbell Hay, *The Scotsman*, 15 February, 1975, p. 26.
7. Seamus Heaney, 'Introduction', in *Sorley MacLean: Critical Essays*, p. 2.
8. For an account of 'The Battle of the Braes', see James Hunter, *The Making of the Crofting Community* (Edinburgh, 1976), pp. 133–40.
9. Karl Marx, *The Revolutions of 1848: Political Writings* (London, 1973), vol. 1, p. 221.
10. The phrase is Ezra Pound's, from 'Hugh Selwyn Mauberley'.
11. Sorley MacLean, *Spring Tide and Neap Tide: Selected Poems 1932–72* (Edinburgh, 1977).
12. Douglas Sealy, 'Literature, History and the Poet', in *Sorley MacLean: Critical Essays,* p. 60. Sealy's historicist readings are invaluable.
13. Terence McCaughey, 'Continuity and transformation of Symbols', in *Sorley MacLean: Critical Essays*, pp. 127–135.

14. Douglas Sealy, loc. cit., p. 59.
15. Sealy, loc. cit., p. 70.

For the Sake of Alba

NAOMI MITCHISON

I am a woman of Scotland,
I have read my history through.[1]

Naomi Mitchison's energy is prodigious almost beyond quantifying measure. With more than seventy books to her credit, her scale of endeavour is self-evident, and as Isobel Murray remarks, 'a bibliography which included her major and minor contributions to books, let alone her major and minor contributions to an extraordinary range of periodicals would be a stupendous and daunting document'.[2] Together with short stories and novels – historical, contemporary and futuristic – there are volumes of memoirs, biographies, work in philosophy, politics and political ethics; books for the young, and plays. As one of the diarists for the data-gathering operation mounted by Mass Observation, Mitchison generated a million words during World War Two.[3] While bringing up a family and running a farm at Carradale, Kintyre, she has devoted time and energy to a life of sustained political activity. After striking up a friendship in the 1960s with an African student who later became paramount chief of the Bakgatla in Botswana, and following annual visits to the country, Mitchison has been honoured as mother to both chief and tribe. In her ninety-third year when I visited her, she was sitting in front of her typewriter nursing grazed and bloodied shins, having just come in from the gardens where she had been helping to prune and tend a rhododendron of which she is particularly fond. She had recently finished an essay about Neil Gunn.

Though it must seem invidious to derive manageable themes from such a body of writing, Mitchison's imagination recurrently focuses upon divided loyalties within communities at times of unprecedented change. Several of the stories in *Beyond This Limit* quarry this metaphorical vein. 'The Powers of Light' charts the emergence from an oppressive tribal existence to a more sustaining primitive community, of two characters; a young woman called Fire Head, who can strike sparks from her hair, and her male companion the Surprised One, a cave-artist. 'The Coming of the New God' acknowledges the efficacy of what a western audience might recognise as witchcraft when it sets African preference for Anglican Christianity against domination by the Boers. The closing tale, 'Remember Me', constructs an unsettling account of attempts at continuance in a post-nuclear Highland village. A story published in 1987, 'The Things From Space', recounts the coming of the first slavers to African shores from the perspective of their uncomprehending victims.[4] A massive novel, *The Corn King and the Spring Queen*, takes the Black Sea as location to explore the processes of individuation within an ancient Scythian people; a transformation effected by the intrusion of the revolutionary kingdom of Sparta. What deepens the resonance of much of this writing is its design upon assumptions and perceptions relating to Scottish experience past and present. More directly, a major historical novel, *The Bull Calves*, constructs a story of ideological self-discovery leading to reconciliation when a Gleneagles family conceals a Jacobite fugitive just after the Rising of The Forty Five.

Fictive mention of a family in Gleneagles connects us with the Haldane family home at Cloan, and reminds us that Naomi Mitchison's genealogy intersects in forceful ways with English power. Viscount Richard Haldane, her uncle, was Lord Chancellor in Asquith's government, and her father was the distinguished Oxford scientist J. B. Haldane. But she added an entertaining dimension to this lineage when, at the end of our interview, she read an excerpt from 'The Historie of Squyer Meldrum' by the sixteenth century Scots poet Sir David Lindsay of the Mount. The episode concerned Meldrum's visit to a lady's estate, and his subsequent courtship of her, 'ane lustie ladie ... Quhais Lord was deid short tyme befoir.' The wooing proceeded and Naomi warmed to her narrative. Seeing the squire's door open, 'this fair Ladie' entered his chamber on the pretence of retrieving a box:

Bot that was not hir erand thair.
With that, this lustie young Squyer
Saw this Ladie so plesantlie
Cum to his Chalmer quyetlie,
In Kyrtil of fyne Damais broun,
Hir goldin traissis hingard doun.
Hir Pappis wer hard, round and quhite,
Quhome to behald wes greit delyte.
Lyke the quhyte lyllie was hir lyre;
Hir hair was like the reid gold wyre;
Hir schankis quhyte withouttin hois,
Quhairat the Squyer did rejois.
...
I can not tell how thay did play;
Bot I beleue scho said not nay.
He pleisit hir sa, as I hard sane,
That he was welcum ay agane.[5]

The woman in question was Marjorie Lawson, the Lady of
Gleneagles and, at the time of the fortunate squire's visit, early in
1515, widow of Sir John Haldane of Gleneagles, killed at Flodden
two years before. Marjorie was the daughter of Richard Lawson,
Justice-Clerk and Provost of Edinburgh. Not only ancestry, I felt,
but also a certain historical pedigree for liberated attitudes was
being established.

In *Small talk: Memories of an Edwardian Childhood*, Mitchison
records her earliest self-identifying memory:

It was bright and bobbing. Out of my dark cave I reached for
it. My hands wavered up to it. It came nearer. Did I catch it?
The importance was the attempt. My brother's long fair hair
was cut before he was six old, which means that I, under the
hood of my pram, was under a year old. But me.[6]

Where, then, did that life begin on Hallowe'en in 1897?
   [NM] *I was born in Randolph Crescent, Edinburgh. My parents
were Scots on both sides with a touch of Irish; and I think a little bit
further back a touch of Jewish – it's very important, I think, to have*

*a little bit of that Jewish valuation. I was a schoolgirl in Oxford,
where my father was then working, hoping to become a professor
and never actually becoming it. But it was in my mother's parents'
house that I was born.*

Though its genealogy is well-known, I wondered about the
Scottish provenance of the Haldane name.

[NM] *It was always a joke with us that we said it was really
Haftan. It was somebody we thought would be a nice ancestor, a
Haftan who came over from Norway. He died by falling through
the roof of the salmon's house.*

And did Gaeldom figure in her family tree?

[NM] *No. There's no Gaelic at all: we were all good Lowlanders.*

The opening poem in Mitchison's sole published volume of
poetry, *The Cleansing of the Knife*, called 'The House of the Hare',
taps into memories of a four year old girl gleaning corn with older
women. Already mingling images of escape from prescription, of
fruitful paganism in the figure of a young Ceres, and of self-
development, it traces a movement away 'from house of the
Haldanes':

> Of work and thinking and prayer
> To the God who is crowned with thorn,
> The friend of the Boar and the Bear

and into a different kind of time:

> The day that I built the corn-house,
> That is not built with prayer,
> For oh I was clean set free,
> In the corn, in the corn, in the corn,
> I had lived three days with the hare. (p. 1)

[NM] *It is based on the idea that the boar and the bear were the
male elements, the ones which were dominant. The hare escapes
them, and so does the young girl, but it was also something that I
felt very strongly, and that I remember happening – though of
course it didn't happen.*

A striking of symbolic, sometimes mythic resonance from richly
textured personal experience is characteristic, and touches epic
qualities in her title poem 'The Cleansing of the Knife'.

Towards the end of 1937, Mitchison bought the house at Carradale where she has lived ever since.

[NM] *I was very much part of a family, and was really depending on others. Coming to Carradale wasn't a choice of my own. In fact it was a combination of my cousins, who were all devoted to fishing, and my own family. The estate turned up with a house which had been left empty for some time and an estate including a shooting forest and moor and a fishing river! I didn't at all want to take this on. Remember this was 1936. But my husband and the older boys were very keen about it. All three loved river fishing; Dick [her husband] had always been keen, and now Dennie and Murdoch [sons] caught their first salmon: and I didn't mind coming there for summer holidays. Then it became more and more of a pull and also more interesting as one got to know a few people. But to begin with, I wasn't much involved in Scotland, much more with what was happening in Europe, and getting people out of Germany.*

Many of the poems chart that developing sense of encounter and identification with the community there.

> You stand before me rocking as the boat rocks
> From the unaccustomed ankles, the knees in the grey
> rubber thigh-boots,
> The swaying hips, dancer, oh dancer to the
> sea's moving,
> not mine now (p. 2)

Though addressed to a particular individual, and as such a celebration of desire, 'The Alban Goes Out: 1939' also celebrates herring fishing, focusing upon people in one boat but involving the rest of the Carradale fleet.

Closeness and danger soon suggest the necessity of camaraderie: 'How can we think of our neighbours except in a neighbourly way', (p. 5) and when the labour begins in earnest, rhyming participles catch the stress and flow of work at sea:

> Men and engines grunting and hauling,
> The nets dripping, the folds falling;
> The spring-ropes jerking to the winches' creaking
> Wind in by fathoms from their sea-deep seeking
> Steady and long like a preacher speaking. (p. 6)

[NM] *I went out as often as I could. This was in the late thirties, mostly the year before the war. I'd made friends with many of the fishermen and they took me out, so I was able to see the whole thing. This was ring-net fishing, where one boat pays out the net and another takes it in. They make a great circle then they come together and haul in the nets with whatever engines they have helping them. It's a pretty heavy thing and a very impressive sight. The great point about ring-net is that it is harder to do. You have to know much more about fish. If you use one of those drag-nets, you take all the fish there are, the little ones can't get out. You're spoiling everything, and people know it. Some are even talking about going back to ring-nets.*

And who was the 'you' to whom the poem is addressed?

[NM] *That was someone I was very fond of. With a lot of people here I had a sort of love-relationship, in the way that I wanted to see what they were like underneath: to get rid of the class thing and just see them as people.*

As a working paradigm of collective self-help, the experience was to feed into poems on other occasions. But in the meantime, 'The Scottish Renaissance in Glasgow: 1935' derives potential out of grimly realised urban experience:

> So that a man, fearful, may find his eye fixed on tomorrow.
> And tomorrow is strange for him, aye,
> full of tearings and breakings,
> And to the very middle he feels his whole
> spirit shaken.
> But he goes on. (p. 12)

Had the poem been suggested by any particular event?

[NM] *No, I think just talking to people, seeing that ideas were moving. There was a lot of interesting talk around at that time, and I could begin to see the old horrible Glasgow disappearing. When I first went there with my father, oh, I suppose I was fifteen, he was doing one of those big sets of lectures and the weekend we were there it appeared as if everyone was drunk. There was nothing else for them to do. And then when I came back there were the same people going out and doing things, often climbing. Of course, at that time Glasgow had a left-wing Council and they had begun, at least, to pull down the worst bits, and new buildings were going up. I felt things stirring.*

Those feelings spilled over into Mitchison's own locality, and 'Adoption of a Parliamentary Candidate, Lochgilphead: 1939', still tracing desire as a sub-text, opens:

> We are beginning to make something
> That was not here before.
> *I will be true to you.*
> Or maybe that was here once
> But died and must rise again. (p. 12)

Then, during the war years, 'The Farm Woman: 1942' takes heart from seeing 'in a film the Russian women working/ On the land they had made their own'. (p. 17). How inspirational had Russia been?

[NM] *Tremendously. I mean, we got it all wrong. Well, not all wrong. But I had been to Russia, with the Fabian Society. We all thought it was wonderful. We were just unable to see what was happening to an awful lot of people.*

Yet in her memoirs, *You May Well Ask*, Mitchison quotes from her diaries to suggest that during her 1932 visit, she was not so easily taken in. 'I was critical as well: "a lot of Sparta about all this."'[7]

During the war years Mitchison was living at her usual furious pace: mention of 'The Burial of Elie Gras', (p. 18–21) an elegiac composition on wartime exigencies, led to memories of Carradale at that time.

[NM] *Elie Gras was one of the many French resistance fighters; there was a very well-organised underground. And sometime during the war, when things had broken down in France, I took in several French people who'd had a hard time. Because they were the ones who had been keeping on with war they had been tortured by their own people. I got them here just to look after them; I was quite good at healing people. Some of them had been excommunicated and I was able to arrange for a Catholic priest to come and take them back into their Church.*

Meanwhile work at Carradale continued, as 'The Farmer and her Cows' (p. 18) testifies, and 'Then' looks back wistfully to earlier days of relaxation, contrasting them with present attentiveness to news of the war's progress:

Oh the evenings of song and dancing,
Brush of the kilt and touch of partners –
Dust on the pipes and the dancers dumb.
Now I twist the knob of my programme,
Cold as fairies the voices come. (p. 21)

By '1943', with German armies comprehensively defeated at
Stalingrad, a nervous, tentative optimism seemed possible:

Furl yourself, flower, become bronze, stealthy, crested,
Watcher from pastures. Oh watch a little, plover,
Nor be too glad this spring. (p. 21)

A sense of the relative calm at Carradale potentially threatened by
movement elsewhere is registered as disturbed sleep in the poem
'Kintyre' (p. 25); and 'On a Highland Farm' constructs an image
of woman as hunter, figuring Mitchison out in the Grounds of
Carradale at nightfall, armed with a gun and distinctly uneasy as
she waits 'for the marauding deer/ That tore my potato drills':

In a world made insecure
For me as for the deer,
Between a horror and lure
Where reason could be undone,
In a wood of wind and fear. (p. 26)

[NM] *It was pre-war, though we knew the war was coming. I
had one gun and the keeper was there. Nice young chap; survived
the war, too. It was pretty wild down there, and we were just
waiting. I don't think I got the stag, though I think probably Eddie
[the keeper] did. The deer were an awful nuisance, but I've never
shot a stag myself. I used to go out with a gun, but as often as not
[laughs] I just didn't feel like killing anything.*

The poem 'Living in a Village' reverses that hunting image to
explore a recurrent concern; the ambiguous position of a left-wing
laird subjected to local envy and suspicion. Animal imagery shifting
to the carrion-crow suggests a pervasive structure of feeling in the
community:

Living in the big house is being
The big stag, the twelve-pointer,
Watched on, edible, spied and lied to,
from burrows, runways, witch-twisted bushes, and most
From the hoodies' rock where the observant, the cautious,
the hungry hoodies
Feed upon small game still, hoping for bigger,
And bide their time. (p. 27)

[NM] *Well, I always felt I was doing it much better than I
actually did. I mean I was enthusiastic and full of go at that time. I
believed in politics much more. People warned me that I was in the
wrong position and that everything was twisted by my being the
laird. We tried very hard, but it was difficult establishing anything
like a solid relationship. And yes, I think it a recurring image. I
would think that I was very much more accepted than I probably
was.*

But wild-life in the area could also trigger imaginative associations of release, and with the way her own writing roots itself in
contemporary observation. Watching a grey heron take flight, 'Up
Loch Fyne' leads to a prayer-like conclusion:

May my own squat and spear-beaked mind
Fishing and gulping its needs among weedy statistics
Or in the dazzle of everyday reflections and refractions,
Sometimes take wing and re-create a myth. (p. 27)

In common with the heron, fishing was an important preoccupation
of hers, and 'Three Poems' were dedicated to the Highlands and
Islands Advisory Panel.

[NM] *I was a member of the Panel, and initially we started off by
saying what we knew most about. I said I knew most about fishing:
so I went with three others to I think practically every place where
there was a pier and a few fishing boats, all around the Highlands
and Islands. It was a good time, that.*

A significant time, too, since Mitchison was assisting in the
development of the economic infrastructure for Scotland's fishing
industry. These activities did not, though, inhibit reflections upon
darker elements in Scottish history, as 'Duncraig' demonstrates:

But behind the bens
Is another ben
And behind sorrow
Is the mother of sorrows. (p. 28)

Then, 'The Highland Scene: The Great Fault' articulates the effects
of the Clearances. Its opening line, 'There is a loch of tears with
great monsters in it,' catches the lingering grief of that historical
process, and leads in the third stanza to lines of troubled meditation:

Here stands reflected mountains of ancient guilt,
Half bare, half forested with witch-loved spruces.
Along their flanks a narrow road has been built,
From end to end trailing its own abuses. (p. 33)

I wondered whether, given her social status, there was any sense of
personal guilt in 'The Highland Scene'.
   [NM] *No, I don't think so. It's much more because the land on
the north side* [of Kintyre] *is an area where good people had been
badly treated. There was, I suppose, a slight class thing, but it was
mainly about that particular place.*

With 'The Cleansing of the Knife', many of Michison's concerns
come together. Both elegiac and lyrical, and involving personal as
well as historical registers it ranges across moods of regret, frustration, meditation and activity to end affirmatively. The opening
section, 'Why do we lift the Glass?' begins in dream with sugges-
tions of ritual, then expands to stereotyped impressions of an earlier
order where 'courage and song and laughter/ and the plaids go
swirling wide'. This concealment of oppressive hierarchies is an
image which may be said to signify the poem's true subject:

But the common man must hunt
For the black shells in the sea-weed
Between a tide and a tide. (p. 39)

In imaginative challenge to English domination by force of arms,
Scotland's heroes are invoked to stir a contemporary readership
into 'making action rise out of fear' (p. 40). But the historical

blighting of an independent nation produces a remorseful brooding
in this long opening section. Looking back upon the depletion of
domestic resources, the poem reflects that what was once a possible
future is now folded into history:

> No need now of the double sight,
> They are scattered as a blown stack
> through a long and a wild night.
> Tears will not bring them back. (p. 41)

Typically, that history is related to its effects upon Mitchison's
immediate locality:

> Between Minard and Carradale
> You will see the dark, squared walls,
> Sheep-folds that tell an ill-tale
> Of ruined steading and byre,
> Lost homes where once was loving and laughter.
> But the folk went far from Kintyre
> And the thatch came down with the rafter.
> Landlord's doing, yon.
> Are you angry, Donnachadh Bàn? (p. 41)

This opening section also questions the efficacy of poetry in
opposing Calvinist rigour. 'No act of ours, no love nor faith nor
prayer/ Can change predestined fate,/ Lighten our muckle fear'
(p. 42). But a recurrent refrain here also projects the dangerous
attractions of alcoholic oblivion, with the closing lines of 'Why do
we lift the Glass?' warning against the fatalism attendant upon
maudlin nostalgia:

> When a thing is used for life
> At fixed and life-giving seasons,
> For a breaking of barriers
> To the music all should play,
> Then it is water of life.
> It is not that today. (p. 44)

Continuing a clear-headed opposition to any 'soft daze or self-
pity/ And self devoted tears', the second poem, 'What can we see?',

grapples with problems of a 'past that must not be forgotten/ For all our wish to forget'. The rebirth of 'Scots indeed' requires a repudiation of historical romance and a new ability to:

> Peer back as Scott did once
> But clearer than ever he did,
> Seeing our folk in bond
> In a poor and a hard land,
> But slowly getting freed
> Through their own thought and sweat. (p. 45)

This 'steady righting of wrongs' moves into contemporary history with the third poem, 'Carradale to London: Blood Promise', which records the swearing of an oath between the speaker and Donnachadh Bàn as she goes south 'to the war' taking with her the knife that is their token of loyalty. The mingling of lovers' blood beneath the knife-blade forms another image which runs through the sequence, uniting personal and national devotion.

In the following poem, 'What are you doing?', Hitler's depredations are implicit, and Mitchison calls for appropriate kinds of leadership: 'Scotland will need to be led,/ But never by one man only':

> Now no one talker and fighter,
> But leaders here and there
> With sense and honour and pride,
> Men and women of Scotland
> Through city and countryside,
> Waking their fellows to think
> And act like Scots indeed. (p. 49)

The ballad-rhythm here suggests affiliations with older traditions of orality. But its moral imperatives qualify any easy ascription of Mitchison's socialism into ideas dominant at the time. If, in verse form, her sentiments seem with hindsight rather too trustful, her healthy suspicion of centralising control was rooted in concrete experience. In 1941, difficulties she encountered in the task of improving the fishing industry under wartime conditions led to this: 'It's all just part of this bloody planning business that has got at everything, the sacrifice of the individual and the small community.

It has got at socialists too.'[8] More recently, she has emphasised immediate responsibilities and relationships as the bedrock of wider senses of connexion. 'One's got a loyalty presumably to one's family to start with, and then it widens out to one's village, one's town, one's country. Perhaps to being a European, and finally, I suppose, to being a human being.'[9]

Across her writing, Mitchison elaborates complex responses to the idea of citizenship – 'We act because we must/ And I needed to be there' – and the bombing of Glasgow is directly recalled in 'Blitz on Clydebank 1941':

> My eyes are blinded
> By the grey plaster dust
> Of a smashed house in Partick,
> Where a boy's body lay. (p. 50)

In an elegiac turn, the poem contemplates change and loss as well as a shared culpability:

> We must take the weight of the blame:
> Clydeside is Scotland's shame
> And was, before they came
> With the death cross on their wings. (p. 52)

It turns, too, to thoughts of a new beginning, and of the difficulties of reconstruction within existing social relations, before invoking more transcendent senses of human communion:

> For our souls are not our own,
> We are held by future and past
> And the love and care of our friends.
> We can never be alone. (p. 53)

Reconstruction begins in the mind and memory, and 'The Cleansing of the Knife' suggests ways in which a differently conceived past might shape and advance present possibilities. The recurrent love-promise between a man and a woman becomes sign and symbol of dedication to widely encompassing relationships, within which Mitchison can call, with no trace of irony, for male leadership.
    [NM] *Yes. Men are quite human.*

The unobtrusive acceptance of her own womanly awareness seems never to have been afflicted by the difficulties and problems which beset some of her younger contemporaries. Privileges of birth and status, she acknowledges, were a considerable advantage, but she recalls something else, too, and laughs with the memory.

[NM] *I was lucky – in some ways. I went to a boy's school in Oxford to start with, where I was the only girl. That was probably good for me. And I was always treated as a sensible person.*

In her self-assurance, Mitchison conceives of Scotland as the spirit of woman, and closes the sixth poem, 'Shifting the Sand', by addressing a call for the necessary patience beyond human reach to:

> Alba our mother,
> Who, waiting, knows
> The needs and hearts of her children,
> The inner light and the stir.
> As, times, I too am patient,
> Finding past shift and blur
> Of a Whig-twisted history,
> The things that were done to those children,
> And, through their pains, to her. (p. 57)

Mitchison's distinctive mingling of the intimate with the expansive achieves a kind of apotheosis in the hymn to spring, 'The Green Braird of April', at the mid-point of her sequence:

> The thoughts toss with the words,
> Reaching from here and now,
> Tumbling and wild like the farm birds,
> The peewits over the plough:
> Thoughts of Scotland and of taking courage,
> How you might be if you chose
> – If only a man could choose,
> Choosing right, how to be and whose! – (pp. 57–8)

These things entail struggle and, continuing the political education of the addressee – another main sub-text through the sequence – the poem 'They did it' urges a lifting of horizons 'past Scotland, past the home light,/ Far out to Stalingrad' to learn desired modes of transformation from the experience of others:

They did it, who began,
lighting Iskra, the Spark,
From the same discouragement
As mine from which I write. (p. 59)

Iskra was the newspaper through which Lenin had argued his case.

[NM] *It did seem at that time as though Russia was the place to
look up to. In many ways it was. It had endured a terrific invasion,
worse than Napoleon's, and it was beaten down almost as near the
capital as it is in* War and Peace. *We didn't know about many of the
things that were going on, and if the Soviets hadn't resisted, Nazism
might have been able to walk all over us. It was Hitler's big mistake.*

Struggle and frustration were also locally engendered both politi-
cally – 'The bold and exact plan/ Lacks money, lacks more the man/
With courage to speak and strike/ As the timeous moment comes'
(p. 60) – but also in personally hurtful ways, through the 'Village
snigger and chatter/ Over me or Donnachadh Bàn' (p. 61). Local
recriminations and suspicions form a worrying echo from poem to
poem. 'Yon woman,/ Here from the Big House' (p. 55) and culmi-
nates with:

Fear of the Big House,
Shadow of all that has been,
Class hate worse than clan,
Hate of the Big House
Sundering woman from man.
Time that old thing ends –
Ah, could we not get ending it!
The dead pain from the past
Coming between friends
And all I had hoped to do
For Scotland, and for you,
And myself and Carradale. (p. 67)

[NM] *One couldn't easily have the same kind of intimacy, the
same kind of expressed love, perhaps, because there was always this
barrier. It was worse, of course, in the village, because there I was in
the* Tigh Mór [the Big House], *and that in itself made for difficulties
… . It's less so now, because I've needed help more, and there are
some people in the village who have always helped. During the early*

years of the war, when they heard I was on Hitler's Black List, they
said 'Och, we'll take you over to Canada!'

A sense of waste, in 'Fashing and Working', whether caused by
the dumping of herring in the absence of buyers, or by 'bairns ... in
our schools,/ Savagely not learning,' leads to a question and a
refrain:

> Did we think, did we intend,
> Putting sheep here in the stead
> Of our own hill cattle,
> To spoil what we could not mend?
> Alba our mother, what have we done to thee? (p. 64)

Earlier reference in the same poem to John Knox sows the seed of
another reformation, based upon the need to repudiate a culture
which enslaves the present through its mystifying connexions with
the past:

> Must we be thirled to the past
> To the mist and the unused shieling?
> Over love and home and the Forty-five
> Sham tunes and a sham feeling?
> Must we be less than alive,
> Must we lurk in half light? (p. 65)

In measured response, 'The New Song' proposes a cleansing of
the knife:

> Scraping away the grime
> And tears of centuries
> And blood of treacherous killings,
> a little at a time. (p. 70)

Throughout the nineteen-forties Mitchison continued with a range
of political activities.

[NM] *There was a Scottish Convention going on then and I was*
very keen about it. Neil Gunn and I were always writing to one
another; organising meetings. We were fairly deep in. I thought at
that time of a complete break with England, and yet it was very

*difficult because I would say to myself: 'Well, we really haven't been
touched by the war at Carradale, and I don't want to give up
England when things are difficult.' I was down there from time to
time during the Blitz, and you felt a tremendous love of London. It
was as though one were thinking with two different parts of one's
mind.*

'The Cleansing of the Knife' ends with a poem called 'Work and
Love' which looks to an awakening from the dream with which the
sequence opened. There is no slackening of personal or political
constancy. 'The old scar skins over/ But the shape of the cut stays,/
As stays the strength of the promise,/ As stand the hills of Scotland'.

Transforming Wordsworth's lines, 'Getting and spending we lay
waste our powers:/ Little we see in nature that is ours',[10] the poem
turns to a theme of regeneration:

> At last, and at long last
> There will be getting and spending
> For the sake of Alba, our mother,
> There will be hope and life,
> The pibroch over the hill
> And the fiery cross of good will,
> And I see my poem's ending
> And the cleansing of the knife. (p. 72)

[NM] *I think it's gradually coming; getting into the habit of
doing things on our own. And we'll all see this funny building
they've got being used for a kind of parliament. I don't think it's
going to be quite as simple a sort of break and rearrangement as we
thought about in the forties. There was a time when I thought that
this would all come when I was able to take part. Unfortunately,
one goes on getting older and things haven't yet crystallised. Quite
often I see my old friends from the Scottish Office who all say that if
only they were still there they could really make things hum: that
the people there now are no good, and so on. I had so much backing
from the Scottish Office at that earlier time.*

Irrepressible to the end, Mitchison added that the Scottish Office
'was also, of course, the best place in Edinburgh to have a cheap
lunch.'

Notes

1. Naomi Mitchison, *The Cleansing of the Knife & Other Poems* (Edinburgh, 1978), p. 39. Subsequent citations will be given parenthetically.
2. *Among You Taking Notes ... : The Wartime Diaries of Naomi Mitchison* (London, 1985), edited by Dorothy Sheridan.
3. *Beyond This Limit: Selected Shorter Fiction of Naomi Mitchison* (Edinburgh, 1986), edited and with an introduction by Isobel Murray, p. vii.
4. Naomi Mitchison, 'The Things From Space', *Chapman*, ix (Spring 1987), pp. 131–3.
5. *The Works of Sir David Lindsay of the Mount* (Edinburgh, 1934), edited by Douglas Hamer, vol. II, pp. 171–2. For biographical information see vol. III, note to lines 864ff., pp. 203–6.
6. Naomi Mitchison, *Small Talk ... : Memories of an Edwardian Childhood* (London, 1973), p. 9.
7. Naomi Mitchison, *You May Well Ask: A Memoir 1920 – 1940* (London, 1979), p. 188.
8. *Among You Taking Notes*, p. 126.
9. *Beyond This Limit*, p. viii.
10. *William Wordsworth: The Oxford Authors* (Oxford, 1984), edited by Stephen Gill, p. 270.

Such Clarity of Seeming

NORMAN MACCAIG

> Landscape and I get on together well
> Though I'm the talkative one, still he
> can tell
> His symptoms of being to me, the way a shell
> Murmurs of oceans.[1]

In his 79th year at the time of the interview, the poet regarded by many as Scotland's laureate was kept as busy as ever fulfilling a diary of reading engagements under the auspices of the Scottish Arts Council's 'Writers in Public' scheme. 'I am,' MacCaig reflected humorously, 'looking forward to retiring from retirement.' In constant demand for public readings over many years, he possesses a seemingly inexhaustible ability to strike off utterances which connect immediately with his audience's unexpressed reflections and perceptions. Whether he's noticing 'The goat, with amber dumbbells in his eyes' (p. 71); or, as a cock struts by, that 'one can almost see/ the tiny set of bagpipes/ he's sure he's playing' (p. 316); that 'the daddylonglegs helicopters/ about the room' (p. 321); or that 'a butterfly, crazy with wings,/is trying to go in every direction at once' (p. 381), the precision of MacCaig's rhythms invites us back into the minutiae of life, sharpening our recognitions and amplifying our senses of the world. Given his professed attraction towards correspondences, these rhythms coordinate MacCaig's perceptions in particular ways. As one reader suggests, MacCaig's alertness to the proportions of things results in a highly structured verse. 'These are

its natural proportions, if rhythm in a work of art can be a simile for
rhythm in nature itself. The rhythmical arrangement is the poetic
equivalent of a natural scene: a metre of landscape.'[2]

While he delights in proposing novel identifications for things
around him, MacCaig also registers depths beyond the immediately
perceptual to produce a poetry of 'visual unexpectedness which is
his fingerprint or signature'.[3] At the 'End of a cold night' for
example, '... a spell is broken; suddenly Time scratches/The hour on
its box and up flares a new day' (p. 31). Or consider how closely
focused is the eye which asks, in 'Rain on fence wire' (p. 90):

> What little violences shake
> the raindrop till it turns from apple
> to stretched-out pear, then drops and takes
> its whirling rainbows to the ground?

MacCaig's 'lust of looking' (p. 82) achieves memorable definition
as the poem turns to a bird's foot plucking fence-wire at the
moment of flight, thereby vibrating a chord of movement, simultaneously into the air and down to earth:

> Was it the world itself that quaked
> Enormously beyond my knowing?
> Or tiny claws, that perch and shake
> From yards away a rainbow down?
> No difference ... I look and see
> The dry wings flirt, the small ounce soaring
> And with its leap a shower of drops
> Flames down, released into the grass.

MacCaig often appears happiest when obeying Aristotle's injunction to give instructive pleasure. 'Here is the world about you,'
he seems to say, 'while you are able, scrutinise its intricate meas-
ures.' Partly as a consequence of this, his imagination registers
concerns with 'being' and 'nothingness', with time and transience,
which echo in the mind to sobering effect. A celebration of being is
pervasive in his writing, but the figure which death makes as it flits
through MacCaig's pages is also chillingly engraved:

A hand dangles
from a chair arm;
and a man's head droops.
The night outside creeps into it. (p. 413)

'The old conspiracy of space and time' (p. 13) is one which haunts
his writing. And it is a theme which can produce images of unaccustomed concretion. 'Wreck', (p. 16) considers a 'hulk stranded in
Scalpay Bay':

Twice every day it took aboard
A cargo of the tide; its crew

Flitted with fins. And sand explored
Whatever cranny it came to.

That silting of the sand in the ship's remains, so slow as to be
virtually imperceptible, enables the poem's final meditation, a ges-
turing of movement within an aeon of time:

Its voyages would not let it be.
More slow than glacier it sailed
into the bottom of the sea.

Norman MacCaig's own world and time is initially defined by
Edinburgh, where he was born in 1910. He grew up in Dundas
Street, living in a top flat above the chemist shop his father owned.
He remembers moving house when he was still at school.

[NM] *Straight across the road to another top flat. And later we
moved to Howard Place, opposite the Botanic Gardens. I think by
that time I was at the University.*

That was in 1928, and MacCaig read Classics. He went on to
spend a year at Moray House College of Education, training to be
the schoolteacher he remained for thirty-four years. He always
wanted to be a schoolteacher and could never remember there being
another profession in his mind. but he did not have the same
assumption that he was going to be a poet.

[NM] *I got interested at school, of course, because the teacher,
Puggy Grant, asked us either to write a composition or a poem by*

next Wednesday. And, with my sturdy Scottish pragmatism, I thought to myself – well, a poem's shorter. So I wrote my first poem then – got interested, and started writing, writing, writing.

His first volume of poems had been published during the Second World War, and an enquiry about these circumstances led to a digression concerning MacCaig's imprisonment in Edinburgh Castle.

[NM] *I was a conscientious objector, and when I was called up, I was supposed to go to Ilfracombe to a unit in the Pioneer Corps. I wrote to the head chap and said 'I'm not coming, but if you want me I'm generally in by midnight.' And eventually I was collected – it was after midnight – by a couple of policemen who stuck me in a local gaol near the house. The next day or so, a corporal and private came and bundled me off to the Castle, where I was imprisoned. At the Tribunal I had made it clear that I was willing to join the Royal Army Medical Corps, but that I wasn't going to kill anyone. Some time after our arrival at Ilfracombe, they put us on a job in a tank depot. I don't know what we were supposed to do there because I refused to go. And I was court-martialled. In Aldershot no less. And they were very fair. I was drummed out of the army with contumely.*

It was while he was in the army that his first volume of poems was published – poems which MacCaig would now prefer never to have seen the light of day.[4]

[NM] *A collection of terrible poems – semi-surrealistic. I have a phrase for them: every poem is a 'vomitorium of unrelated images' … which nobody could understand. Routledge and Kegan Paul published them during the war. A friend of mine asked to see this terrible book, and when he gave it back he said the only thing about them that was ever of any use to me, spoken or written. He said 'There's your book, Norman, when are you publishing the answers?' And I came to what was left of my senses: struggled on my hands and knees along the rocky road to lucidity and comprehensibility – which took me a good few years. Any fool can be obscure, but to be lucid is hellish difficult.*

Several years ago, during his time as Edinburgh University's first writer-in-residence, MacCaig had maintained at a seminar that he was not a writer who went through draft after draft of poem to produce a final polished version. Yet he achieves the kind of lucidity on the page that must always look hard worked for, and it was natural to wonder about his process of composition.

[NM] *Well, I can tell you what happens, I can't explain it. I feel like writing a poem the way you feel hungry or thirsty. And if it's possible, I sit down always in this particular chair, and with a particular size of blank paper, no lines on it. And I have not an idea what's coming. Not a clue. And very quickly into my head comes a memory of a place or an event or a person or all three. But far more often it's a short line, a short phrase – four or five words, nothing extraordinary about them. Down it goes, and the poem trickles down the page until it's finished. They come very quickly, very easily. I'm asked 'how long does it take you to write a poem, Norman?' And I say 'two fags'. Sometimes it's only one. And I can't work on them. I never write a second version, as most poets do – three, four, five, six, ten sometimes. I just can't. I don't want to. I'd rather try to write another poem. And often they come out without any changes. You'd think I just copied them. Now the snag of course is, I write a lot that don't please me. They're duds: they don't come off: boring; dull. And about twice a year I look through what I've written and throw them out. I suppose I put five or six out of ten in the bucket. But they come so easily, and I write such a lot.*

Pressing him further about this simply had the effect of bringing out his sense of fun:

[NM] *Someone once asked Philip Larkin 'what gave you the idea of using the toad as a symbol for work?' 'Genius,' Larkin replied.*

But he accepts that for many people this is difficult to believe:

[NM} *After all, most poets have two or three versions at least – sometimes a dozen. I never did that.*

How then did he account for the purely formal accomplishment of his writing? But the mischief was in him now.

[NM *Well, it's my Gaelic origins, you see – they're great formal-ists the Celts.*

Gaeldom was, though, something to which we would return in our conversations, and what began as a humorous aside soon developed into something more.

[NM] *The Gaels are very formal in their arts, even where there is not much, as in sculpture, but did you ever see anything more formal than a Celtic cross? Same with their great music: the pibroch is extremely formal. And you know, I always loved form, which I think may be one of the reasons I took Classics. That, anyway, in turn encouraged this admiration for form. So that I didn't often write a poem that was formally bad.*

Though for many years he did not re-read Classical Literature, as
reference and allusion it enters his own writing in a variety of ways.
He has always considered arcane reference to 'figures that nobody
ever heard of and languages that nobody can speak' to be 'bad art
and bad manners'. Unlike Pound, the allusive web which Classicism
weaves in MacCaig's poetry is characterised by an affable,
invitational tone and structure, as though one part of his intention
sought to domesticate these legends and gods, bringing them back
down to a realm of more immediate, recognisably human, discourse.

[NM] *That's right. They were an appalling shower, the classical
gods – lecherous, treacherous, bad-tempered, cruel; they were fear-
some! They're just enlarged people. So I take the mickey out of
them. Also, though, I'm quite careful, if I write about classical
figures, either real ones or legendary, mythological ones, I very
much restrict the choice to names which even today are known to a
lot of people.*

MacCaig's populist perspective upon Classical characters may
well carry with it possibilities for more localised application. Scotland has its own experience of subjection to 'enlarged people', not
excluding its own clan aristocracy, and MacCaig's ironic treatment
of legendary pride is not without contemporary resonance. His
witty play with the traditions of Classicism indicates his own refusal
of subordination to those narratives privileged as canonically sacro-
sanct. MacCaig frequently uses myth in both popular and colloquial sense, to signify a tale or account that is not strictly factual.
On other occasions, though, MacCaig will use the concept of myth
to indicate the human imagination, with poets figuring as early
mythologisers.

[NM] *Well, myths are very important. Whether you believe in
them or not, they are.*

His use of the terms of myth and mythology has an often
arresting vitality. In a poem like 'Apparition', for example, the poet
climbs Ben Stack, to the north of Lochinver, in Sutherland:

At the cairn I turn round and scan

the jumbled wilderness
of mountains and bogs and lochs,
South, East, North and then – West
– the sea

Where a myth in full rig,
a great sailing ship, escaped
from the biggest bottle in the world,
glides grandly through the rustling water. (pp. 424–5)

Apprehended so directly, what might 'myth' signify in such a context?

[NM] *It all goes back to the old clipper days, with everyone trying to be the fastest from Britain to Australia: the 'Cutty Sark' – those great ships, which had become a sort of myth.*

So it was the reality within and underneath the myth that he wished to bring back into focus?

[NM] *Yes, and to see this beautiful – I don't remember how many masts it had, but it was a real, full-rigged ship in this wilderness of a place. It was like something from another time.*

Years earlier, 'The rosyfingered' (p.14), from the first volume of the *Collected Poems*, used Homer's habitual mode of reference to the dawn to bring the mythic back down into the mundane world. Humour enriches MacCaig's working of the theme of the sun rising:

And an old myth tries to heave itself to its feet:
The phoenix newly feathered in the east
Takes wing, blundering; and Phoebus not so fleet
Comes cantering after it, but comes at least.

Agreeing that in this instance he returns to Homer's mythic structure to stress everyday aspects of life, MacCaig's sense of mischief bubbles to the surface again.

[NM] *That's right. Rosy-fingered my foot! Just have a look at it! What's more, that's a mistranslation, though that's always the way it's translated: rhododactylos – it's equally rosy-toed, since dactylos meant both your fingers and your toes!*

Nonetheless, the fascination with metaphor remains a constant; the beauty who walks in the plain field still figures the sunrise as a beautiful woman, with MacCaig substituting metaphor for myth. And, though compromised by its own admiring gaze, the drily witty demythologising of a poem like 'Two Ways Of It', displays similar considerations:

You are no Helen, walking parapets
and dazing wisdom with another beauty

that made hard men talk of soft goddesses
And feel death blooming in their violent wits
With such seduction that they asked no pity –
Till death came whistling in and loosed their knees. (p. 78)

At its close the poem reflects upon 'natural celebration', and it seemed sufficiently characteristic to enquire further.

[NM] *This is me at it again. This woman is not Helen: she's not going to be turned into a constellation by some god or other. She is exactly what she is. In that last stanza, I'm objecting, I suppose, to things in the past being curmudgeonly, mystified and 'rouged'. Helen is a myth, and the poem is written against this mythologising. You are what you are – five foot four inches high, seven stone eight pounds. This is a very recurring thing with me.*

That same plea for human self-sufficiency may help to account for another strand in MacCaig's writing; his usually witty, frequently cutting and sometimes angry references to formalised religion. And this, too, forms part of his constructed poetic, since he had no religious upbringing as a child.

[NM] *I don't think my parents had any belief at all and, as I like to put it, I was born an atheist. It isn't the fact of religion that I oppose, it's what the believers do with it and because of it. There's more blood shed in the history of the world because of religion than anything else. Religion has consistently, even in primitive tribes, caused cruelty, torture, death.*

In his poetry, the assumptions of institutionalised religion are refused in favour of a pervasive humanism. 'Down-to-earth Heaven' makes the point. Since the Christian concept of heaven is itself a construct of the human imagination, the world of the poem displaces it in favour of our own continuing creativity. Both the music referred to and the poem being written are testimony to our shaping and ordering powers. The idea of 'genesis' is also our own conception and practice, demonstrated by the continuing generation of song and poetry. Since secular writing can also value the idea of ceremony (long since appropriated by religious institutions) the poem enshrines a sacramental vocabulary, echoing Biblical and liturgical words and phrases. Passion and reason are united within Art, 'each in its own distinction.' So a different kind of communion is invoked, involving a 'revelation of the ordinary'; a repeated concern in MacCaig's writing, which heals and consoles as it celebrates both creative and created energies.

MacCaig is acutely aware of the almost religious function of metaphor in primitive language as a factor joining poetry and myth. The ceremonial aspects of metre and rhythm are certainly widely accepted, and MacCaig's allusions to myth suggests further affiliations. In 'Between two nowheres', MacCaig uses biblical references to imply the supremacy of poetic language:

> We praise the good God for his creation
> of the universe. – When are the hymns to be written
> in praise of the unimaginable power of the Word
> that first made the chaos that made
> creation possible?

Mythologies which seek to explain the Creation become fit subjects for MacCaig's radically secularising attitudes. Conversely though, an approach which sees in myth vestiges of primordial ritual and ceremony that might give order to personal perceptions and images finds more sympathetic response. At the same time, much of his poetic attention relates to a celebration of the present. These themes are developed in tandem, historical material being used to create a relevant sense of the now.

[NM] *I quite often, I suppose, write exactly about the past and now; and even the future. I despise the future. It doesn't exist until it's now.*

> It's my pretty Now I'm in love with
> that won't stand still
> to be measured. The past
> has gone to a far country; and as for the future
> there's no future in it.
> But my pretty Now, I love her, I love her,
> because she shows herself off to me
> and will always be faithful. (pp. 289–90)

While fidelity to the figure of woman evidently remains a metaphoric constant, there are times when his verse has a distinctly existentialist ring to it.

> My own self
> Is what surrounds me and it trembles

With my own winter. I hang in ragged
Branches and echo like these grassy cobbles. (p.139)

[NM] *Well, there was a time when existentialism was a kind of*
craze-cult, and I read some existentialist books at that time. The
only philosopher I read with any interest was Kierkegaard, who
really was a kind of founder of existentialism.

Early and late with MacCaig imagistic precision is placed at the
service of a sensuous probing not only of how we read meaning but
of how things come to signify what they do.

[NM] *I often mention Suilven, but I'm well aware it's only a*
lump of sandstone. I don't put my feelings onto it, or extract new
feelings from it. Except that it's a most beautiful lump of sandstone.
That's what it is.

He has always striven for physical accuracy in his representa-
tions, sometimes to an obsessive degree.

[NM] *Take the oyster-catcher. I first described it as having*
yellow legs. That's not true. It has orange legs. But by the time I
realised that, the poem was already published. And that troubled
me for about thirty years, until it appeared in the Collected Poems,
when I changed it.

In his poem 'Notes Towards the Supreme Fiction', Wallace
Stevens uses the phrase 'theatre of trope',[5] and it seems an appropriate description for some of the ways in which MacCaig works in
metaphor giving a dramatic intensity and often a sense of physical
presence to his verbal conjurings. Quite apart from such occasional
echoes of Stevens' characteristic phrasing as 'opulent ululations'
(p. 251), 'lordly magnifico' (p. 273), or 'dandified gluttony' (p. 310),
there can be few poets who have introduced the word 'mind' into
their work as variously as MacCaig has, often enough in apparent
exploration of the Stevens aphorism: 'what we see in the mind is as
real to us as what we see by the eye'.[6] The idea of 'the poem as the
act of the mind' also brings Stevens into focus.[7] Both poets direct
their attention to the process of perception, subjectively analysing
even the most ordinary-seeming of images. For both, 'seeing is
believing' is the great cliché to be probed, stripped of its
mystifications, analysed and endlessly reconstituted. And Stevens'
eloquent blank-verse testimony to the self-sufficiency of human
consciousness in the poem 'Sunday Morning' would naturally

strengthen and encourage MacCaig's own secular values. It seemed to be a case of genuine poetic interaction on MacCaig's part.

[NM] *When I first came across Wallace Stevens' work, it was the occasional poem here and there in different magazines, because he wasn't published in bulk over here for a ridiculously long time. I was very much attracted to his work. I am not saying I am as good a poet as Wallace Stevens, but I felt a sort of affinity with his persistent – perhaps too persistent – talk about the difference between reality and imagination, and what imagination does to reality. He was all for what the imagination does to it. I don't go that far; in fact rather the opposite. But I felt this interest of his in reality and imagination, and his notion that everything has to be a fiction. And when the books began to appear, I read them gluttonously. I read books about him, and was fascinated. I still think that he's a great poet, but my direct interest in him stopped quite suddenly. I was saturated, you know, I'd read enough.*

One area where it seems he was able to turn American precept to Scottish account lies in Stevens' attitude to poetry as a satisfying of the human desire for resemblance, expressed with clarity in *The Necessary Angel*:

> Poetry is a satisfying of the desire for resemblance. As the satisfying of a desire, it is pleasurable. But its singularity is that in the act of satisfying the desire for resemblance, it touches the sense of reality, it enhances the sense of reality, heightens it, intensifies it. ... It makes it brilliant. When the similarity is between things of adequate dignity, the resemblance may be said to transfigure or to sublimate them. Take, for example, the resemblance between reality and any projection of it in belief or in metaphor. What is it that these two have in common? Is not the glory of the idea of any future state a relation between a present and a future glory? *The brilliance of the earth is the brilliance of every paradise.*[8]

MacCaig forges a distinctive voice, yet it is interesting that one of the abler contemporary American critics of Stevens makes a remark which can as accurately apply to the Scottish writer. 'For [MacCaig], however, poetry always remains lyric poetry, as late Romantic theory (if not always the poetry) had defined it – the poem as short verse utterance (or sequence of such utterances) in which a single speaker expresses, in figurative language, his subjective vision, a truth culminating in a unique insight or epiphany that unites poet and reader.'[9]

MacCaig's closely focused attention to the fictionality of metaphor is recurrent:

> – But how hard it is
> to live at a remove
> from a common wall, that keeps out and
> keeps in, and from water, that
> saves you and drowns you.
> But when I went on to notice
> that I could see the pair of them
> as a trickling wall or as a wall
> of water,
> it became clear that I can describe only
> my own inventions. (p. 163)

Again, perhaps relating to Stevens' insistence that: 'Every image is a restatement of the subject of the image in terms of an attitude',[10] MacCaig here accepts that 'Every image is an intervention on the part of the image-maker.'[11] No matter how careful the scripted attention to detail, a part of the poetic process will always be that 'a transference has been made' (p. 165). And MacCaig's reference here to Aristotle's *Poetics* is pertinent, where our familiar sense of metaphor as 'the application to one thing of a name belonging to another thing' is categorised. Aristotle states: 'The transference may be from the genus to the species, from the species to the genus, or from one species to another, or it may be a matter of analogy. As an example of transference from genus to species I give "Here lies my ship," for lying at anchor is a species of lying.'[12] In high spirits, MacCaig the sometimes surreal classicist, places Aristotle's example of metaphor upon a metaphorically unsteady slope:

> A ship sails clean out of its metaphor
> And birds perch on no simile; and Time
> Breaks all the rules of reason and of rhyme. (p. 53)

In such circumstances, a poet can only embrace the shimmer of signifiers almost as an act of defiance against their own duplicities

> I won't give up being deceived by landscape's
> Likenesses and incorrigible metaphors. (CP p. 290)

Little wonder, then, that 'A Sigh for Simplicity' (p. 322) laments in comic vein:

> If only I could see a hazelnut without thinking
> of monkish skullcaps. Does the fishing boat at the pier
> Really rock like a bear? Is a mussel really *bearded*?
> It's time I put the lady moon on my blacklist.
> I groan and think, if I were only Adam
> To whom everything was exactly its own name –
> Until one day the other appeared, the shameless
> Demander of similes, the destroyer of Eden.

Language itself becomes a permanent temptress towards the next created likeness, and the figure of metaphor as seductive woman reappears. It has been suggested that 'MacCaig looks on metaphor with such suspicion precisely because of his outstanding gift for it, and only this innate scepticism can prevent him from slithering into facility. ... Indeed, the impossibility of any truly detached perspective is felt as a tragedy in much of MacCaig's work'.[13]

In a famous utterance, Wallace Stevens declared that 'the final belief is to believe in a fiction, which you know to be a fiction, there being nothing else. The exquisite truth is to know that it is a fiction and that you believe in it willingly'.[14] Both Stevens' systematic privileging of fictionality, and in his substitution of it in place of Christian prescription, MacCaig might be seen to agree. But having ironised the master narrative of Classicism and rejected that of Religion, it is hardly to be expected that MacCaig would readily subscribe to any formulation concerning belief, and his Scottish scepticism further complicates the American's transcendental sweep. It seems at times to be a scepticism nurtured by the absence of territorial security: 'That transcendental One I don't believe in. / How give it birth with no place to conceive in?' (p. 292). In 'Ego', MacCaig expresses his existential doubts in navigational terms:

> Tree
> And star are ways of finding out what I
> Mean in a text composed of earth and sky.

> What reason to believe this, any more
> than that I am myself a metaphor. (p. 45)

MacCaig's alertness to the conditions of writing makes him both
a parodist and an ally of the post-structuralist fascination with the
coding of language. This argues that everything we know and do is
readable as a text, and so nothing exists beyond textuality. Accordingly, a 'Swimming Lizard' 'twinkled his brief text through the
brown and still' (p. 12), or being pricked by thorns becomes 'I
touch/ the little jagged word, and my torn skin carries your signature' (p. 41). 'Bookworm' (p. 243) makes sport of the idea of
experience as textuality, as does 'Prism', when it reads 'the whole
city/ [as] a code in a foreign language' (p. 248), or 'Sparrow' reading
a blackbird's song as 'writing/pretty scrolls on the air with the gold
nib of his beak' (p. 249). So it is not the case that MacCaig expresses
any fundamental suspicion about the poetic efficacy of metaphor.

[NM] *Not at all. I wrote a wee poem confounding metaphor,
saying I'm sick and tired of it – except that it consists entirely of
metaphor. Which I'm well aware of, because I can't escape from
metaphor and images – I just can't. It's the way my mind goes.*

Rather than Stevens' often assertive mode, then, a characteristic
uncertainty holds sway. In one sense, MacCaig's attitudes may owe
more to the plenitudes and doubts of Wordsworth's 'Tintern Abbey'; with that romantic exploration of the processes of signification: 'Of all that mighty world/ Of eye and ear, both what they half-
create/ and what perceive',[15] finding echo in Scottish expression:

> eyes change what they look at,
> ears never stop making their multiple translations
> and the right hand refutes the meaning
> of what the left hand is doing. (p. 325)

Yet it remains the case that MacCaig considers himself to be a
man of reason.

[NM] *That's why I admire 'mind' so much. Of course no-one really
knows what it means, but often to me it stands for reason, for
accuracy of that physical kind you know – Suilven isn't a phallic
symbol, it's a great lump of sandstone. I'm a great admirer of
reason, though I know it has its limitations.*

Given this ambience of rationalisation in his verse, and MacCaig's often ingenious deployment of poetic conceits, it seemed timely to mention his affection for what are still called the 'metaphysical' poets, the great lyric writers of the seventeenth century.

[NM] *Oh well, I still have that; especially for John Donne. I love him for – well, he's extraordinary. His technique alone is admirable, and the fantastic images and metaphors that he creates. And the straightforward almost prosy way in which he states them – only it's not prose at all, it's poetry. But he just speaks directly out, you know, very forthright in spite of his metaphors and images, because that's the way he thought.*

And earlier in his writing career, MacCaig paid homage to this technique?

[NM] *Early on, I would agree, but not for a long time now. There's one book of mine where two, maybe three poems would make somebody think, 'Aye aye, MacCaig's been reading Donne again.' But that was a long time ago. 'Poem for a Goodbye' [pp. 51– 2] – that seems to me to be 'Donneish'.*

Yet in other ways, MacCaig's relationships with his more direct ancestors was for a long time ambivalent at least. He seems to have spent considerable time finding a creative response for the peopled history of his own past, but, increasingly, they come to occupy significant space in his writing. I asked him about his own genealogy.

[NM] *I don't know much about it, largely because three of my grandparents were dead before I was born and the other one died when I was about eight, and living in Edinburgh. They were all Gaels. I spent three holidays in my teens at my mother's place in Scalpay, off the Isle of Harris. But it wasn't until years later that I began to realise what an important thing these holidays were. They shifted me from thinking that Edinburgh consisted of me and my mammy and my daddy and my sisters. I found on Scalpay my aunties and my cousins. And it did two things. It made me realise that I, like everybody else, come from generations and generations and generations; which was the beginning of an interest, though not a very well exploited one, in actual history. It gave me a channel, a telephone wire to the past, which before that I didn't have at all.*

And MacCaig's father?

[NM] *From Dumfries. But his father was from Argyll – another Gaelic speaker.*

How then did he feel that he related to the world of Gaeldom?[16]

[NM] *Now that's awfully difficult. I know that I feel more at home when I'm amongst the Gaels at Lochinver – never mind the Outer Hebrides – than I do among Edinburgh people, although I've lived here all my days: I really do. I much enjoy the company of Gaels. I feel at home among them – genetics, I suppose. And then, of course, my mother: she was illiterate all her life, yet I never knew anybody who in conversation, without realising it, used metaphors and images as much as she did. If there's any poetry in me, that's where it came from: some of the most astonishing images and metaphors – often very funny. It was just the way she thought, and there's a bit of that in me.*

And his relationship to poetry in Scots?

[NM] *I love the Scots Language. My father lived in Dumfries until he was eighteen, and no doubt spoke rich Scots in those days. So that the Scots language does not in any way feel alien to me, not a bit. On the other hand, I've lived all my days in Edinburgh, and I talk English – did at school. 99% of what I read is in English. English is my language. And if Edwin Muir was right when he claimed, I think stupidly, that no Scot could write good poetry in English because he is not using his ancestral language – why then my ancestral language genetically is Gaelic, not Scots at all, except that wee bit through my father. So if there's any truth whatever in 'the language of the blood', then mine is Gaelic, which I can't even speak! No, English is my language, just as it is the language of almost all Scots people these days. The number of people who speak a rich Scots – Oh you'll get them in Aberdeenshire, but hardly anywhere else.*

Given the ways in which McCaig has combined his role as the poet of Edinburgh's urban landscape with his imaginative possession of the Assynt region of Sutherland, he has earned the right to claim representative status for his writing. While he has spent a lifetime extending Scottish experience in terms of the country's landscape, flora and fauna, Assynt in particular comes to symbolise a Scottish territory deeply cherished and powerfully preserved.

[NM] *I cycled all over Scotland, with a tent, when there was no tourism really. I started in my teens, and I poked into all the corners of Scotland, and I fell in love with that particular area. In the first place I was attracted to it just because it is so beautiful – and also it's scattered and splattered with trout-lochs – my other passion! And also, at Achmelvich near Lochinver there is a beautiful bay with white sand and sand-dunes – wonderful for children, and after the war, we had two very young children. So we started going there, and have gone back every year since.*

The whole area becomes a significant literary *topos* in MacCaig's writing, a landscape of the mind where exploration and articulation at many levels can take place.

[NM] *The groundwork on which the mountains there stand are made of a hard, hard, hard rock: I'm told it's one of the oldest rocks on the earth's surface – Lewisian gneiss. It's all over the Hebrides, the west coast, the Highlands. Very hard, comes in different colours, grey, greenish, purplish, that change with the light.*

His longer poem, 'A Man in Assynt', (pp. 224–31) from his 1969 volume *A Man in my Position* is interesting for several reasons, not least its free verse form which combines with orchestrated developments of theme and image. In fact, a move away from closed forms had begun earlier with the volume *Surroundings* in 1966.

[NM] *It was totally unconscious. I had written in strict form, metre and rhyme – often wavering metre, often para-rhyme – but strict form all the same. And one night I sat down to write a poem – felt like it – and the damned thing came out in free verse. Of course, I got interested in the form. I wrote for a good while in both free verse and strict form, but as the years passed, I've been writing more and more in free verse.*

How did 'A Man in Assynt' come to be written?

[NM] *The poem was written because Scottish Television ran a series of fifteen-minute programmes called 'Poets and Places'. Iain Crichton Smith did Lewis, George Mackay Brown did Orkney, Sidney Goodsir Smith did Edinburgh, and so on. They asked me to do one on the Lochinver area. And I said no. I don't write long poems. I even added, I don't like reading long poems, why should I write one? Well that series finished, and in the autumn of that year they had another, shorter series, and they approached me again. I said, 'Well, I'll have a shot, and if I don't like it, you won't get it.' I sat down one night and wrote the whole poem; just as if someone were dictating it to me. The reason wasn't brilliance and genius and cleverness: it was all there waiting to be spoken. So I spoke it.*

The interest in history, to which MacCaig had earlier referred, becomes the subject of the poem. From the 'Glaciers, grinding West' in the opening line, the structure modulates to its closing stanza where:

                                                 the scraping light
         whittles the cloud edges till, like thin bone
         they're bright with their own opaque selves. (p. 230)

'A Man in Assynt' comprises a meditation upon Highland time and
identity, weaving themes of possession and dispossession into a
celebration of imaginative independence. From figures and moments 'clear and tiny in/ the misty landscape of history' comes the
suggestion that 'up from that mist crowds/ the present', before its
interconnexions, shaped as phrasal repetition and choric echo,
confront difficult continuities:

         Or has it come to this,
         that this dying landscape belongs
         to the dead, the crofters and fighters
         and fishermen whose larochs
         sink into the bracken
         by Loch Assynt and Loch Crocach? –
         to men trampled under the hoofs of sheep
         and driven by deer to
         the ends of the earth – to men whose loyalty
         was so great it accepted their own betrayal
         by their own chiefs and whose descendants now
         are kept in their place
         by English businessmen and the indifference
         of a remote and ignorant government. (p. 226)

Since it marks a shift in perception and perspective in MacCaig's
writing, I wondered to what extent 'A Man in Assynt' represents his
own coming to terms with history, even a laying of historical ghosts.[17]
    [NM] *Sutherland, the county, the whole of it, was the most
shamefully treated in the Clearances. And it's a beautiful, beautiful
countryside. But it's also very sad, because there are hardly any
people in the place. And you keep coming across ruins of what used
to be crofts, in the most unlikely places, from a time when the
population was much bigger than it now is. So it's a sad landscape,
in that way. You can walk for miles and miles and miles and miles
and never see a house, let alone a person. It's got that sadness in it,
and you can't help being afflicted by that history in that landscape,
because there it is under your very eyes.*

History and topography come together in MacCaig's more recent work, achieving senses of permanence, durability and security.
'Old Highland woman' is a case in point:

> She has come here through centuries
> of Gaelic labour and loves
> and rainy funerals. Her people
> are assembled in her bones.
> She's their summation. Before her time
> as almost no meaning. (p. 417)

'Crofter', too, can answer its own question with a quiet, wry
confidence:

> What's history to him?
> He's an emblem of it
> in its pure state. (p. 432)

Upon reflection, might MacCaig accept that the struggle towards
lucidity has not always entailed such stark effects of simplicity?

[NM] *Oh well, I don't mind poems being a bit difficult. I hate
poems being obscure. A good difficult poem is trying to say something which is difficult to express and to understand. But an obscure
poem is bad writing. That kind of obscurity always brings to my
mind a remark in a Peter de Vries novel, where a man and wife are
talking about a friend. The man says, in his accent, 'Oh he's got a
head on him; if he says something it's worth thinking about.' And
his wife made the splendid reply – 'Oh I don't know. He's very
profound on the surface, but deep down he's shallow'.*

The depths and shallows of MacCaig's poetic endeavour mingle
to such different effect that his own question from 'The Streets of
Florence' suggests appropriate continuities:

> I, then? What am I
> a continuing creation of? What Hebridean
> island and what century have I failed
> to escape from in the dangerous journey
> from my first great rendezvous to the one
> I have still to keep? (p. 147)

Notes

1. Norman MacCaig, *Collected Poems: A New Edition* (London, 1990), p. 297. Subsequent quotations are marked CP and given parenthetically.
2. Valerie Gillies, 'A Metre of Landscape', in *Norman MacCaig: Critical Essays* (Edinburgh, 1990), edited by Raymond Ross and Joy Hendry, p. 146.
3. Douglas Dunn, '"As a Man Sees ..." – On Norman MacCaig's Poetry', *Verse,* vol. 7, no. 2, p. 55.
4. Norman MacCaig, *The Inward Eye* (London, 1946).
5. Wallace Stevens, *Collected Poems* (London, 1955), p. 397.
6. Wallace Stevens, *Opus Posthumous* (ed. by Samuel Fench Morse) (London, 1959), p. 162.
7. Ibid p. 240
8. Wallace Stevens, *The Necessary Angel* (London, 1960), p. 77 (Emphasis added).
9. Marjorie Perloff 'The Supreme Fiction and the Impasse of the Modernist Lyric' in *Wallace Stevens: The Poetics of Modernism* (Cambridge, 1985), ed. by Albert Gelpi, p. 51.
10. *The Necessary Angel*, p. 128.
11. Ibid p. 129.
12. Aristotle 'On the Art of Poetry' in *Classical Literary Criticism* (Harmondsworth, 1985), trans. T. S. Dorsch, p. 61.
13. Christopher Whyte, 'This Trash of Metaphor: on the Poetry of Norman MacCaig', in *Norman MacCaig: Critical Essays,* pp. 90–1.
14. 'Adagia', in *Opus Posthumous*, p. 163.
15. *William Wordsworth* (Oxford, 1984), edited by Stephen Gill, p. 134.
16. For a further exploration of this theme see John MacInnes, 'MacCaig and Gaeldom', in *Norman MacCaig: Critical Essays,* pp. 23–37.
17. Two essays which discuss these emphases in MacCaig's poetry are by Douglas Dunn in the issue of *Verse* cited at note 3 above, and by Raymond Ross in *Norman MacCaig: Critical Essays,* pp. 7–21.

Living in the Utterance

EDWIN MORGAN

> Like Chaucer,
> like the beginning of an
> idea,
> like the hinge of a
> horizon.
> *Iain Crichton Smith*

Unlike those ancient map-makers who marked territory beyond the limits of the known world with 'Here be dragons', such boundaries in Edwin Morgan's imaginary cartography hold no terrors. They serve instead to trigger his invention. Back and forth across time and space, the connexions he forges between known worlds of experience and those previously unexplored have extended the territory of scripted English in quite spectacular ways. From squibs to sonnets, from love poetry to limericks,[1] from Anglo-Saxon alliteration to Russian translations, from the Middle East to the Pacific Islands, he shapes voices for artists and aliens, for hyenas and a crack in glass. Given such scope, Denis Donoghue's testimony that 'the force of Morgan's imagination is its variousness'[2] can read almost like an understatement.

Born in Glasgow in 1920, Edwin Morgan grew up on the South side of the city, in Pollokshields then Rutherglen, going to Glasgow University when he was seventeen. He can remember writing for his school magazine at the age of eleven or twelve, but before that can recall his mother laughing when he danced around the house as a child chanting silly rhymes he had made up.

[EM] *I think that might have been the beginning of it. I like that idea, anyway, a mixture of rhyme and song and dance all coming together.*

His first volume, *Dies Irae*, is marked by an apocalyptic rhetoric described by one reviewer as a 'puritan-gothic' stylistic mode.[3] There is, at any rate, an Old Testamentary ring to some of his early work.

[EM] *There is, and I suppose it does go back to the upbringing I had. My parents weren't really what you would call religious, but they were church-going, with a strong sense of right and wrong, and I was fairly strictly brought up, going both to church and to Sunday school every week. You had to do it, and I got to know the Bible very well because I had to learn large parts of it by heart. Bible-imagery stays in your mind, whatever your beliefs eventually become, and when I was writing these apocalyptic things, like the one about the atom bomb, it came out in terms of religious imagery:*

> Shall the trumpet sound before the suns have cooled?
> Shall there not be portents of blood, sea-beds laid bare,
> Concrete and girder like matchwood in earthquake and
>   whirlwind?
> Shall we not see the angels, or the creeping ice-cap, or
>   the moon
> Falling, or the wandering star, feel veins boiling
> Or fingers freezing or the wind thickening with wings?[4]

That first volume also contains imitations of Anglo-Saxon that are more than merely technical exercises.

[EM] *When I was taking the English degree at Glasgow, Anglo-Saxon was a large part of the course, almost a back-bone to it. It was compulsory, and I was one of the few who liked it. I loved the Anglo-Saxon poetry, and so got fairly well into the language. I've always liked heroic poetry and I admired the heroic and stoic tones of Anglo-Saxon. I think a mixture of that and its curious elegiac, melancholy quality hit me very strongly. I also admired it from a technical point of view. It was one of the first things that showed me the use of different kinds of metre. This wasn't a regular beat at all, but it had rhythm, wonderful rhythm, and that appealed greatly.*

As an undergraduate, Morgan also studied Russian and French and his life-long attraction to European poetry began.

[EM] *At school I encountered no modern poetry at all. And then it all burst upon me: a great series of impacts. It was a sudden discovery, between the ages of seventeen and eighteen, of twentieth century poetry. In French studies I read the French symbolists, Baudelaire, Rimbaud, and Mallarmé; I liked Baudelaire particularly. In the Russian classes I first read Mayakovsky, whom I translated later. I remember being impressed, too, by the American Hart Crane.*

Clearly, frontiers were already crumbling. And yet it remains a curiosity that apart from his translations Morgan writes very little in Scots. Those translations, though, mark significant extensions of the Scots tongue into international relationships, and it is interesting that he should call his volume of translations of Mayakovsky *Wi the Haill Voice*. In Mayakovsky's poetry Morgan felt the presence of a kindred spirit, and, in his introduction he quotes approvingly Mayakovsky's dictum that 'poetry – all poetry! – is a journey into the unknown'.[5] In similar vein he quotes from the Russian's essay 'How Are Verses Made?': 'Innovation, innovation in materials and methods is obligatory for every poetical composition.'[6] 'In that essay,' Morgan comments, 'innovation joins careful craftsmanship, a feeling for the age, and a commitment to social struggle as one of the prerequisites for modern poetry.'[7] The remark applies equally to his own work. As far as the choice of Scots is concerned, Morgan says this:

> There is in Scottish poetry (e.g. in Dunbar, Burns, and MacDiarmid) a vein of fantastic satire that seems to accommodate Mayakovsky more readily than anything in English verse, and there was also, I must admit, an element of challenge in finding out whether the Scots language could match the mixture of racy colloquialism and verbal inventiveness in Mayakovsky's Russian.[8]

As the translations show, Scots met the challenge successfully. Why, then, has Morgan not made more use of Scots in his own poetry?

[EM] *I started off writing in English, and it seemed the most natural way for me to do it. In the late forties, when I tried Scots, mostly for translations, it seemed that the poets being translated did go better into Scots than into English – Mayakovsky and some translations from Heine. They went very well into Scots and I enjoyed using it, trying it out, accepting the challenge. I was tempted to write more in Scots because at that time what people call the 'second wave' of the Scottish Renaissance was in full flood, and it was tempting to fall in with that. But I could never make it my main thing. It goes back to a sense of just what your own voice is. This is not the whole answer because I know, for example, that Sydney Goodsir Smith was able to force himself to use Scots, though it wasn't his natural voice, really, at all. So it's not a clear-cut thing. In my own case it is simply not so compelling to use Scots as perhaps it is to some other people.*

An endless curiosity with other poets and other languages (besides Russian and German, Morgan has translated from French, German, Italian and Spanish and, with some assistance, from Hungarian, too), combines with a restless formal inventiveness to suggest that there might be a deep need to avoid constriction within any one mode.

[EM] *I think there was probably something of that. I did not want to restrict myself to carrying on a Scots tradition. I didn't look at it in that kind of way. I didn't put myself to school with MacDiarmid or with any of the earlier Scottish poetry. It was there and I enjoyed it, but it wasn't what compelled. Even during my last years at school, and at university, I was feeling my way gradually into other ways of looking at things. It's hard to say why this should be so, except that perhaps it has something to do with being an only child. I think perhaps an only child gets the imagination going more than someone who belongs to a large family and so is interested straightaway in immediate relationships. With no brothers and sisters you can't do that. So you look out at things, look up at the stars, go out into the garden and wonder about things, creep up into the attic or whatever.*

The strong vein of creative eclecticism in Morgan's writing draws on many sources. At times his literary radicalism calls William Blake to mind, with both poets sharing an attraction to created worlds of libertarian possibility. Morgan's poem 'The Fifth Gospel' begins:

I have come to overthrow the law and the
prophets: I have not come to fulfil, but to overthrow.

and continues:

> I have not come to call sinners, but the
> virtuous and law-abiding to repentance. (p. 259)

[EM] *Blake was certainly one of the poets who made an early impact on me and I still like him a lot. The method he has of often turning ideas inside out or casting a very strange light on accepted ideas appealed to me strongly. So I did go out to Blake, I'm sure of that.*

'Twilight of a Tyranny', (p. 345) sets polyphonic speech against figures of oppression, and in comic vein 'The Mummy' makes its serious point not only by direct reference to Ozymandias and the mummy's gagged response, '– M' n'm 'z 'zym'ndias, kng'v Kngz!', but in the ironically pacifying words of welcome spoken to the preserved corpse of Rameses II:

> – Yes yes. Well, Shelley is dead now.
> He was not embalmed. He will not write
> about your majesty again. (p. 398)

[EM] *I like Shelley, yes; both the political element in 'The Mask of Anarchy', which I remember enjoying as a student, and also 'Prometheus Unbound' which moves right out into the universe and asks serious questions about where power really resides.*

In a variety of ways, and to different ends, a constant concern in Morgan's poetry is with the abolition of constraints. Using forms of concrete poetry he will playfully deconstruct, in 'Levi-Strauss at the Lie-Detector', a line from *The Savage Mind* – 'any classification is superior to chaos.' (p. 354) Taking as its first line a quotation from the *Tractatus Logico-Philosophicus*, 'the world is everything that is the case', 'Wittgenstein on Egdon Heath' (p. 355) performs a similar operation. Then, the poem 'The World' repudiates an incipient negativity in this deconstructive turn:

> I don't see the nothing some say anything
> that's not in order comes to be found,

and proposes instead:

> Imagine anything the world could, it might
> do; anything not to do, it would. (pp. 346–9)

Raising serious questions about the colonising power of language, 'The First Men on Mercury' comically plots the triumph of non-sense-speaking aliens over English-speaking astronauts who land upon their territory. Speakers of Glaswegian demotic, and perhaps Scots more generally, might read an optimistic parable into the performance.

The range of Morgan's sympathies suggests an urgency for social transformation. Looking at the poor and uncared for in Glasgow, for example, prompts this response:

> Hugh MacDiarmid forgot
> in 'Glasgow 1960' that the feast
> of reason and the flow of soul has ceased
> to matter to the long unfinished plot
> of heating frozen hands. (p. 290)

Certainly, orthodox forms of political instrumentation are found wanting, as 'On John MacLean' makes clear. Quoting from the Glasgow socialist, the poem proceeds:

> 'I for one will not follow
> a policy dictated by Lenin until he knows
> the situation more clearly.'
> Which Lenin hadn't time to,
> and parties never did. (p. 350)

But at its close the poem rescues the aims and aspirations of MacLean's radicalism, quoting the Clydesider again:

> MacLean was not naive, but
> 'We are out
> for life and all that life can give us'
> was what he said, that's what he said. (p. 351)

It seems, then, that in Morgan's writing we encounter something like an anarchist aesthetic.

[EM] *I think there is something like that – anarchist or libertarian; I think it's probably true. It fits in with the fact that I don't really like systems of thought or systems of belief, and I don't find myself worried by this. Some people have thought that there is a search for belief in my work, but I don't really think that's true. Quite often I take up the idea of a search or a quest, maybe in a longish poem or in a sequence, but I don't think of it as being a quest for a system of belief. I just like to think of things as they are and bring as many of them as I can into my poetry. If I were asked whether I had a philosophy of life, I just couldn't describe such a thing; I don't really have one at all.*

> There is no paradise
> (who could believe in such shadows?) but
> what there is can be so nearly so
> I'd give the wilderness no other name
> if you were there. There is no paradise
> but you, that's all I know, here or to come. (p. 507)

Whether in concrete poems, sound poems, computer code-poems, Newspoems or limericks, there is a constant play and wrestle with language, probing it for other ways of seeing, pushing it into varying shapes and forms. Wasn't there a problem here, perhaps a problem with language itself, in that it is rule-bound, whereas Morgan, despite his devotion to the sonnet, seems always to be on the lookout for new ways of transgressing rules?

[EM] *I don't think of language as in any way static. I know it's an ordered system in the sense that we can all use it and understand each other: but in writing, particularly in poetry, I see it as a very extensible and explorable system. Some of the experiments you undertake if you are dealing with language will turn out not to be useful, may be cul-de-sacs. But we have to take that risk, and other things you discover will be useful, and will extend your instrumentation. Hugh MacDiarmid used to speak about the human brain being largely unused. I'm sure that's quite true, and I think language is like that too.*

In this writing Heisenberg's 'Uncertainty Principle' becomes a guiding metaphor:

> It seems this is a world of change, where we,
> observing, can scarcely fix the observed
> and are unfixed ourselves. (p. 337)

Morgan's insistence that the best parts of a poem often spring from what he calls 'lightning discoveries that fly into the mind, unplanned, from sources that may be remote from the ongoing discourse of the poem'[9] is evident in much of his work, and he has recorded his feelings about the ways in which poetic construction departs from conventional, rule-bound procedures:

> Doubtless everything in the universe has a cause, but in the heat of composition the causes, the concatenations, are like a chain that melts *into* being instead of out of it. And there are few things stranger than that. If we lose sight of the strangeness, we lose sight of the poetry.[10]

The extraordinary diversity of Morgan's talent is certainly evidence of a powerful release of energy; and this energy, encoded and revealed by such literary strategies, may relate partly to the self-denial which Morgan's homosexuality compelled him to in the decades after the War. Looking back upon this, he has acknowledged some of the ways in which such repression may have contributed to his work:

> Creative activity of any kind is not hindered by pressures and difficulties and tensions, in fact it's often helped by these things, so I don't think one should rush to get rid of all one's problems in the hope that this will lead to better art. I don't think that this would necessarily be true.[11]

In spirited resistance to restrictions upon the freedom of the imagination, Morgan proposes connections and correlations which destabilise the security of any assumed 'norms'. 'Surrealism Revisited' merges linguistic boundaries to extend the poem's space. Challenging our conceptions of the possible, he juggles with syntax to disturb our senses of the fitness of things: 'A clockwork orange by Fabergé fell out of a magpie's nest and ate/ humble pie./ A brazen yelp escaped from a condemned gasholder and was torn to/ pieces in a fight between scavengers and demons' (p. 411). To different effect, we read in the third stanza of 'Pictures Floating from the World':

> Two old painters
> jailed for representation
> have escaped: the sirens

shriek for them, the black
sleek cars are out
in magic realism. (p. 407)

His 'New Year Sonnets' spring similar surprises;

Satan was squatting with his lurid tuba,
potting a blackly incandescent coda.
Hell is improvisatory. (p. 407)

[EM] *It gets you into impossible situations now and again. But
people say that we can't go faster than the speed of light; well, that
just sets me wondering* [laughs]. *Or to take another example:
professional linguists are fond of putting forward what they call
impossible sentences – 'you can't say that in English!' I would like
to accept the challenge and devise a context whereby you* could *say
that in English! I don't think there's anything you can't say, that
wouldn't make sense if only you could devise a context for it. That
kind of thing is in my work a lot, I'm sure.*

As part of this attraction, Morgan seeks to unsettle habits of
mind whereby objects, phenomena, including other poems, are
assumed to be ready for human recognition. One of a series of such
reconstructions, 'Variations on Omar Khayyam' sows phrases and
moments from Fitzgerald's translation of the *Rubaiyat* into its own
reworking, allowing these echoes to chime in the reader's mind as
the texture of the narrative is re-woven. It comes as a surprise to
realise that the opening we have encountered is a film version –
'almost like life' – of the story, being watched by astronauts travel-
ling through the cosmos:

Outside the ship
asteroids sparkled, hurtled; behind it the train
of its flotilla swung past Mars, all space
its battered caravanserai. (p. 504)

Those astronauts, unruly and creating mayhem as their craft probes
the unknown, are themselves being tracked on a screen suspended
for 'one moment in annihilation's waste'. So the moving finger
which inscribes Morgan's poem confounds received ideas about
time and space, prompting us to question the mode of existence of

any literary text and even the nature of language itself. The studied intertextuality of Morgan's *Collected Poems* calls to mind Foucault's insistence that 'the frontiers of a book are never clear-cut. Beyond its internal references and its autonomous form, it is caught up in a system of references to other books, other texts, other sentences: it is a node within a network.'[12]

Comparisons between ancient voyages and futuristic travel recur, but I was struck by the attraction to those kinds of effects which bring surrealist practice to mind. Morgan reached behind him and from among several books on the subject pulled down Herbert Read's 1936 edited collection *Surrealism*, well-used enough to need an elastic band to hold it together, laughing as he responded.

[EM] *Obviously I was interested. When I was at school I took art as one of my main subjects. I only went to university at the very last minute: I was always intending to go to the School of Art, then something changed my mind. At that time, around 1937–38, surrealism was at its height, really; it was in the air, and being discussed. So yes, there's something there.*

Read's book includes Paul Eluard's essay 'Poetic Evidence' which proclaims that surrealists:

> are all animated by the same striving to liberate the vision, to unite the imagination and nature, to consider all possibilities a reality, to prove to us that no dualism exists between the imagination and reality, that everything the human spirit can conceive and create springs from the same vein, is made of the same matter as his flesh and blood, and the world about him.[13]

Morgan is a multi-media poet in the sense that he incorporates into his own inscription signifying systems of different kinds: tapes, television, video and, centrally, film. Filmic influences enter not only as subject-matter but technically, in the way that his images can flicker and flash in a seamless continuity, one to another, even when warning about the nuclear obliteration of all signification:

                              We've endured
the frames per second thing but a
reality that rolls off in vapours
is still on the cards and when it's all

up we needn't be surprised with the rushing
gravestones and skyscrapers, thrown out
like a Harra of slags. (p. 310)

'Five Poems on Film Directors' (pp. 362–5), is further evidence of a
continuing fascination.

[EM] *I've always enjoyed film and I remember being taken by
my parents at quite an early age to what they regarded as 'good'
films. So I was able to see some of what are now classics of the
cinema. Fritz Lang's* Metropolis *made a strong impression. I saw
more and more when the Cosmo Cinema opened in Glasgow just
before the war, what is now the Glasgow Film Theatre. It was a
great fascination to discover, as the Russian revolutionists kept
saying – Lenin was a great believer in film – to discover that here
was, really, the art form of the twentieth century. And it was quite
hard in a way for poetry to compete with the effects of the greatest
films being made. I felt that quite strongly, and you have to be true
to your reactions. As a succession of pictures, film combines art
with story-telling, yet at the same time producing totally new
effects, which you wouldn't see anywhere else, certainly not in the
theatre; effects which came from the purely technical aspects of how
you use a camera. That interested me, too, because although I'm no
great photographer, I've always taken a lot of photographs; so from
that angle I felt I was very much at home with this kind of thing.*

Composed as fragments of tape-recordings playing in a distant
galaxy, 'Memories of Earth' reveals how aliens have been affected
by the courage and cruelty they witness on their visit to this planet.
The manner in which they enter our universe owes something to
contemporary zoom-lens effects:

> The stone we are to enter is well marked,
> lies in a hollow and is as big as my fist.

As they undergo this process it seems that the stone expands,
forming a landscape which:

> explodes upwards, outwards, the waves rise up
> and loom like waterfalls, and where we stand
> our stone blots out the light above us, a crag
> pitted with caves and tunnels, immovable

yet somehow less solid. We climb, squeeze in
and one by one tramp through the galleries
till we have reached the designated cavern,
fan out on the dim rubbly floor, and wait.
We shrink again – accelerated this time.
The rubble's a mountain-range, the shallow roof
a dark night sky in infinite soft distance.
The gallery we came by's like a black
hole in space. Off we go across the plain
into the new foothills. (p. 331)

At this stage of the narrative the visitors have not even entered our universe, so it is a relief to realise that alien astonishment at what they are witnessing matches our own:

                                    Surprise
comes from old microstructure thinking.
We must stop that.

These defamiliarisations allow us to see our own planet through unaccustomed eyes.

    [EM] *The main idea in the poem is the contrast between the very ordered society that the people leave when they shrink to get into our universe, and what they see of change here, and of suffering, which they don't have in their world. They're deeply affected by it, and when they return they set about changing their world because they see other things of importance. The poem has something to say about perfectly ordered societies, and whether or not this is a good thing.*

    Since the visitors' time and ours can never be in phase, they experience human history as an eternal present, thus linking inter-galactic travel with the earliest of earth's voyagers:

The sun begins to walk on the Pacific.
And now we see and come down closer to
a speck that does not fit that emptiness.
A thousand miles from land, this black canoe,
long, broad, and strongly built, with high fine prow
much ornamented, and many oars, drives
forward steady across the zigzag sun-prints...

By the gunwale a cock crows.
Whatever far landfall is their goal,
known or unknown, or only hoped-for, they
have crossed dangerous immensity
Like a field, and dangerous immensity
to come lies all about them without land:
their life is with waves and wind, they move
forward in ordinary fortitude,
and someday they'll steer through that Southern Cross
they only steer by now. (p. 338)

[EM] *The part I thought I'd done best in that poem was the bit
about the Pacific voyagers. They were quite extraordinary. These
Polynesians or Melanesians would be casting off into pretty well
unknown seas, going for hundreds and perhaps even thousands of
miles in what to us would be rickety boats. The risks they took, and
the kinds of hopes they had were just as great as the risks and hopes
of the astronauts we have today. That kind of connexion appeals to
me very much. In the early days of life on earth you sail by the stars.
Our job is to sail through them.*

Although they can involve speculations on post-nuclear desola-
tion, his science-fiction metaphors reveal a general optimism, in
that they open new areas for the imagination. Nothing imaginable is
necessarily beyond human capacity: 'What is that infinite hope/ that
forces a canoe upon the waters.' (p. 339).

[EM] *All of these things are a part of the human story, the human
adventure. I don't think we are necessarily bound by what is here
about us on earth. We may be at the moment, but I'm not sure that we
always will be. In one of the poems, 'A Home in Space' [p. 387], I
take up this idea, that once we land on and eventually, presumably,
live in and have children on other worlds, and then look back at earth,
will we always be nostalgic for it, or are we ourselves evolving into
creatures who can live contentedly on other worlds? I like to think
of that process going on as far forward in time as we can imagine.*

Morgan's own capacity for new poetic departures was demonstrated again when he published his long sequence *The New Divan*
in 1977. Collage-like, and by turns autobiographical, historical and
futuristic, the sequence ranges widely from its defining location in
the Middle East.

[EM] *Though we were there in wartime, the sequence goes right back to history and pre-history. It also goes forward beyond the was to include the kind of violent incident you would have in more recent times, perhaps in the late sixties.... Parts of the sequence come from my own experience over there, other parts are invented characters, not me at all. Probably all of them are based on something that I saw or heard, but much of it is fictionalised into bits of story-telling. I don't think there's a continuous story; I didn't see it as that, certainly. There are bits of narrative here and there, and maybe they do impinge upon one another. But the poems are based upon people I met or knew and just slightly built up into fictional characters.*

The Persian poet Hafiz, invoked in the first poem and appearing from time to time thereafter, serves as a kind of model, but did Morgan have a clear idea of its arrangement when he embarked upon the sequence?

[EM] *No, I didn't have a clear vision of what it was going to be like, it grew as it was written. I quite soon got the idea that it was going to be a hundred poems, but although it doesn't have much structure in an overall sense, it does have a beginning and an end, and I think the middle one is probably important in this respect: that was slightly arranged. But apart from that, I didn't want too much structure. I spent almost the whole of the war in the Middle East and got to know something about their arts, and this word Divan is used by them in ways not common with us. From its meaning as couch or sofa, the same word is also used for a council chamber. And the other meaning is a collection of poems. It's the same word and comes from the same meaning in that the poems are all sitting talking together, as it were, in these collections. They can sit where they like on these sofas, these divans, but there's something going on between each of these poems, there's some kind of mysterious conversation going on between them. In Middle Eastern Divan poetry they like this idea. They are not driven quite so hard as we in the West drive our readers. In things like, say,* The Divine Comedy *or* Paradise Lost *you are driven along and you can't escape. Of course you admire their structure, but once you get in there you've got to go on to the end. But in Divan poetry they say no; let people wander among the groves, play a flute, watch a fountain, meet someone and not see them again, that kind of thing. And yet they maintain that this poetry is not so chaotic as you may think. I*

*know it's chaotic in a way, but from that perhaps you get something
which you don't get from the more straightforward driving method.
This appealed to me, perhaps because of what we were saying about
the libertarian element in my writing. But I make a slight compro-
mise, because I do give it some structure: It's slightly Westernised,
it's not entirely of the East.*

If, then, we accept the invitation to wander through these poems,
we will see and hear sights and sounds of the desert and its characters, its towns and villages: meet an old man under a date-palm,
attend a banquet, witness a funeral or go to a bazaar:

> The power and the glory walked
> here? Buy some statuettes,
> blue and white, nothing looking
> blander ever shot from the mould. (p 316)

A mirage shimmers to fine effect:

> Paradise in prospect,
> after sand, after sand, after sand. Hungry
> for vision yet thirsty for water, we're gleaming
> sweaty ancient pilgrims that go softly
> past mirages. With
> thought withdrawn from emptiness
> a while, we watch the flickering meadows. (p. 328)

Trips to archaeological sites, or the experience of a camel-caravan
combine with images of futuristic import ('ships like peacocks/
spread vanes near Mars, wear out, become souvenirs'), to compose
an intertextual meditation on love and death, time and change. In
the stream of discourse that arises from the sands of the Middle
East, it becomes apparent that: 'Many and great delusions is the
history/ of the desert' (p. 306). Homosexual relationships ('not in
King's Regulations, to be in love') are recalled with comedy but also
with affection, while amid:

> Domes, shoeshines, jeeps, glaucomas, beads –
> wartime Cairo gave the flesh a buzz,
> pegged the young soul out full length. (p. 328)

The emotional infrastructure of an autobiography is elliptically plotted and pieced, and the sequence also comprises war poems:

> Swiftly
> the thud of land-mines brings confusion
> to the Canal. One star moves, drones. Position
> on a map's the universe. The night is Rommel's tree:
> searchlights cut it, history the secretion. (p. 328)

[EM] *Partly it was a kind of delayed war-poem. I never wrote my war-poem during the war. I tried, but I couldn't write a thing during those years. I must, though, have been storing up all sorts of images and memories. They came out during the seventies probably because the Middle East was in the news so much; it had become again a focus of interest, and these things came rushing back into my mind very strongly.*

One of the pleasures of this text is the way in which it composes its meditations on larger themes. Not religious in any accepted sense, as Morgan makes clear in the final poem:

> For you
> and me, the life beyond that sages mention
> is this life on a crag above
> a line of breakers (p. 330)

the sequence nonetheless reaches beyond its immediate contexts.

[EM] *I was in the desert for a large part of the war and in times like that it can be a dangerous and unpleasant place. But desert landscapes do give you long thoughts, you know. I felt very strongly the appeal which so many others have felt before me. There's no doubt, it lingers in the mind. If it's peaceful and you're out in the desert at night you certainly are aware of the vast extent of stars which in our islands you can hardly ever see. But the skies there are so clear, and so black; you can see all these constellations, and you have thoughts that are on the verge of what you might call religious. And while they're not exactly that, you can begin to understand why mono-theism – Islam after all means submission – did arise in those parts.*

The free-flowing structure of *The New Divan* seemed to relate more to developments in American poetry than to anything happening in England.

[EM] *I had enjoyed what the Beat Poets had done earlier, in the late fifties; I could see why they were reacting against academic poetry in America. Although it's another country and another tradition, Ginsberg, Corso and Ferlinghetti loosened up my way of looking at things. Robert Duncan, later, with* The Opening of the Field *[1969] made some kind of impact. I'd been writing in a fairly tight, perhaps rather rhetorical, somewhat old-fashioned kind of way until the mid-nineteen-fifties. Then after that I felt that there was some kind of liberation coming.*

Edwin Morgan's position in contemporary Scottish poetry has a number of differing facets, but across the arena of his various imaginings particular aspects recur. 'Ingram Lake or, Five Acts on the House' (1952) and 'The Whittrick: A Poem in Eight Dialogues', first published as a whole in 1973 but written in 1961, are early evidence of something that develops into a staple of Morgan's writing; the preferred form of the dialogue and monologue.

[EM] *I've always liked the idea of a poet being able not just to speak in his or her own voice, but to project into other kinds of existence. One of my earliest poems, written when I was still at school, fifteen or sixteen years old, was a poem like that. It was called 'The Opium Smoker' and was a study of a man dying of opium addiction in the Far East. I liked to imagine that character. He comes from the islands of Polynesia and ends up in some kind of Chinese opium den. So this kind of imaginative attention does go far back with me.*

His concern with the development of voices has produced a remarkable body of verse, and in 1986 Morgan drew upon this experience, and upon his interest in other media, for the construction of his sequence *From The Video Box*. The sequence is arranged in small groups, each treating different aspects of viewing, from scratch video to satellite broadcasting. In one way the poems can be read as an updated televisual version of *The Canterbury Tales*, presenting an electronic series of figures in a variety of cadences. What had drawn him to the idea?

[EM] *I began it from having watched the 'Right to Reply' programme on Channel Four Television and being interested in the method. Eventually I came to the conclusion that I would like to write something that would be a kind of equivalent in words but would be different in the sense that it opens the whole thing out*

*imaginatively. I wouldn't write about actual programmes: my
people would go into the box to talk about unreal or impossible
programmes, or something that isn't a programme at all. This
actually happens; television people would confirm that individuals
go into the video-box in Glasgow just to get something off their
chest. This, too, appealed to me. You mentioned Chaucer – I love
Chaucer, and I love presenting characters. I'm a kind of non-
dramatist dramatist: I don't write plays, but I've a strong dramatic
instinct. I like to dramatise everything, I do feel that. And in
presenting characters I try to make them as distinctive and real as I
can in a short space, to give them all the life I can. So you've twenty-
seven different people going into the box, and each one is meant to
be alive, so that you can actually see that person.*

The reader does see them, and the poems range from the hilarious to the disturbing. The first three, for example, record a sup-
porter of book-burning in ancient China, a horrified viewer of the
burning of the library at Alexandria, and a pompous librarian who
has just seen the British Library go up in flames. Whether it is a
camp male seeking help to find his lost cat or a macho Glaswegian
who not only exposes his erect penis for a wager, but draws
attention to an anatomical curiosity of which the 'lassies never
complain but', Morgan's ear for the turn of phrase and trick of
speech which typify individual utterance is impeccable.

Within this achieved plurality of address, one of Morgan's
voices roots itself recurrently in the city of his birth, to focalise
diverse forms of attention. The celebrated poem 'Glasgow Green'
takes Scottish poetry into areas it has normally shunned, dramatising a nightmarish incident of homosexual violence in its plea
for compassion, reclamation and renewal. Still exploring urban
terror, the 'Instamatic Poems' (1972) freeze with unnerving
realism such images of violence as a young couple being pushed
through a shop window which the hoodlums responsible then
proceed to loot:

> In the background two drivers
> keep their eyes on the road. (p. 217)

[EM] *When you live and grow up in a city you know it fairly
well: you know that there are, as in all large cities, dangerous parts,
dangerous times, and places that are best avoided. This was particu-*

larly true of the old Glasgow I grew up in, which is obviously
different from today in the sense that it was then very dark, with
sooty buildings and a great deal of fog. At night it was a sinister
place even around the city centre and the small streets that lead off
from it. It was quite Dickensian at night and that atmosphere was
part of it. And Glasgow, of course, still has its problems.

The sequence of ten 'Glasgow Sonnets' included in his 1973
volume *From Glasgow to Saturn* offers the fullest exploration of
this theme, with urban blight and economic decline creating contexts of deprivation for human misery. This is a grim emotional
landscape, which tests Morgan's ability to enter traditional form
and leave it cadenced with the brutish rhythms of modernity. The
third sonnet's tenement shark preying upon the homeless poor gives
the tone:

> 'See a tenement due for demolition?
> I can get ye rooms in it, two, okay?
> Seven hundred and nothin legal to pay
> for it's no legal, see? That's my proposition,
> ye can take it or leave it but. The position
> is simple, you want a hoose, I say
> for eight hundred pound it's yours.' (p. 289)

Explicit in a different direction, a sympathetic anger in the octet of
sonnet five, assesses the human cost of de-industrialisation:

> 'Let them eat cake' made no bones about it.
> But we say let them eat the hope deferred
> and that will sicken them. We have preferred
> silent slipways to the riveters' wit.
> And don't deny it – that's the ugly bit.
> Ministers' tears might well have launched a herd
> of bucking tankers if they'd been transferred
> from Whitehall to the Clyde. (p. 290)

The half-caught echo of obscene expletive in 'bucking' suggests an
effort at control, and the overall impact of driving corrosive matter
against precious form has been finely expressed by Douglas Dunn:
'"Glasgow Sonnets" especially creates an atmosphere in which each
poem feels like a verbal fist in which the immediacy and passion of

his concerns squeeze the form until its pips squeak.' He goes on to remark that 'some passages ... feel like revolutionary speeches delivered on the premises of a hostile terrain.'[14]

But when the impulse to self-government crashed in the Referendum fiasco of 1979, Edwin Morgan was moved to produce his most ambitious and accomplished sonnet-sequence to date. The fifty-one poems of *Sonnets From Scotland* (1984) construct a space-time continuum from Scottish pre-history to kinds of speculative future. I wondered whether for this undertaking he had any sense of its narrative form when he began.

[EM] *Only slightly, I think, though it has more structure than 'The New Divan' in that it has a time-sequence. The first one written was 'The Solway Canal' which was, obviously, connected with Scotland's identity and place, its reality or non-reality as a nation. And the idea of that, and what developed from it, was a reaction to 1979 and the failure of the Referendum to deliver any kind of an Assembly. There was a sense of political numbness after that. I had been hoping that there would be an Assembly, and the sense of let-down was very strong. But despite that, or maybe even because of it, the 1980s have been a very prolific period for Scottish writing, both in the novel and in poetry. I felt impelled to write a lot in the eighties and this sequence was the first fruits of that. It represents both a determination to go on living in Scotland, and a hope that there might be some political change. And to write about such things too.*

Though the volume includes intimations of future promise, a sense of disappointment is conveyed in sometimes harsh imagery with evocations of Scotland's primeval formation in the opening poem – 'drumlins black as bruises were grated off like nutmegs' – giving way to memories of crustaceans in the second, 'diving in the warm seas around Bearsden', and stumbling upon a nest of sharks lurking in the deep:

> They themselves were dark,
> but all we saw was the unsinister
> ferocious tenderness of mating shapes,
> a raking love that scoured their skin to shreds. (p. 437)

Following on from evolutionary developments in the 3rd, 4th and 5th sonnets, deep in the ancient forests of 'Silva Caledonia', the

sixth proposes a resurrected utterance for people the speaker cannot
see:

> Yet men,
>   going about invisible concerns,
>   are here, and our immoderate delight
>   waits to see them, and hear them speak, again. (p. 439)

The seventh draws upon an old Scottish legend to excavate the
theme of betrayal, with 'Pilate at Fortingall'.

If 'The Solway Canal' were ever to be constructed it would, like
the Caledonian canal further to the North, link western seaways to
the North Sea, but this time dividing Scotland along its border with
England. Futuristically, the sonnet so named takes us on a hydrofoil
journey along it, in the company of Southern incomers:

> a wizard with a falcon on its wrist
> was stencilled on our bow. (p. 455)

The image combines a suggestion of Viking invaders with a figure of
occult mastery. By a series of such oblique hints and insinuations
the sequence constructs a complex political testament. In the pre-
ceding sonnet, a similarly futuristic scenario is envisaged for the
discovery of a coin inscribed 'Respublica Scotorum'. The date has
been worn away where:

> as many fingers had gripped hard
> as hopes their silent race had lost or gained.
> The marshy scurf crept up to our machine,
> sucked at our boots. Yet nothing seemed ill-starred.
> And least of all the realm the coin contained. (p. 455)

Time is flowing both ways in this sequence, and the star of good
fortune shines to striking effect upon a vision of Glasgow as a city of
the future in 'Clydegrad' (p. 456).

Back in history, meanwhile, Scottish republicanism forges links
with an historic English counterpart in another sonnet, 'Thomas
Young, M. A. (St Andrews)' – the Scot who was John Milton's
tutor:

Yes, I taught Milton. He was a sharp boy.
He never understood predestination,
But then who does, within the English nation? (p. 442)

[EM] *I found it interesting that Milton was getting that kind of
Calvinism at such an early age. But I also had in mind Milton's
sonnets. I've always liked those sonnets, and think they're underrated.
He showed that you could use them for political purposes, so there's
something of that behind the sequence, too. I have, though, tried to
avoid the obvious trap of writing about the famous figures and events
of Scottish history. And when I do bring in a figure like Robert Burns,
*['Theory of the Earth' p. 443] *I put him in a new context, talking to
a famous geologist in Edinburgh. It may have happened, who
knows? But I liked the idea that there might be something between
them, which might not be seen by someone who just knows Burns.*
    Another character brought in is Edgar Allan Poe, who visited
Glasgow as a boy. The sonnet ends 'To Arnheim, boy, Arnheim!',
and the reference is to Poe's story 'In the Domain of Arnheim'.
    [EM] *The story is basically about landscape gardening, but when
Poe goes into landscape gardening it becomes something else; about
somebody going gradually into a very strange and beautiful landscape with wonders unfolding before his eyes. It stuck in my mind,
and it stuck in the mind of the Belgian surrealist René Magritte, who
has a painting called 'The Domain of Arnheim', so there you are!*
    Sonnets From Scotland is a rewarding experience. Morgan's
creation of conversational idiom seems to glide serenely through the
technical accomplishment of each sonnet and this is a mark of the
volume's distinction. The sequence becomes something of a paradigm for varied possibilities, where each text displays an integrity of
its own. They present us with a poetry of the democratic intellect, a
poetry whose open society of self-contained techniques proposes a
creative revolution in our expectations. When, in the final sonnet,
visitors from another planet register their reluctance to leave this
territory, the sequence connects traditional concerns of past sonnet-
cycles with its ambitions for a political awakening:

If it was love we felt, would it not keep,
and travel where we travelled? Without fuss
we lifted off, but as we checked and talked
a far horn grew to break that people's sleep. (p. 457)

Notes

1. Edwin Morgan, *Tales from Limerick Zoo* (Glasgow, 1988).
2. Quote from the back cover of *Themes on a Variation* (Manchester, 1988).
3. *Stand*, vol. 2, no. 3, p. 70.
4. Edwin Morgan, *Collected Poems* (Manchester, 1990), p. 25. Subsequent quotations are given parenthetically.
5. *Wi the Haill Voice: 25 Poems by Mayakovsky* (Manchester, 1972), translated into Scots by Edwin Morgan, p. 10.
6. Ibid. p. 10.
7. Ibid. p. 10.
8. Ibid. pp. 16–17.
9. Edwin Morgan, *Nothing Not Giving Messages* (Edinburgh, 1990), edited by Hamish Whyte, p. 222.
10. Ibid. p. 222.
11. *Nothing Not Giving Messages*, p. 162.
12. Michel Foucault, *The Archaeology of Knowledge* (New York, 1972), p. 23.
13. *Surrealism* (London, 1936), edited by Herbert Read, p. 175.
14. Douglas Dunn, 'Morgan's Sonnets', in *About Edwin Morgan*, (Edinburgh, 1990), edited by Robert Crawford and Hamish Whyte, pp. 75, 77.

An Impression of Continuity

GEORGE BRUCE

> To make a start
> out of particulars
> and make them general
> *William Carlos Williams:*
> *Paterson: Bk IV*

The opening poem of *Sea Talk*, 'A Song for Scotland', is in some respects uncharacteristic of the rest of the volume. It includes generalisation and political commentary, as its closing lines make clear:

> A song for Scotland this,
> For the people
> Of the clearances,
> For the dead tenements,
> For the dead herring
> On the living waters.
> A song for Scotland this.[1]

Yet in other ways it is typical of Bruce's procedures, with youthful memory responding to adult recapitulation. The opening line, 'A skull shoots sea-green grass from its sockets', startles natural life and continuity out of traditional *memento mori*, and echoes forward to an image-pattern which comprises a reflective sub-text for the working of Bruce's imagination. In 'Sea Talk: To a Buchan Fisherman' we read:

Here is the image of your skull.
Who will tell upon the shingle beach
Which the shell splinter and which the particle of the skull
long bleached by the flow and the ebb? (CP p. 12)

'Good Wishes for a Departure' begins:

Town now step into your heart –
From the fine white rabbit's skull
At the sea's edge, sea-beaten and wind searched
To the faces of men set by storm
And the hope of haven hereafter. (CP p. 50)

A retrieval of natural sculpture differently perceived, relates to the
crafting of sparsely structured poems, and as 'Song for Scotland'
proceeds, the parallelling of transience and decay with life and
survival is repeated:

The oar rots on the beach.
The skua breeds on the cliff. (CP p. 1)

But for a poetry avowedly of the North East, what was the
relevance of 'the people/ Of the clearances'?

[GB] *The first thing to say is that although that poem is placed
first in the book, it was actually the last one to be written, and so
was more reflective than the others. It incorporates a wider range of
imagery though they all have the threat of death in common. The
oar rotting on the beach – the boat lost and a useful implement left
to decay; and the skua – a sea-bird I saw in the Shetlands pursuing
other birds to make them disgorge the fish they had caught, which
was then consumed by the skua; it fed on carrion. The people of the
clearances had their way of life destroyed. The dead tenements
relates to the terrible unemployment at the time. 'The dead herring/
on the living waters' comes from something I saw, with my father,
and it hurt me more than anything, and him too. We had gone
down to the docks to see the boats come in laden with their fish, and
the price wasn't high enough. Whenever that happened, the skippers would take their boats out again and dump their catch back
into the sea. The hope was that this would drive up prices for the
next day's catch. But there's something else, too. Together with*

hymns from the Baptist Chapel next door to our house, the first communal singing I can remember hearing was in Gaelic. The majority of the gutters and packers of herring came from the western ports and Islands. They sang as they gutted the fish, which they sometimes did until late into the night. My father visited them in their homes in Stornoway or Mallaig: he knew about them and the history of the Highland people.

It was an unusual family background, and George Bruce, born in 1909 in the port of Fraserburgh on Scotland's exposed North East coast, is voluble with memories of it. His family controlled the oldest and one of the largest herring curing businesses in the area, and the Baptist Church next to which their house stood on Victoria Street had been built with the help of money given anonymously by his grandfather.

[GB] *Yes, he was a Baptist. It appears that around 1880–1890 he was worth a quarter of a million or so. None of which he told anyone. We lived sparingly while he was busy secretly building churches, and also contributing major funding to the building of the south pier at Fraserburgh, for the safety of the fishermen.*

In Bruce's recall of an organic community, his own family developed patterns of behaviour based upon a benevolent, paternalist capitalism. These provided a model for relatively humane social relationships which, although rendered obsolete by subsequent economic evolution, remained and remains a sustaining paradigm. Liberal in temper, Bruce's father encouraged his sons to explore their own potential, and actively promoted discussion of a wide range of ideas.

[GB] *Although we were living on the periphery, out on the edge of things up there in Fraserburgh, the sea takes you places. My grandfather had opened up trade with the Baltic, and at the age of ten my father was sent to Germany to learn the language. At home, all about me, were books, and I remember at about the age of eleven or so, next to my bed was the whole of Byron's poems. So at least I was well up on sexual things by the time I was twelve. On the same shelf were the Waverley novels, so I had read many of these by the age of thirteen, and Dickens and Lord knows what else.*

Bruce's second volume, *A Man Of Inconsequent Build*, introduces the Scots idiom which achieves continuing definition. The medium, though, is absent from *Sea Talk*, yet as a child Bruce had often heard Scots.

[GB] *There was absolutely no distinction made between speaking in Scots and speaking in English. Whenever the foreman came into the house, my father would speak naturally to him in the dialect of the area. Nobody ever said one was better than the other. In school and at home we generally spoke a variety of English: very differently accented, a different cadence and movement of the voice – one might call it a dialect of English. But in the playground and at all times with companions we spoke the Doric, that is to say Aberdeenshire Scots. There was, anyway, no discouragement of speaking Scots in the house at all. Bear in mind, too, that my mother used to sing a lot of Scots songs.*

What then were the problems associated with Scots that so inhibited Bruce at an early stage?

[GB] *To begin with, there was a total block because of the wide popularity of Charles Murray's verse. This was a mush in literary terms from my point of view, and at an early stage that became a serious barrier. Another reason was a feeling that Scots belonged to the country and not to the sea, that it was inward-looking and belonged to a shut-off place. Then, of course, I was brought up under the influence of F. R. Leavis, and Scots was just not a language of use. For a combination of these reasons, Scots was unavailable to me. And this remained the case until the 1950s by which time I had a changed attitude. Even though I had read MacDiarmid's Scots poems as early as 1932, it never entered my mind for one moment to write in Scots; not until I had several other situations under control, and when I found the need to do so. That need occurred at the point at which I was risking going beyond blunt statement, beyond the identification of the fact. It occurred after we came into the more settled climate following the war, when desperation, both public and personal, had lessened.*

This can be seen in a poem like 'Sumburgh Heid' where onomatopoeic display evokes turbulent seas around the southern tip of the Shetland Islands:

> Rummle an' dunt o' watter,
> Blatter, jinkin, teun an' rin –
> A' there – burst an' yatter
> Sea soun an muckle an' sma win
> Heich in a lift clood yokit. (CP p. 54)

It may be that the equal status accorded to English and Scots in his childhood home enabled the mingling within individual poems of dialect speech with standard English. 'Late Springs this North' inserts Doric chorus into English utterance, while 'The Island' weaves dialectal elements into a still dominant English.

But it seems beyond question that the significant poem for this aspect of Bruce's development is 'The Singers', which contrasts the decorums of Homeric allusion with the home-spun rhythms of regional dialect. Its opening invocation harks back to schoolroom memory.

[GB] *At school in the third year, I take Greek, and this is how the first Greek lesson begins, with the teacher saying '"Thalassa", that's a good word for the sea isn't it?' Of course we were all of us associated with the sea; in one way or another it virtually took over the whole of our lives. So I came to read the Greek account of how Xenophon's army got lost and had to ask for directions. When they finally came to the sea again, with one great voice the Greek army shouted 'O Thalassa! Thalassa!' At the same time, remember, our schoolteacher is telling us how good and significant is our own word 'sea' – that sea we all piddled in and took so much for granted.*

In the poem, this previously unsuspected relationship between the mundane and everyday and Classical inscription emerges:

> We did not know that our sea, debauched
> by old men's pilferings, sullied by piddling boys,
> Was not unsimilar to Homer's ocean,
> Our bitter, treacherous coast reminiscent.
> We did not know the music of the Ancient World
> Whispered with its spindrift at our back door,
> offered its strange acclamation with wintry thunderings
> For all who would hear.

The marine equivalence is one parallel being drawn; another connects domestic rhythms of Scots song with Homer's preferred metaphor for the new day breaking:

> *Hist ye, Meg, the baited lines*
> *And hist ye, lass, ma s'wester.*

> 'The rosy-fingered dawn' – we had no eyes for the dawn –
> And the music was there waiting. (CP p. 62)

These connections are registered, now, in terms of celebration:

> Here a land of rock and little soil
> But held from the invader.
> What is won with difficulty is twice ours
> And twice over again worthy of song,
> And the songs are with the black capped tern
> On the wide waters and with the swinging gull
> in the rebuffed wind. (CP p. 63)

By 1977, when he wrote 'Scots Bard', 'Scots Haiku', and 'Urn Burial: (R.I.P. Scots Tongue)', song-worthiness is accepted: the deployment of comic irony speaks with an established security and a confidence of voice:

> It wis hardly worth peying for
> a casket,
> the body wis that peelie-wallie,
>
> nae bluid in't
> luikit like a
> scrap o' broun paper
>
> papyrus mebbe?
> nae gran eneuch
> for that.[2]

Bruce used Scots, too, for a series of poems about paintings, most of which hang in the National Gallery of Scotland. As preamble to the series, 'An Interview With Rembrandt' achieves comic effect by using standard English for the interviewer and Scots for Rembrandt's replies, with English posing questions of abstract, metaphysical import and the painter answering in such a down-to-earth way as to leave the interrogator bemused and uncomprehending: 'There was a pause./ I could hear heavy breathing./ I thought he might have been a little more revealing.' (P p. 44). In contrast, the Scots of 'Rembrandt in Age' can express a sense of wonder stripped of affectation, while 'The Nichtwatch' registers the extraordinary presentation of ordinariness:

They cam in tae get pentit, bleat wi' pride,
padded burghers – ('burghers' did ye say?
Weel let it staun at that the whiles.')
Rembrandt gets on wi the wark. (P p. 46)

Why bring Scots into play with a Dutch Master?
[GB] *First of all, Scots is much nearer to Dutch than English is.
It's quite astonishing what you can do with Scots in Holland. So
there's something approaching almost a natural congruity. And
apart from that there's the sheer desirability of the homely quality
in Rembrandt. For such purposes Scots is infinitely warmer
than English. Because of that achievable intimacy, Scots does the
job in a way that English just couldn't; and it also has something
of a texture of roughness that is an added advantage for such a
subject.*

This is the East coast with winter
Written into its constitution
And so is productive of men
Who do not wait for good
In case there is none. (CP p. 76)

It was, however, with his English verse that George Bruce caught
critical attention. Its direct and immediate identification with place
elicited a chorus of approval. For Kurt Wittig, 'It is hard as the
rocky foreshores of Bruce's home',[3] and John Speirs sees it as being
'distinguished by a bareness, an asceticism, a tautness and terseness
of diction and rhythm.'[4] Considering its geographic area of origin,
Roderick Watson agrees that 'its clear light and its harsh coast are
reflected in the linguistic austerity which [Bruce] chose for his first
collection, *Sea Talk.*[5] We know that Bruce is attracted to 'a spare
language trusting that it gathers to itself more than the statement it
evidently makes', and Alan Bold, who quotes this remark, goes on
to say that the poems 'are taut with the tensions of the sea-town'.[6]
John Speirs is of the same opinion. 'These poems are not in Scots
and yet they are not English poetry; they could not be more distinctively Scottish. They are the way a particular Scotsman talks, individually so, the talk of one born and bred a Scotsman of a particular
locality, the North East Seaboard.'[7]

My house
Is granite
It fronts
North,

Where the Firth flows,
East the sea.
My room
Holds the first

Blow from the North,
The first from East,
Salt upon
The pane. (CP p. 3)

Yet this stripped, unadorned utterance turns to an expression of love at the close of the poem, and Bruce has written elsewhere that 'one could not praise in terms of the exploited and commercialised language of the "heart", nor could I come to terms with the introverted interests of the Aberdeenshire dialect, which had become a vehicle for the cosy nostalgia of Charles Murray. I began with the laconic statement of "My House".'[8]

[GB] *This was the first poem, and the others in* Sea Talk, *written around 1940 have the same line-length. At that time I was in a deep despair. Through the 1930s I saw the certainty of war coming, and I didn't see it simply as Hitler's war. I saw it as the inevitable culmination of the political immorality of what was going on in Britain – the neglect of the unemployed among other things. Having been brought up in a vital community in the North East, and having been sustained by that community, now I was feeling that I was nothing. The poem came out of a necessity to hold despair at bay, because of the utter misery I was feeling then. The initial impulse was a determination not to go mad. So. It is 1939–40 and I am a teacher in Dundee High School. I love teaching but the conditions under which I am teaching are absolutely intolerable. It is December and I come out of the school into the dark to catch my train home. It's the black-out, remember, and a man stumbles towards me, drunk. Then a woman offers herself to me, and I just think 'The Waste Land'. On the train I find myself stopped from attempting to write another 'Waste Land' – indeed I had begun. Absolutely*

*stopped. I don't believe I have ever felt at a lower ebb in my life.
Then I realise that I am writing these words – 'My house/ Is granite/
It fronts/ North'. I was able to feel 'there is reality in this – there is
reality in my house.' In my desperation the firmest image I could
come up with was stone.*

One of the models for Bruce had been the lyrics of William
Carlos Williams and, in particular, Williams's insistence upon keeping his eye firmly upon the object in view and borrowing no word
from either left or right of it.

[GB] *I was drawn by the decisive limitations Williams put upon
himself, the discipline he placed himself under.*

Disparaging the coining of similes, Williams remarks 'it is in
things that for the artist the power lies, not beyond them.'[9] As
Paterson was later to proclaim:

> – Say it, no ideas but in things –
> nothing but the blank faces of the houses
> and cylindrical trees[10]

[GB] *I had become entirely distrustful of anything that smacked
remotely of Romanticism. In fact I had become distrustful to such
an extent that at this stage I could hardly believe in any objective
reality outwith myself. But we did indeed live in a granite house,
and even now I can remember the wind howling like mad around it.
It took this traumatic experience of going down into total despair to
set something going, for me to tap into something and know, 'This
is it.' Then I knew, technically, what I had to do.*

If the value of Carlos Williams in this process is self-evident,
it seems reasonable to speculate that in addition, at a time of
profound psychological depression, Bruce was also reaching back
into memories of his own childhood for support and inspiration.
Remembering the child he once was, Bruce has written: 'He sought
for objects which defined themselves, which had their own independent existence, which could be seen and touched, as could the
herring scales, which became fixed in the mat after my father had
come in from the yard, where the herring were cured, with the scales
on the soles of his boots.'[11]

[GB] *It's all due to Pound and William Carlos Williams, who
gave me the means. I knew perfectly well that behind me lay these
two, and it didn't matter terribly. The first thing that Pound taught*

me was that it was possible to make poetry out of very unpoetic material. He showed me that you can sensitize that kind of material in such a way that it becomes poetry. It certainly wasn't his philosophy that appealed to me, but I could admire his technique.

Of Bruce's poem 'The Sculptor' T. S. Halliday writes, 'we encounter an imagery foundational for his own aesthetic: 'The man who handles/ Bronze, clay, wood, stone,/ Praises the durable,/ Makes marble the moment.' (CP p. 29)

> My father came home,
> His clothes sea-wet,
> His breath cold.
> He said a boat had gone. (CP p. 4)

In an autobiographical essay Bruce remarks upon the line 'He said a boat had gone', and goes on to explain that it 'had already been purified, not by the poet, but by a community which required a spare, athletic language for survival's sake, and in this case words which would convey terrible news quickly and with a minimum of emotion. Such a phrase puts the writer in the right place, that is to say out of the way so that the light can shine through the words, so that the thing itself speaks.'[12] It becomes a curiosity, then, that Bruce's style is generally accepted as being particularly appropriate to the North East, yet its existential formation springs from a clearly remembered and all but destructive angst at a specific time. Had he been aware of its literary definition of locality when he first wrote?

[GB] *A problem with this is that up there it didn't exist before me in English. Up there, too, the general reaction was that my writing was foreign to them, that my poetry was not poetry. So perhaps inevitably, it seems to me that the kind of reaction that people now have of the North East, through my poetry, is in a peculiar way a recognition of my poetry. But let's look at it the other way round. There is the most remarkable and clarifying light in and around the North East of Scotland. The reasons for this are elementary – the micaceous granite in the buildings, the vast sea, all of this creates a most intense brightness. So while my poetry is not true to the literature of the North East which preceded it, it is true to the actual facts of the area. There is of course the other factor that in a sea-born life of fishing you have to speak quickly and clearly – you might otherwise drown. Perhaps we all hammered out our conso-*

nants because otherwise you might not be heard. Anyway it was
part of the way we spoke the language.

There is in this earlier work a pattern of tensions between a
desire to put down 'the thing itself' without adornment, and an
expression which resonates beyond that simplicity. At times this can
strike out a music plangently at odds with popular impressions of
Scotland's traditions:

> This is the land without myth –
> From the crown of this low hill
> To the useful country receding East
> To the rectangular towns we have built;
> Coast towns, granite pavemented, with drinking troughs
> For the animals, electric standards, kiosks,
> Large gasometers and excellent sanitation. (CP p. 10)

[GB] *In fairness, it should be said that it was a land without*
myth. There were very few myths. In the land to which those
fishermen return, there aren't any giants. In order to keep alive
you've got to keep your eyes on the facts: otherwise you die. It is
brute reality on both the sea and the land. People died making a
road across Buchan, because of the bog that it was. Everything had
to be won. We had no time for myths.

> Here are neither mountains nor dark valleys
> Here the shadow's length is man, or the tree
> That is his, or the house he has built.
> Years back the stones were lifted from the fields,
> The animals driven to their holes, the land drained.
> Dug, planted, the ground pieced out.
> The heather was beat. The crop grew
> On the hill, The paths were trod.
> The land was peopled and tilled.
> This is the land without myth. (CP p. 11)

Alexander Scott pointed out that while the last line quoted is
repeated six times in the poem, the one verse paragraph it does not
conclude is the one concerning the sea.[13] At least in that area of
promise and endeavour, mythic potential is acknowledged:

> The crab scuttles on the sea floor,

> Hook dangles, net opens to the tide,
> The boat's keel is still or moves
> With the greater water movement.
> Between the thumb and the first finger
> The weighted line. (CP p. 10)

[GB] *Again, though, you can see in 'A Land Without Myth' a kind of continuing mistrust, where even adjectives are suspect. But the identification of the object in that curiously dramatic way relates itself to Duns Scotus, and to Vico.*

Duns Scotus has an immediate relevance to Bruce's work, and is remembered with academic humour in one of the poems inspired by a visit to Australia:

> 'As Duns Scotus said,' said the Prof.
> 'objects may possess individualities
> peculiar to themselves. This thisness,
> haecceitas, should be a central interest
> in your papers. Evidences are expected
> as witness to your conclusions. (P p. 5)

The poem 'De Stael's Wall', with its opening: 'Fact. Registration', had earlier testified to the power and dominance of the fact:

> Yet you achieve object, that, no more:
> object achieved – wall. Finished
> as you were in the fictive act –
> to make order. (CP p. 96)

But the influence of the Italian philosopher Giambattista Vico seems both deeper and more extensive. A fundamental principle of his, known as the verum-factum principle, held that people know only what they make. 'The true is precisely what is made.'[14] This would have an obvious appeal, given the nature of Bruce's writing. But Vico exercises a wider pull on the Scotsman's imagination.

[GB] *Vico's holism, his notion of society as an organism, was an endless concern of mine. That idea, I realised later, had been an influence all through my childhood years at home. There's a passage in Vico which I encountered many years ago in a book by Sam Beckett.* [Reading from Beckett's Introduction] 'Giambattista Vico

*was a practical roundheaded Neapolitan.... His treatment of the
origin and function of poetry, language and myth ... is as far
removed from the mystical as it is possible to imagine.*'[15]

In 'Sea Talk: to a Buchan Fisherman', Bruce explores Vico's
notion of organic metaphor, linking human and natural activity in a
variety of ways:

> Night holds the past, the present is manifest in day,
> In day activity, but night shuts the door –
> And within the mind hints of your old powers,
> Recollections of your associate, the sea. (CP p. 12)

A pattern of imagery integrates the human and the elemental: 'Sea
gives tongue to greater/ Fears'. We witness the East wind 'Disclosing
the stone ribs of the earth' and watch the sycamore's 'dwarf fingers'
bend to the west, while:

> The kirk looks graceless, a block house
> to defy the last snort of winter,
> The house shouldering the sea. (CP p. 14)

Gradually a linguistic construction of organic relationships, domin-
ted by the sea, is defined:

> Between these your feet are shaped, your hands helped
> By water, pebble, cliff and sky.
> Blue rocks nose above the sand about your feet,
> Feet expert and attentive to the ship's swing.
> Your hands like women's in their dexterity,
> Never fumble needle or net, rope or wheel.
> The small words of sea talk, the mumbling
> and knocking at the little boat's side. (CP pp. 14–15)

Elsewhere, Vico suggests that 'the nature of institutions is nothing but their coming into being at certain times and in certain
guises'. George Bruce, writing at a time when he had no confident
sense of his own identity, inclines towards a similar sense of his own
formation, in the poem 'Inheritance':

> This which I write now
> Was written years ago
> Before my birth
> In the features of my father.
>
> It was stamped
> In the rock formations
> West of my hometown.
> Not I write,
>
> But, perhaps William Bruce,
> Cooper.
> Perhaps here his hand
> Well articled in his trade. (CP p. 2)

Counter-balancing this tendency towards a sometimes biographical historicism, another life-long attention of Bruce's has been a celebration of the moment, intimating not only evanescence but also permanence:

> Bone, cheek, all tangible,
> All touched by time,
> Touched by the sculptor's art
> Make marble the moment. (CP p. 29)

If 'Two Love Stories' ends with a hope that memory can make it possible 'to find the moment of making/ where there is neither time nor place', (CP p. 86) 'Butterfly' concludes with 'Every moment is goodbye to every moment/ but the beam of the mind holds butterfly.' (CP p. 84)

[GB] *I think it's something to do with the urge to stop time. Perhaps that is what every good work of art or poem does. Because of my acute sense of the fragility and transience of life, it is the moment's durability that attracts…. When you create a poem, it seems to me, though it is an enlargement, nevertheless it is a single moment that is being celebrated.*

In Bruce's 1987 collection, *Perspectives*, though there is, as 'The Witness' put it, 'an impression of continuity' (P p. 61) with his earlier work, a sense of enlargement is also registered in a greater willingness to expand in narrative. The four poems which compose

'The Desert: for Hugh MacDiarmid' are evidence of this. Described by Bruce as 'a furiously anti-political poem because of the way politicians fragment and cheat on life', the detail and conviction of the poem's fourth section show him occupying different territory. And there is a similar extension in the 1986 poem which grew out of a visit to Australia, 'Aborigine with Tax Form'. But as the poem meditates upon the Aboriginal naming of an environment, we are carried back to Bruce's earlier work:

> 'Warringin' – wild dog, the teeth are bared
> in the word: dried grit, sharp stone in the word,
> and the land stretches its bone in an eternity of distance.
>
> (P p. 64)

[GB] *When I was in Australia, one of the people I met was an aborigine whose surname was Watson. Her grandfather was a Scot. She told me about the experience of aborigines in Australia, and I told her about Gaeldom in Scotland. That encounter forms part of what lies behind the poem.*

Notes

1. George Bruce, *Collected Poems* (Edinburgh, 1971), p. 1. Subsequent references are marked CP and given parenthetically.
2. George Bruce, *Perspectives: Poems 1970–1986* (Aberdeen, 1987), p. 77. Subsequent references are marked P and given parenthetically.
3. Kurt Wittig, *The Scottish Tradition in Literature* (Edinburgh, 1958), p. 301.
4. John Speirs, *The Scots Literary Tradition* (London, 1940) 2nd edition, 1962, p. 17.
5. Roderick Watson, *The Literature of Scotland* (London, 1984), p. 432.
6. Alan Bold, *Modern Scottish Literature* (London, 1983).
7. Speirs, loc. cit.
8. *As I Remember* (London, 1979), edited by Maurice Lindsay, p. 27.
9. Ibid, p. 234.
10. William Carlos Williams, *Paterson: Books I–V* (New York, 1963), p. 14.
11. *As I Remember*, p. 26.
12. George Bruce, 'Words of a Poet', p. 5.
13. Alexander Scott, 'Myth-Maker: The Poetry of George Bruce', *Akros*, vol. 10, no. 9, pp. 37–8.

14. Giambattista Vico, *On the Most Ancient Wisdom of the Italians, Unearthed from the Origins of Latin Language* (New York, 1988), translated by L. M. Palmer, p. 46.
15. Samuel Beckett, *Our Xagmination Round his Factification for Incamination of Work in Progress* (Paris, 1929), p. 4.

Unlocking Time's Labyrinth

GEORGE MACKAY BROWN

> To the mind's eternity I turn,
> With leaf, fruit, blossom on the spray
> See the dead world grow green within
> Imagination's one long day.
> *Edwin Muir*

An introductory note to George Mackay Brown's 1989 collection *The Wreck of the Archangel* proposes that a thematic recurrence of voyages should not be surprising. 'Orkney lay athwart a great seaway from Viking times onwards, and its lore is crowded with sailors, merchants, adventurers, pilgrims, smugglers, storms and sea-changes. The shores are strewn with wrack, jetsam, occasional treasure.'[1] Connections between Orkney's geographical position and Viking expeditions from an earlier epoch articulate a history, both maritime and agricultural, have focused Brown's attention from the beginning. Combining myth, history, legend and personal memory, he probes the roots and origins of the Orcadian community. His poetry takes inspiration from and weaves variations upon, *Orkneyinga Saga,* the medieval chronicle in which Orkney is the central place of action. According to its most recent translators, the Saga has a special significance for the people of Orkney, 'having become ... what might be called their secular scripture, inculcating in them a keener sense of their remote forbears and sharpening their awareness of a special identity'.[2]

Given his religious cast of mind, Brown might warm to poetry as secular scripture. He has written of folklore that it is an attempt 'to

come to terms with certain mysterious matters in a people's surroundings and circumstances.'[3] 'Mystery', from its original Greek
suggestion of religious ceremony, retains that connotation in the
medieval 'Mystery Plays', also based upon scripture. It is appropriate that religious references attached to legendary and historical
event and personality should form a back-drop for Brown's work,
given that the *Saga* introduces Christian redemption into the world
of pagany. In the words of its latest editors, the *Saga*, like a great
deal of such medieval history, 'deepens the sense of continuity by
pushing back into a mythic or legendary past'.[4] That, too, would
hold particular attractions for Brown, in whose writing a mythicising tendency is evident.

[GMB] *I think the Sagas involve the basics of narrative. All the
essential structures of narrative are there. Any other kind of writing
is an elaboration on their simple, streamlined way of telling a story,
without lengthy descriptions of characters, and with everything
superfluous stripped away. I liked that very much. My own writing
is much more decorative than that, but I think that must come from
the Celtic element in me. I'm sure it does.*

Born in 1921 in the small sea-port of Stromness on the south-west
of mainland Orkney, George Mackay Brown has not often ventured
into the wider world. He did, though, in 1951 go for a year to
Newbattle Abbey, a residential adult education college near Edinburgh. Edwin Muir was then warden, and the encounter was important for Brown's advancement as a poet.

[GMB] *He gave me great encouragement. When we were there
we had to write a monthly essay: it could take any form, it could be
a poem, a story, anything really, and Edwin was very helpful. In
fact he sent one or two of the poems I sent him to magazines like the*
New Statesman *and* The Listener. *I wouldn't have done it myself,
but Edwin did it. One of them* ['The Exile'[5]] *was published, and
that was a great thrill of course. I write very differently from him
and it was tremendous having his support at that early stage.*

Though poor health made things difficult, Brown returned to
Newbattle in 1956 prior to entering Edinburgh University in the
same year. He graduated in 1960, and returned two years later to
spend time as a graduate student working on the poetry of Gerard
Manley Hopkins.

[GMB] *It was an immediate, instinctive attraction. It was the new way that he did things, and the strangeness and vividness of it.*

In 'Pied Beauty', Hopkins sees the glory of God in Creation's variety, in a 'landscape plotted and pieced – fold, fallow, and plough;/ And all trades, their gear and tackle and trim.'[6] These terms of celebration exert a natural and continuing appeal. Occasionally, a line appears in a Brown poem which might take its impetus from the nineteenth-century Jesuit: 'Hoof-fast Njal bore his manseed wombfurled waveward'.[7]

In his sprung-rhythm reconstructions of Old English, Hopkins at times used its alliterative patterning, and Brown, too, will rework Anglo-Saxon cadence: 'Fareth a shadow to the ghostly feast-halls.' (FP p. 6). The opening poem in *Fishermen with Ploughs*, 'Building the Ship', is a case in point:

> Logs throttled a mountain torrent.
> A goatherd gaped on the lumbering tons.
> Saws shrieked, sputtered, were sharpened, sang.
> Dunes were pale with strewment of boards.
> Seaward a keel was set.
> Sprang from that spine a vibrant cluster of ribs.

[GMB] *I read Anglo-Saxon at Edinburgh and I liked it very much – after I got over the initial difficulties. But* Beowulf *and other poems like* The Seafarer *and* Deor, *I was very interested in. I was quite taken by it all. We had to do it as undergraduates, and I approached it with some dread. I remember I wasn't looking forward to it because I'm a rather lazy person, and I don't like to exert myself. But I just had to apply myself, and once I got into the grammar, I think I enjoyed that part of the course better than anything else. It was a wonderful feeling of getting right down into the roots of words and language.*

Given this feel for linguistic origination, were there any ways in which his own poetry related to the world of Gaelic writing?

[GMB] *I never think about these things at all, though I know there must be a Celtic influence through my mother who was a Gaelic speaker from the North of Scotland, and I'm sure some of her mental attitudes and the whole culture of that ancestry has come into me somehow unconsciously. I know it's there, right enough, in the imagery and so on, but I never consciously think about it.*

And poetry in Scots?

[GMB] *Of course, they don't speak Scots here, really, though naturally there are quite a few Scots words. But the language derives originally from Scandinavian and Icelandic. It's all been filtered since through the English language, but it retains quite a few of those earlier characteristics. You see, Scotland only came into Orkney's story fairly late, around 1497, when Orkney was incorporated into Scotland. So we don't feel entirely Scottish. It's a very different history we have here.*

Brown's myth-inspired interpretations sometimes reveal a contemporary Orkney, but the world of modern development is not something that appeals to his imagination at all.

[GMB] *I think it's ruined Orkney life, though it has improved it materially and financially. The people have never been better off in those terms, but something has gone out of their speech and their character. Although this might just be an old man talking, when I was a boy and then a young man, Stromness was full of what we call characters, individuals with their own quirks and eccentricities – very marked, some of them. But that seems to be quite ironed out now. Everybody is striving to be as like his neighbour as he can be: so that's gone from contemporary Orkney life. Or at least, it seems to have gone. But it's maybe just that I'm a recluse and I don't see as many people as I used to.*

How, then, does he account for the fact that in his portrayal of Orkney life, many of his characters are also memorably constructed from the present?

[GMB] *I don't know; but it might be because the contemporary part of my poetry isn't set in contemporary Orkney at all, in which I find very little that is poetic. It's always set in my childhood, when I was maybe twelve or fifteen years old. It's always seen in the 1920s or 1930s; pre-Second-World-War, anyway, because then everything was very vivid and alive. The whole community seemed to be vibrant in a way that it isn't now. But that, too, as I say, might just be an old man talking. I do have a vivid memory, I suppose, and when I was a boy I used to love to listen to the old men talking in that speech, and the women too. And I still remember it vividly. Yet I can't remember what they said along the street yesterday nearly so well. I think what I do is go back to a child's memory and a child's experiences. What you get is an older man remembering a child's experiences.*

Writing in 1940, Edwin Muir recalled: 'The Orkney I was born into [in 1887] was a place where there was no great distinction between the ordinary and the fabulous; the lives of living men turned into legend.' Mermaids were sighted and fairies seen dancing. 'There was no harm in them,' Muir remembers, but 'all these things have vanished from Orkney in the last forty years under the pressure of compulsory education.'[8] Brown is similarly drawn towards characters for whom the magical was still a living possibility.

Under 'Harpoonist', in 'Runes from a Holy Island', we read:

> He once riveted boat to whale.
> Frail-fingered now
> He weaves crab prisons.[9]

Seventeen syllables here suggest an affinity with Japanese haiku, which influenced modernist poetics, and elsewhere the semantic compression achieved in Brown's runic practice gives modernist emphasis to sometimes ancient matter. Yet the rune, originally often the simplest of devices as far as the words used were concerned, and employed from about the fourth century A.D. for inscriptions on such things as weapons, coins, or memorial stones, occurs in Anglo-Saxon poetry as well as Scandinavian and Icelandic sagas. So although Brown's adaptations often relate to modern perceptions, they form a design of scripted continuities. Traditionally associated with incantation and magical practice, the word rune itself meant 'whisper' or 'mystery'. 'Indeed', Brown once remarked, 'what is a poem or a carving on a stone? It was, originally, a spell to make the corn grow, to lure fish into the net; beauty and utility were one.' (PO p. 48). We watch him conscripting these associations into the service of Christian ritual:

> Easter
> Friday, dayspring, a pealing cockerel.
> Haul west, fishermen,
> With flushed violent mouths. (PNS p. 34).

Verbal compression springs its own surprises as the betrayal of Christ by Peter, fisher of men, connects with Orkney fishermen at their redemptive labours on subsequent Good Fridays. But additionally we see Brown extending runic effect into Christian transformation, with metaphor speaking miracle directly:

Saint
   A starved island, Cormack
   with crossed hands,
   Stones become haddock and loaf. (PNS p. 34)

Cormack's miraculous benediction here intimates Christ's administration of the biblically few loaves and fishes to feed thousands.
   But runes also have a specifically Orcadian relevance.
   [GMB] *A rune is an inscription incised on stone, very brief and
laconic: you find them all over Scandinavia. And in Orkney here,
too, especially inside the burial chamber at Maeshowe, where the
walls are covered with them. In 1151, I think it was, some of the
Norwegian sailors who were going to Rome and Jerusalem on Earl
Rognvald's famous pilgrimage, spent a night inside Maeshowe as a
kind of feat of derring-do. They were very forceful, these characters;
they weren't afraid of ghosts or anything like that. But they spent
the time incising very brief poems on the walls: things like 'Ingibjorg
is the most beautiful of the women', and 'Many a proud lady has
come in here low-stooping' – because it was a burial chamber.
Those are examples of runes.*
   In a contrary direction, Kenningar in Skaldic verse were originally more like conceitful thought. Brown explained:
   [GMB] *A kenning is just an elaborate way of saying things. We
were speaking about the laconic nature of Icelandic narrative, but
they have poems too, in quite an opposite mode. They would find
every roundabout way of saying things. The sea was 'the whale's
acre', or 'the swan's path'. And the more ingenious the way of
describing a simple thing, the more highly it was thought of.*
   Perhaps because it appeals to what he has described as the Celtic
element in his make-up, the kenning seems often to be a preferred
construction. 'The Sea: Four Elegies' includes the examples cited
above, and continues:

   She is the Garden of White Roses.
   She is the Keeper of Horses.
   (the Loom also, the Harp with a thousand voices.)
   She is the Giver of Salt and Pearls.
   The Vikings, her closest children, hated the sea.
   She summoned them, twice a year, from plough and love bed.
   They called her, with cold mouths, the Widow Maker.[10]

In 'Stations of the Cross: Nine Variations', the eighth poem, 'Creator', composes a litany which combines kenning elements with biblically-derived liturgical address:

> He is the Pitcher at the fountain.
> He is the Winter Tree dragged by a peasant.
> He is Flax and Wheel and fold of linen. (W p. 54)

Brown's constant search for the sacramental aspects in life and his inclination towards ritualised utterance both find inspiration in the Roman Catholicism to which he converted in 1961. From his mid-teens, he was intrigued by Catholicism's 'majesty and history: the long history of the church from that stark beginning, that incredibly endured through the changing centuries, always adapting itself; enriched by all that poetry and music, art and architecture could give; and still apparently as strong as ever in our grey twentieth century'.[11]

[GMB] *Catholicism is full of material for poets. It's a huge quarry of very rich and beautiful imagery; especially the Mass which is in a way a kernel of all life. I think they've spoiled it with the modern liturgical translations, using thin, flat, modern English.*

Loaves and Fishes (1959), precedes his conversion yet, as its title indicates, is imbued with Christian symbolism. Its opening poem, 'Old Women', connects the Daughters of Jerusalem who 'bewailed and lamented' Christ, with the women of Orkney, while 'The Masque of Bread' invokes central transformations in Christian belief:

> The bread lay broken,
> Fragmented light and song.
> When the first steeple
> Shook out petals of morning, long bright robes
> Circled in order round the man that died. (LF p. 13)

Each poem in the volume calls up a Christian environment of image and symbol, as though in the writing of the book Brown were feeling his way to the coming conversion.

[GMB] *I had thought about it for a long time. It wasn't a sudden jump by any means; it had been pondered for a decade or more.* So the ceremonial aspect was a conscious element in his poetry?

[GMB] *I suppose so, vaguely, yes. It's a part of my mental make-up, and I can't get away from that.*

In *Chapman*, in 1976, Brown described the parable of the sower and the seed as one which illuminated the whole of life.

> It made everything simple and marvellous. It included within itself everything from the most primitive breaking of the soil to Christ himself, with his parables of agriculture and the majestic symbolism of his passion, and death, and resurrection. 'I am the bread of life.' 'This is my body that is broken for you.' That image has a universal meaning for me, especially when I can stand among ripening fields all summer. You will find it at the heart of many of my stories and poems.[12]

Indeed, there is a frequent elevation of the mundane into the parabolic, the crofter into Christ.

> The small boats in the Sound
> Pluck this brightness and that from their nets,
> Our cow watched a black field in March,
> And the green tumults of summer.
> Today she cries over a sudden radiance,
> The clean death of corn.
> Christ, crofter, lay kindly on this white beard
> Thy sickle, flail, millstone, keg, oven ... (PNS p. 78)

As the crofter's labour makes corn serve life's various purposes, so Christ is invited to take and shape the human soul. In a similar procedure, though with greater complications of ritual effect, the final stanza of an earlier poem, 'Elegy', brings myth, death, and biblical narrative into conjunction:

> Now let those risers from the dead,
> Cornstalk, golden conspirators,
> Cry on the careless wind
> Ripeness and resurrection;
> How the calm wound
> Of the girl entering earth's side
> gives back immortal bread
> For the year's dust and rain that shall be man. (LF p. 40)

Brown construes a prayer-like language of exaggerated effect, often luminous and intense, yet also curiously direct, rooting itself in the everyday. As tides roll incessantly, 'the sea grinds his salt behind a riot of masks', (LF p. 14) and drunkenness is described as 'tranced with corn'.[13] To dig peat is to 'tear thick pages from the Book of Fire': (FP p. 40) when a downpour occurs, 'rain let down its silver enchanted walls'. (W p. 29). Of a drowned man, Brown writes: 'They unweave him, mackerel and gull' (W p. 42).

A further dimension in the ritualising of experience recurs in an almost addictive recourse to numbers.

[GMB] *I think that that part of my technique, in stories as well as in poems is to look, say, at an incident or character from seven different points of view, and slowly build them up from there. Seven seems for some reason to be an ideal number for that sort of thing. It's a very important number – the seven days of Creation, following the seven days of the week, and then such things as the seven deadly sins, the seven colours of the spectrum, the five loaves and two fishes of the miracle, the seven oceans and seven continents, Shakespeare's seven ages of man, and so on. It's a mystical sort of number and very practical at the same time, as the old Hebrews recognised when they made the seventh day one of rest.*

By combining these means and effects, everyday experience is transmuted. But this is not simply an idealisation of facts. The grim actualities of a sea-faring existence – consider the number of shipwrecks in Brown's poetry – as well as the violence of Viking depredations, are given due place and emphasis. So, too, is the daily grind of survival: 'I rent and till a patch of dirt/ Not much bigger than my coat.' (W p. 34). What is sought throughout is a resurrection of the human spirit within frequently hostile circumstance. Writing in praise of an account of Orkney's agricultural cycle and parish communal life in the nineteenth century, Brown remarks that in the book, 'labour in the fields was seen as a ritual, a ceremony, a dance of bread'.[14]

In *An Orkney Tapestry*, he describes how the stonemason made the Stations of the Cross for Rackwick's chapel:

> putting blue and red clay and egg-yolk among the shallow scratchings of fourteen stones, so that the passion of Christ along three walls of the church was like the year-long labour of a crofter from furrow to loaf-and-ale. The cross a ploughshare; Veronica a croft girl risen in pity from her spinning

wheel; lance and sword the harvest sickles; the flagellating flails, the grinding millstones and black oxen of execution; the last stone, tabernacle of birth and death and resurrection.

(OT p. 31)

Increasingly, the events of the Nativity become a poetic lode-stone, attracting different treatments. One aspect foregrounds t he innkeeper, who figures prominently in Brown's inclination to domesticate the account, giving it immediacy by introducing conversational cadence. 'King of Kings', (PNS pp. 29–32) is an example of this, and another is 'Bethlehem': 'Straw in the cowshed, that's all I can offer.' (W p. 10).

[GMB] *Yes, the innkeeper does come into several of the poems. I was always fascinated by this part of the Nativity story – why the innkeeper sent them down into his byre or stall below the inn, and whether he was a mean, grasping man. Because his inn would have been very busy, since the tribe of David were coming in to register for what I suppose was some kind of poll tax. I was always interested as a child by the business people in the town, I mean the shopkeepers and the people who dealt in trade and money. And the innkeeper was based upon my memory of them. Besides which, because of my love of beer in my younger days, I got to know many inn-keepers.*

By the time of *Wreck of the Archangel*, Orkney is construed as a possible location for the birth of Jesus. 'The Twelve Days of Christmas: Tinker Talk' ends:

I thought I heard a night cry, a bairn
poorer than me.
A white dream, surely,
...
I saw the shepherds. One
Folded a shivering lamb.
They lingered at the door of the inn.
...
We took plans and mirrors to Hamnavoe.
Three foreign skippers,
The pier heaped with bonded cargoes. (WA p. 96)

As the biblical metamorphosis of God into man is given Orcadian context, Brown's 'Orkney Saga' develops and extends the

potential of myth. The ease with which legend merges into fact seems
to blur boundaries, uniting different modes of perception. Particular words echo from poem to poem, as in a traditional hymnal.
'Bread', 'cornstalk', 'seed', 'honey', 'furrow', 'plough', 'ship', 'whale',
'cuithe', 'ale', and 'jar and tapestry and gold' are examples of such
verbal texturing. 'Harp' is particularly useful in this respect, since it
is a way of not saying 'psalm', defined alternatively by the OED as a
plucking of the strings of the harp, a song sung to the harp, or any
song of a sacred character. Devolving from biblical precedent, each
of these usages is germane to Brown's practice at one time or
another. Coupled with his attraction to the kind of verbal elaboration associated with the Skaldic kenning, these repetitions intimate
a harmony within and beyond each poem.

A comment made in another context speaks relevantly to this
element in the writing:

> It is the word, blossoming as legend, poem, story, secret, that
> holds a community together and gives meaning to its life. If
> words become functional ciphers merely, as they are in white
> papers and business letters, they lose their 'ghosts' – the rich
> aura that has grown around them from the start, and grows
> infinitesimally richer every time they are spoken. They lose
> more; they lose their 'kernel', the sheer sensuous relish of
> utterance. Poetry is a fine interpenetration of ghost and ker-
> nel. (OT p. 22)

As Viking incursion, historical event and the cycle of Orkney's
land- and sea-based existence recur, the 'rich aura' to which Brown
refers is represented in an overall narrative. The names of characters
reappear from poem to poem, simultaneously personalising and
generalising them. Historic Rognvald Kolson, sometime Earl of
Orkney, walks on farms known to the fictional characters Halcro,
Mansie and Peero. In the figure of Saint Magnus, potent symbol and
inspirational ikon across a range of Brown's writing, Icelandic
ancestry links forward to Catholic canonisation. Different versions
of his death signify more than simple repetition. The formal stylisa-
tion of 'Saint Magnus in Egilsay':

> They lured you there, a gentle enemy.
> bow your blank head. Offer your innocent vein.

a red wave broke. The bell sang in the tower.
Hands from the plough carried the broken saint
under the arch. Below, the praying sea
           Knelt on the stones (LF p. 39)

is later rehearsed in the vernacular of a lyric addressed to Magnus's
executioner:

'Lifolf,' they sang, 'here's better butchering –
Come up, come up!'
'The lords get hungry after a hunt,' said Lifolf.
he washed his hands in the burn.
He went in a slow dance
Up to the blank stone in the barren moor. (WA p. 15)

Echoes of Pilate add significance to the martyrdom.

In another instance of figural return, the first time that we
encounter the legendary Thorfinn, he is set to leave an Orkney
where 'every casual car was the Black Maria'. (LF p. 15) Each of the
eight poems which comprise 'Fisherman and Boy' is addressed to
Thorfinn, and a coda reads:

Thorfinn, you will learn more in Orkney
Than Mansie did
Who made seven salt circles of the globe. (YW p. 45)

[GMB] *Thorfinn is a Scandinavian name, and one of the great*
Earls of Orkney had that name. He was the grandfather of Saint
Magnus, and he was also a first cousin of Macbeth. In Thorfinn's
day the Earls of Orkney were beginning to intermingle with the
Royal House of Scotland, making alliances. He went on a pilgrim-
age with Macbeth; they rode over the Alps to Rome together, where
Macbeth threw money to the poor people – maybe trying to atone,
but more likely because princes were expected to be givers of gold.

But perhaps the most memorable of Brown's creations to figure
in the kind of cross-textual linkage he favours is Ikey, the Orkney
tinker. It is only when we hear the words of 'The Scarecrow in
the Schoolmaster's Oats': 'I do not trust Ikey the tinker./ He has a
worse coat', (FP p. 61) that we recall Ikey's words from an earlier
volume:

Mansie at Quoy is a biddable man.
Ask for water, he gives you rum.
I strip his scarecrow April by April. (YW p. 39)

That poem, 'Ikey on the People of Hellya', is one of the ways in
which Brown presents characters from a remembered Orkney, and
'Ikey's Day' defines a tinker's existence:

A ditch awakening.
A bee in my hair.

Egg and honeycomb,
Cold fare.

An ox on the hill,
Bulls, ploughman, ploughshare.

A sharp wet wind
And my bum bare.

A fish-brimming corn-crammed house,
But a hard door.

Chicken, thief, and a crab
Round a blink of fire.

A length of bones in the ditch,
A broken prayer. (FP p. 46)

Runic compression here gives a charge to the poem as a day in a life
becomes a life as one day: the 'hard' door that will not open to share
the plenty inside lending purpose to the almost comically acknowledged theft of a chicken for survival. The starkness of the final
image is quietly forceful. The poem 'Tinkers' (PNS p. 37) is further
evidence of an abiding interest.

[GMB] *Tinkers don't really exist any longer, though there were
plenty of them when I was a boy, and I was half-scared of them and
half-fascinated at the same time. There was something slightly
menacing, dangerous, about them, and yet they had a kind of vividness and picturesqueness too. They somehow fit into the complex of*

characters I'm attracted to.

As well as characters, historical event figures in the cycles of recurrence which Brown constructs. With his tinker's superstition, Ikey will 'not go near Merran and her cats'. He would:

> Rather break a crust on a tombstone.
> her great-great-grandmother
> Wore the red coat at Gallowsha. (YW p. 39)

'Witch', in a later volume, perhaps recalls that very incident:

> And there at a steep place, Gallowsha,
> Among tilted bottles, fists, faces
> – a cold drunken wheel –
> James saw the hangman put his red shirt on Wilma. (FP p. 25)

[GMB] *There was a great witch-hunt in Orkney in the seventeenth century. I don't know how many women there were who were condemned as witches, but Gallowsha was the place in Kirkwall where they were burnt; strangled first and then burnt. They stood them on a pile of faggots and someone applied the torch and up they went. It was a hellish thing.*

Resurrecting Scandinavian experience and threading it both into his island's history and into a continuing present, Brown also reconstructs versions of event from those hinterlands where history shades into legend. His 1976 volume, *Winterfold* includes eight imitations of the 'Norse Lyrics of Rognvald Kolson'. 'What I have tried to do', says Brown in a note, 'is preserve some of the gaiety, savagery, piety of the originals.' (W p. vi). Recounting Rognvald's Mediterranean attack upon a high-sided ship called a dromond, carried out while *en route* for a Jerusalem pilgrimage, the sixth lyric is written in praise of Audun, the first warrior to board the African ship and execute his grim reaping:

> Black sheaves
> fell on the dromond.
> Flame-bearded Audun
> Was complete gules.
> Erling's Audun
> Through fire and blood
> Bound his red harvest. (W p. 24)

In a volume published thirteen years later, a poem called 'Pilgrimage' re-works the event. Opening with 'the ship of Earl Rognvald,
first of fifteen,/ Gold-encrusted, left Orkney in autumn', it shapes a
compressed record of the entire journey to the Holy Land, with
syllabic rhyming and a running 'l' composing internal music:

> Endured salt of betrayal; burned
> a tall-masted Moslem dromond, but lost
>   Her molten gold to lobsters. (WA p. 20)

At times there is no obvious way of determining the precise status
of reconstructed event. When, for example, in 'The stone Cross', we
read: 'at dawn Havard sighted a hill in Ulster', (W p. 51) is there an
intended reference to actual historical incident?

[GMB] *No. The Vikings were always raiding into Ireland and
England and down as far as the Scilly Isles. These people from
Orkney were terrible; I tell you, they were just pirates, you know.
Once the fields were ploughed and sowed, away they went in their
long ships and harried in the Atlantic and the Irish sea. Monasteries
were what they went for to begin with, and churches, because that's
where the gold and silver was, and they were undefended. So those
places always had a rough time of it. In Lindisfarne they had the
famous chant:* 'A furore Normanorum libera nos Domine – *from
the fury of these Northmen deliver us O Lord.' It's that kind of raid
the poem is based on.*

There is a similar discursive blurring to precise effect in
'Buonaparte, The Laird, And The Volunteers', (FP pp. 31–2) which
simulates the tone and temper of an actual document from a laird to
Lords of the Admiralty as the poem presents press-gang barbarism,
though no such document was consulted in its composition. On the
other hand, apart from being carefully dated ('The Opening of the
Tavern: 1596', 'The Fight Between Sven and Pedro in William
Clark's Ale House: 1599') the poem 'William and Mareon Clark'
shows every sign of being purely an invention of Brown's imagination – which of course it largely is.

[GMB] *It was a legal document published in 1967 in a book
about Stromness; I hadn't seen it before. But it's a kind of title-deed
of the first recorded house here in Stromness, at the far end of the
bay. It was an inn; they had applied to the Earl of Orkney to build
an inn. That was the real beginning of Stromness, I think. Before*

that it must have been just a scattering of fishermen's huts, bothies and what have you. But by that time sailing ships were taking shelter here. That's why they built an inn; they wouldn't have built it for the local fishermen and farmers, who sat at their own fires and ate their own produce.[15]

There are yet other occasions when human event and Christian symbolism come together in a way ideally suited to a poet of Brown's temperament. Saint Magnus is perhaps the major example, but another occurs when the title poem of *The Wreck of the Archangel* tells of the seemingly miraculous survival of a single infant:

> One thin cry
> Between wavecrash and circling wolves of wind,
>   And there, in the lantern pool
>   A child's face. (WA p. 2)

Was this unlikely event true?

[GMB] *Oh yes. It was an emigrant ship, bound for America, I think. As far as can be gathered it was wrecked in a winter storm off the island of Westray. Everybody was drowned, but this child was found on the shore. The ship's port of registration must have been Archangel, so they must have been people from the Baltic, or from Russia itself. Anyway, that child was brought up on one of the crofts and eventually got married. But since at first they didn't know anything about him at all, they called him John Angel, after the ship. And that Angel family was still in existence in Westray until a while ago, when the name died out.*

So we are presented with a mythopoeic vision of human continuity. *Fishermen with Ploughs* is the most explicit example of this, announced as 'a poem cycle' and constructing its epic project with a diversity of forms.

And if we go back to beginnings, we can already see some of the structural attributes of Brown's preoccupations. The first poem of *Loaves and Fishes* connects biblical precedent with Orkney life. It is followed by 'That Night in Troy' where Classical epic suggests appropriate parameters for an Orkney history yet to be told. Then 'The death of Peter Esson' sews a modern Orcadian into the developing design. Esson was the man for whom Brown's father, a postman but also a part-time tailor, worked, and so the poet's own genealogy is connected. 'I liked Peter Esson's shop – a cloth-smelling

cave.'[16] Following this, 'The Masque of Bread' constructs the first of
many Christian apotheoses of experience, with a dead man seeking
answers in an afterlife. 'December Day, Hoy sound' offers an initial
evocation of localised climate and topography. 'Thorfinn' brings in
a Viking before 'Themes' summarises Brown's poetic conspectus:

> Tinker themes cry through
> The closes of my breath –
>   Straw and tapestry shaken
>   With keenings of love and birth;
> Odyssean corn returning
> Across furrows of death;
>   Women scanning the sea;
>   Ploughmen wounding the earth. (FP p. 16)

When I asked about contemporary poets to whom he had responded, Brown said that he liked some of Auden and Dylan
Thomas, but significant figures had been Eliot and Yeats. In
Orkneyinga Saga, Saint Magnus serves the same purposes for
Brown as Cuchulain of Irish legend did for Yeats. As a framework
for action and event in Brown's mythic narration, the imaginative,
legendary, historical and existential structures of Orkney experience prove amply sufficient. But the term 'myth' is not one that he
readily uses. He is more inclined to oppose 'the facts of our history
– what Edwin Morgan called The Story' to 'the vision by which
people live, what Edwin Muir called their Fable'. (OT pp. 1–2).
These are the elements from which Brown forges his own inscription, and as Alan Bold rightly suggests, in Brown's work 'the Story
is constantly moving towards Fable'.[17]

   'Some of the poems in this book', says Brown in *Winterfold* 'are
swatches cut from here and there in the one weave of time.' (W p.
vi). And of the characters whose history he traces in *Fishermen with
Ploughs*, he comments: 'essentially their lives were unchanged; the
same people appear and reappear through many generations.'[18]
Brown has contrived a linguistic texture for the sweep of history.
Edwin Muir once remarked that 'the life of every man is an endlessly repeated performance of the life of man',[19] and this seems as
true for Brown's perspectives. In one sense his writing becomes a
kind of seamless tapestry, where what happened in Orkney forty
years ago happened seven hundred in the past.

[GMB] *I believe that is indeed so. It is the way that I work and I think that that is the way things happen.*

Notes

1. George Mackay Brown, *The Wreck of the Archangel* (London, 1989), p. ix. Subsequent references are marked WA and given parenthetically.
2. *Orkneyinga Saga: The History of the Earls of Orkney* (London, 1981), translated by Herman Palsson and Paul Edwards, p. 9.
3. George Mackay Brown, *Portrait of Orkney* (London, 1988), p. 111. Subsequent references are marked PO and given parenthetically.
4. *Orkneyinga Saga*, pp. 11–12.
5. George Mackay Brown, *Loaves and Fishes* (London, 1959), pp. 36–7. Subsequent references are marked LF and given parenthetically.
6. *Poems and Prose of Gerard Manley Hopkins* (London, 1963), edited by W. H. Gardner, p. 30.
7. George Mackay Brown, *Fishermen with Ploughs* (London, 1971), p. 4. Subsequent references are marked FP and given parenthetically.
8. Edwin Muir, *The Story and the Fable* (London, 1940), pp. 12–13.
9. George Mackay Brown, *Poems New and Selected* (London, 1971), p. 33. Subsequent references are marked PNS and given parenthetically.
10. George Mackay Brown, *Winterfold* (London, 1976), p. 30. Subsequent references are marked W and given parenthetically.
11. Alan Bold, *George Mackay Brown* (Edinburgh, 1978), p. 11.
12. *Chapman*, vol. iv., no. 4, Summer 1976, p. 23.
13. George Mackay Brown, *The Year of the Whale* (London, 1965), p. 25.
14. George Mackay Brown, *An Orkney Tapestry* (London, 1973), p. 15. Subsequent references are marked OT and given parenthetically.
15. An account of this is given in *Letters From Hamnavoe* (Edinburgh, 1975), p. 21.
16 *As I Remember*, p. 13.
17. Alan Bold, op cit., p. 51.
18. *Fishermen with Ploughs*, Prefatory note.
19. *The Story and the Fable*, p. 54.

To Have Found One's Country

IAIN CRICHTON SMITH

> The island is the anvil where
> was made
> the puritanical heart.[1]

Iain Crichton Smith was seventeen years old when he first read Sorley MacLean's *Dàin do Eimhir* (*Poems to Eimhir*), and although he couldn't fully understand the book at the time, he remembers the impact it had on him.

[ICS] *It showed me that poetry could be written about modernity, it least in relative terms – it was about the Spanish Civil War. Before that, the Gaelic poetry that I'd read wasn't liberating in the sense that it didn't go beyond the Highlands. That was the main thing that interested me then, quite apart from the beauty of the language and the sound. Here was a book of poems presenting a specifically twentieth-century exploration of the crisis between a private world which we inhabit and a public world which is waiting for us to enter. I saw this tug-of-war between the public and the private as being central. MacLean certainly made the leap from inside the Highlands to outside and beyond; a transition which is felt on the pulses. The poems were existential, too, in that Sorley had life-choices which he had to make.*

It was not until he was about thirty-five that he discovered MacDiarmid.

[ICS] *I found the Lallans difficult, of course; for me it's a learned language. But I found this poetry, too, a liberating experience. I felt that the two were akin, in some deep sense, Sorley and MacDiarmid. They represented an incredible challenge.*

Although he was born in Glasgow (in 1928), Iain Crichton Smith moved to Lewis before he was two years old and there he grew up in a Gaelic-speaking, Calvinist community until at the age of seventeen he went to Aberdeen University to study English and Celtic.

[ICS] *I dropped the Celtic because they were concentrating too much on the language and as a native speaker of Gaelic I found this boring.*

He then became a school-teacher of English for twenty-five years, three of them at Clydebank High School and the remainder at Oban, after which he moved to Taynuilt, in Argyll, to become a full-time writer. The spirit of place, concerning an island complicatedly loved and left, though forming nonetheless an ever-returning imaginative presence; the effects of growing up in an enclosed community deeply imbued with Calvinist theology, and a complex and highly-charged relationship with the Gaelic and English languages combine to construct recurring leitmotifs in Crichton Smith's poetry. Throughout, and no doubt due in part to the determining pressures of his upbringing, one aspect of his creative engagement is characterised by a repudiation of romanticised images of the Scottish Highlands and Islands. 'At the Highland Games' is one of many poems which reveal a deep-seated antagonism to the tartan gallimaufry, figuring as it does, the poet walking:

> among crew-cuts, cameras, the heather-covered rock,
> past my ancestry, peasants, men who bowed
> with stony necks to the daughter-stealing lord

and seeing:

> Stained pictures
> of what was raw, violent, alive and coarse.
> I watch their heirs, Caligulas with canes
> stalk in their rainbow kilts towards the dance.[2]

[ICS] *It's very simple, I think, to idealise the Highlands. I've read so many awful books by visitors who come and talk about the sunsets and about the kind of people who live in the Highlands. I don't romanticise because my feeling is that the people in the Highlands are like people everywhere else, except that they are subject to different conditions. It's been very damaging for the*

*Highlands to be looked on as if they are different kinds of people
from the rest of the world – which they're not.*

Those different conditions combine to produce particular effects
in Crichton Smith's poetry. His verse often refers to the actualities
of Lewis as being harsh climatically and religiously unyielding: in
many ways an environment inimical to poetry. Out of this recalci-
trance a taut and vital music is made. 'Poem Of Lewis' concludes:

> They have no place for the fine graces
> of poetry. The great forgiving spirit of the word
> fanning its rainbow wing, like a shot bird
> falls from the windy sky. The sky heaves
> in visionless anger over the cramped graves
> and the early daffodil, purer than a soul,
> is gathered into the terrible mouth of the gale (SP p. 3).

Yet the second of 'Eight Songs For A New Ceilidh' affirms that:

> it was the fine bareness of Lewis
> that made the work of my mind like a loom full of
> the music of the miracles and greatness of our time. (SP p. 59)

Such transformations of apparently uncompromising material are a
distinguishing feature of this writing.

[ICS] *It's an interesting thing as far as Gaelic poetry is concerned,
this century, that most of it has come from the Protestant islands to
the North. And I associate Lewis with an austerity both in religion
and in landscape which acts as a kind of honing for what I'm doing.
It's almost as if in these islands to the North, you have to fight, in a
way, to create poetry.*

So this historical terrain, and the severe religious perceptions
associated with it, work to prohibit any nostalgic recapitulation of
Highland theme and experience?

[ICS] *Oh it does. If you're honest with yourself, it does.*

Crichton Smith produces a mode of writing which contrives to be
as gracefully cadenced as it is relentless in its pursuit of lived
experience.

> The sky holds
> us and the dead, our flesh and the old stones,
> some of which are bare of writing.

Imagine how in winter the wind howls
round the unwritten stone, unglamorous, poor. (SP p. 188)

Against such a background, and weaving an intertextual theme
from poem to poem, adherents of Calvinism are seen as:

emblems of sombre sundays,
with their hard black hats that bite into their brows.
They are a frieze against a pulsing landscape,
against a sky of free and moving cloud. (SP p. 189)

Alert to the difficulty of penetrating closed minds, or of dislocating
closed systems, Crichton Smith approaches the religious bigotry of
leaders in Calvinist communities in a variety of ways; the richness
and diversity of his own paths of enquiry directly exposing the
blinkered vision of theirs. Having thus earned the right of direct
condemnation, he uses it to telling effect:

I accuse
these men of singleness and loss of grace
who stared so deeply into the fire's hues
that all was fire to them.
Yes, to this place
they should return. Cheeks have the fire men
choose.   (SP p. 15)

The intrusion of gaiety into the world of hooded, puritanical
rancour is registered in 'Young Girl':

Will you speak disparagingly of the diamond because
of its glitter or the sea because of its radiance?
There is a white ship among the boats and among the
black hats there is a crown. (SP p. 55)

Given the prevalence of such oppositions in his poetry, the influence of
religion upon Crichton Smith's own development becomes of interest.
  [ICS] *My mother was very Free Church, but I think I must have
rebelled against that very early, though I certainly did go to Sunday
School, I remember, when I was young. In fact I don't think I was
ever in Church on Lewis.*

But the deep-seated and damaging influence which such rigid beliefs exercised upon others brought to mind an episode after he had moved to Oban, and went to see a film which the local minister had shown mid-week in the church hall.

[ICS] *My mother was talking to another old woman later that night, who was saying 'That was a terrible thing there,' and I thought they were talking about the starving millions of India which had been the subject of the film. But they were talking about the fact that the minister had put the film on in the church hall. The starving millions had made no impression on them at all. I thought again, 'My God, if there's a religion that can create that kind of effect in people then there must be something definitely wrong with it'. And I feel this about the Calvinist religion and the Free Church in whose ambience I grew up: that the kind of God in which they believe is the kind of God, to put it bluntly, I would find abhorrent if he were a human being.*

These feelings crystallise in a corrosively ironic poem, 'The Iolaire' (SP pp. 225–6), which enters the mind of a minister to see how he might cope with the wreck on Lewis in 1919 of a ship in which over two hundred war veterans perished.

[ICS] *This brought me face to face with the adequacy or otherwise of art. In that part of the world there has always been a cleavage, given the kind of church we have, between art and religion, where art is condemned as a species of vanity. I think there's always deep within me a dark signal saying that art isn't enough, that there must be something greater. At times I feel that what I'm doing is important, and at others that it's vanity. That's why I keep fighting against religion. I simply couldn't imagine a God who, if he could control anything at all, would allow two hundred people to be drowned on their own island on New Year's morning after they'd spent four years in the war.*

Yet 'At The Sale' suggests a slightly different order of feeling:

How much goes out of fashion and how soon!
The double-columned leather-covered tomes
recalls those praying Covenanters still
adamant against Rome's
adamant empire. (SP p. 97)

And the complications of his fascination with Calvinistic rigour can include attitudes of envy and admiration, as well as repudiation:

> That was great courage to have stayed as true
> to truth as men can stay. From them we learn
> how certain truths can make men brutish too:
> how few can watch the bared teeth slow-burn
> and not be touched by the lumps of fire they chew
> into contempt and barrenness. (SP p. 15)

[ICS] *For a long time I was ambivalent about the Free Church and about people like the Covenanters: that on the one hand there was something inhuman about it; on the other that it was attractive to an adolescent that there were people who knew exactly where they stood. It's not at all like our society, which is more like Hamlet's society in many ways, in that we don't really know what to believe. I think there's always been that slight ambivalence.*

That ambivalent structure of feeling may relate in turn to Crichton Smith's deep relationship with his forcefully religious mother, and also the old women who figure so prominently in his verse. 'Face of an Old Highland Woman' sets the tone for this aspect of his writing, with its suggestion of an intense correlation between enduring religious personality and an uncompromising geography:

> There's no grace
> of any Renaissance on the skin
> but rocks slowly thrust through earth
> a map with the wind going over stone
> beyond the mercies of Nazareth.
> Here is the God of fist and bone
> a complex twisted Testament
> two eyes like lochs staring up
> from heather guarded by a bare wind
> beyond the art and dance of Europe. (SP p. 30)

Though they live an often joyless and harsh existence, these women register too as figures of impressive strength. Had the source for these images been, in fact, his own mother?

[ICS] *Yes. And the puritanical, Calvinist women I met when I was in Lewis. I realised, talking to these women, that they were much stronger than men. On the other hand, I never heard my mother say she was sorry for anything. I don't think I've heard any of these women say they were sorry for anything. Because of this Calvinistic strength, they knew that they were right. So I felt a kind of stubbornness in them, and at the same time this feeling that they would go on to the end, that it would take an enormous amount to shift them. I remember the kind of feeling I had talking to my mother, from the conflict between the strength of her religion as opposed to my own atheist ideas. I was always struck by these two things: the strength that could derive from a real belief in an ideology, and at the same time an unreasoning stubbornness.*

> Your set mouth
> forgives no-one, not even God's justice
> perpetually drowning law with grace. (SP p. 29)

Like black hats, bibles figure and refigure in this writing. But whereas the black hats invariably signify a shadow cast across natural potential – 'black hats darkly sailing on a sea of roses' (SP p. 57), bibles can register in a plurality of ways. Certainly they can and do invoke the tyranny of life-denying prescription:

> I have to live
> where the black bibles
> are walls of granite,
> where the heads are bowed
> over eternal fire. (SP p. 13)

And more recently, 'Farewell To My Brother' recalls how:

> the Bible was a hard wall
> which we climbed over
> to touch the consolations of the heart.[3]

But when the poetry connects bibles with natural phenomena, striking effects of a transfigured text and of alternative possibilities are achieved. 'To An Old Woman' conjures memories of her wedding-day:

You remember other days, a sermon as direct as a
bullet a summer pouring around a church, a gold ring
and the testimony of roses opening summer like a new
Bible in your memory. (SP p. 56)

[ICS] *I think what has happened to me is that the religion which
I intellectually object to has become internalised in some deep
sense, so that I use a symbolism which is imbued with it; which is
a difficult situation. So even though I am intellectually against
religion, I still find that my poetry is penetrated by symbolism from
the Bible.*

A further dimension to Crichton Smith's espousal of secular
values is suggested by references to Glasgow. This may be coded as
that city's soccer rivalry between the religiously identified teams of
Rangers and Celtic: 'Divided city of the green and blue' (SP p. 168),
or 'Glasgow's ruinous land of green and blue' (SP p. 179). It may be
presented more directly in the colours which identify a Catholicism
of Irish provenance and its rival Protestant associations as when the
impressive 'Orpheus' ends with the recognition that this is the place
with which Orpheus must continue to engage:

that he must love them not as in a dream
but on this smoky field of green and orange. (SP p. 197)

[ICS] *At times I think of Glasgow as being a theatre for warfare
between the two religions. My position now simply is that I'm
beginning to think of religion as having caused more damage than
it's worth, and that religious dogma probably has been the single
most damaging thing that civilisation has created.*

These defined positions find extension in a suspicion of history.

[ICS] *Well, I've often been ambivalent about history, too,
because I feel that sometimes history can be used simply as a
metaphor, and that is too easy. What many people do, if they are
not inside a particular culture, is choose certain facts out of an
enormous number of facts and put them together in a historical
fashion. And Scotland has suffered from bad history of this kind.
But what I like to think about is a kind of history lived on the bone
rather than an intellectual construction, which is why I think that
poets and writers are better historians, often, than the professionals,
though of course we need both.*

A response like that helps to account for the poem 'Lenin' (written, surely, with one eye to MacDiarmid), with its ironic warning that it is:

> Simple to condemn
> the unsymmetrical, simple to condone
> that which oneself is not
> ...
> when the true dialectic is to turn
> in the infinitely complex. (SP p. 32)

[ICS] *I think what happens is that if one imagines a whole range of what might be possible, then ideology in this sense cuts off certain elements and casts them away because they won't fit. And there is something here that is antipathetic to poetry. There's not enough raggedness left of all our powers.*

'Lenin' closes with lines of particular relevance to the stance and attitude of Crichton Smith's poetry, preferring over the 'chair of iron' upon which Lenin sits, a moving on:

> into the endlessly various, real, human,
> world which is no new era, shining dawn. (SP p. 32)

'Next Time', a poem addressed to Ulysses, concludes:

> Next time, do this,
> salt bronzed veteran
> let the tapestry be unfinished
> as truthful fiction is.[4]

The exaltation of difference, whether political or religious, assumes, itself, ideological significance; 'Jean Brodie's Children' catches in its final stanza a word which is echoed to fruitful effect elsewhere:

> Mistresses, iron in their certainty,
> their language unambiguous but their lives
> trembling on grey boughs. (SP p. 93)

One of the strategies devised by Crichton Smith to loosen the grip of dogma is a metaphoric merging of the unlike, where terms of similitude collide with those of diversity. In this writing, 'the hare shakes like a lily' (SP p. 71), 'Weasels quiver like the northern lights' (SP p. 75), 'This April day shakes memories in a shade' (SP p. 167), and in 'The Departing Island' we read:

> Strange how it's like a dream when two waves
> passed, and the engine's hum puts villages out
> of mind or shakes them together in a waving fashion.
> (SP. p. 87).

There is a repeated inclination towards the kind of conjunction which eschews any prescriptive clarity:

> as deer so stand, precarious, of a style,
> half-here, half-there, a half-way lustre breaking
> ...
> like daring thoughts, half-in, half-out this world,
> as a lake might open, and a god peer
> into a room where failing darkness glows. (SP pp. 46–7)

So what is being proposed is the kind of connection which can 'let its leaps be unpredictable' (SP p. 44).

[ICS] *I actually think that the best poetry happens when two or three things come together which one would normally think of as being totally unrelated. I used to read an enormous amount of Kierkegaard, who talks about the leap of faith that one has to make whether in theology or in religious life and there's something akin to that in the creation of poetry; a joining together of things which aren't normally joined together. Scientists do this too. It's the kind of leap that changes something at deep levels, so that we can start thinking in a new way.*

In one of his most remarkable poems to date, 'Deer On The High Hills: A Meditation', Crichton Smith puts into exhilarating practice what he means by such an approach to poetry.

[ICS] *I must confess at the beginning that there are areas of it I don't understand! What came out of the poem in the end was the distance between us and the animal kingdom. It concerns how, in relation to animal nature, we are a Hamletish, divided people; and also I link it up with* Ben Dorain *and the strangeness of the deer in that poem. But I began the poem by linking the deer with nobility*

*dancing on a ballroom floor. You can see this connection – the
ballroom floor is the icy road on which I actually saw the deer one
night coming back from Oban. And there's something aristocratic
about deer, as many people agree, though I don't know what it is.*

We had been talking earlier about Crichton Smith's admiration
for Eliot's 'The Waste Land', and I thought that there might be a
technical connection between Eliot's poem and 'Deer On The High
Hills'.

[ICS] *What Eliot taught me was the way in which you can get a
logic of images. In the nineteenth century we get a logic of narrative,
things like 'The Lady of Shallott', and in Browning to a great
extent. But Eliot taught us that you can get a logic of imagery which
is in a sense pure poetry. Also, 'The Waste Land' is a very extreme
poem; I mean he pushes things to extremes. These are the two major
things he taught me: his use of images and the extremism of his
work. And perhaps 'Deer On The High Hills' is close to something
of the nature of 'The Waste Land' in the sense that what I was doing
was a kind of linkage of images. It's a logic of images, really, and
maybe that's why it's difficult, because in the way that deer leap
about, you have to leap from image to image in order to keep
yourself inside the poem.*

In a different direction, one of the changes rung on the rhythms
of Crichton Smith's work is the intrusion of a distinctive, and
perhaps today unfashionable, use of the Classics in the elaboration
of Scottish experience. The impressive elegy 'For John MacLean,
Headmaster, and Classical and Gaelic Scholar' is perhaps the fullest
statement of this theme, but elsewhere there are moments which
suggest how powerful, if deeply ambiguous, was the attraction of
Classical literature generally, and Roman Virtue in particular.
Watching the last hours of 'Old Woman' as, helplessly dependent
upon the ministrations of her aged husband, 'she munched, half
dead, blindly searching the spoon', the speaker is drawn to that
older civilisation, and to what he perceives as a characteristic
temper and attitude:

> There I sat
> imprisoned in my pity and my shame
> that men and women having suffered time
> should sit in such a place, in such a state
> and wished to be away, yes, far away

with athletes, heroes, Greeks or Roman men
who pushed their bitter spears into a vein
and would not spend an hour with such decay. (SP p. 14)

Looking forward more directly to the elegy, 'Mr M.' laments the
passing of a system of values:

the order's broken. We visit its old stones,
dishonoured consuls visiting Hades
(green fields and ponderous doors)

but there are only ghosts there now.
We clutch your ghostly gown like Orpheus
clutching at Euridice while Pluto
giggles on iron coins. (SP p. 85)

[ICS] *This was a period – it's a number of years ago now, but I
remember feeling it, when I actually felt that the Graeco-Roman
world was more rational than ours. I set against this civilisation the
neon lights of the twentieth century, and I felt that we were entering
a period when we would have no knowledge of history, no sense of
this Graeco-Roman world, and this seemed to me to be tragic. John
MacLean was a representative of what I thought of as Roman
values, but Roman values which were at the same time humane,
because he exercised what you might call a beneficent control over
the school. He wasn't intolerant; he knew every pupil by name, and
he had these tremendous personal virtues which I responded to. I
felt that it must to a certain degree be on account of his classical
training, that he had this sense of benign order. I'm attracted to
order, but I like to work between this sense of order and a sense of
creative disorder. In my earlier work, quite often, the order of the
metre is in tension with what I call the inspiration or the grace
which operates inside the metre. I sway between these two ideas
quite a lot.*

As with so much of his poetry, Classical influences feed back into
his own experience of growing up in Lewis, giving shade and depth
and definition to feelings of opposing kinds.

[ICS] *One of the things that interests me, and it comes up time
and time again is the clash between Dido and Aeneas. I do link this
up with my background.*

He is amused by his perception of Aeneas as 'a kind of Free-Churcher' who turns his back upon normal, human desires in order to create Rome, and laughs aloud at the idea of a Free Churcher creating Rome, but Crichton Smith holds on to the connection.

[ICS] *What I mean is that there is a kind of asceticism in Aeneas, and this clash between the erotic and the authoritarian has always interested me in writing. It appears in my own work, perhaps, in the clash between form and what I call grace or inspiration. So these things are linked in my imagination, and the Classics are real to me, perfectly real, because I see so many things going on in the Classical world going on now; authoritarianism is only one example. I find the position of Virgil himself interesting because he seems to me to be a very vulnerable poet who at the same time is creating an image of an authoritarian Rome. Coming from the island that I come from, things like authority and freedom are important to my imagination.*

> Tender Virgil,
> dead in Mantua,
> in the ice of perfection,
> this is not your land,
> you, exquisite saint
> of the compassionate metre,
> sleep elsewhere ...
>
> From Italy
> you come to our sky.
> It is like shifting from a warm flat
> to a lonely castle
> hissing with ghosts.[5]

With these lines we are brought from the envied warmth of a Mediterranean culture to the image of an isolated individual within a castle corresponding to the figure who more than any other stalks the pages of Crichton Smith's poetry: Hamlet.

[ICS] *The fascination is with him partly as a poet but also as a representative of the kind of person who, when he is confronted with power, cannot bring himself, because he is divided, to destroy that power which he knows to be evil. I think that this permeates*

not just the play, but social reality itself. I suppose, too, it is the
contrast between someone who can only think, and another kind of
person, like Claudius, who fascinates me because he doesn't have
this cleavage at all. The crux is how one can be intelligent enough
to wield that kind of state power and yet appear to have no doubts.
Now I find a personality like that alien and incomprehensible. And
there are so many of them on the world's stage, of whom Claudius
is a prime example – running their countries pretty thoroughly as he
does.

The poem 'Hamlet' develops as its central metaphor a sugges-
tive use of mirror imagery:

> Sick of the place, he turned him towards night.
> The mirrors flashed distorting images
> of himself in court dress, with big bulbous eyes,
> and curtain swaying in a greenish light.
> ...
> I see in the warped mirrors rapiers shake
> their subtle poisons perfuming the hall
>
> reflecting accidents, a circus merely,
> a place of mirrors, an absurd conclusion.
> Images bounce madly against reason
> as, in a spoon, wide pictures, fat and jolly. (SP p. 79)

There are provocative echoes of these terms in *The Notebooks of
Robinson Crusoe*, where poem 33 concludes:

> I shall leave my bare island, simple as poison, to
> enter the equally poisonous world of Tiberius, where
> there are echoes and reflections, a Hall of Mirrors
> in which my face swells like a jester's in a world
> without sense. (SP p. 211)

Hamlet's conscience-stricken isolation in the court at Elsinore
and Crichton Smith's pervasive sense of troubled separation from
Lewis and its artistically unsustaining community begin to achieve
intriguing congruence. In his essay 'Real People in a Real Place' he
has written:

> When one is in harmony with the community then one's
> identity is reflected back from the others by a plain mirror and
> not by the exaggerating or attenuating mirrors that one sees
> in fairs. To be in the community is to be in a home of which
> one's real home is a microcosm: thus it is that when one goes
> out into the wide world one comes back to receive the admira-
> tion of the community if one does well.[6]

Inevitably, then, enigmas proliferate. While Shakespeare sets his
play in a remote pre-Christian past, with England a tributary of the
Danish crown (an historical irony unlikely to be lost on a Scottish
poet), its first scene establishes Christian parameters with
Marcellus' reference to that season 'Wherein our Saviour's birth is
celebrated' (1,i,l.160). But Hamlet and Horatio are students at a
university renowned for a particular school of theology. They have
been studying together at Wittenberg on whose Castle Church
doors in 1517 Luther nailed his '95 Theses'. Wittenberg, as John
Dover Wilson reminds us, was 'the very cradle of the Reformation.
[Hamlet and Horatio] are in fact Protestants, and the point has no
small bearing upon our interpretation of the play'.[7] The point
considerably complicates the figure Hamlet makes for a poet whose
attitudes to subsequent and specifically Highland developments of
the Reformation are pervasively critical.

There are further convolutions and affiliations. Wracked by
doubt and riven by guilt because of that, the young Dane is haunted
as much by the continued existence of Claudius as he is by the ghost
of his murdered father. In a disturbing reversal, murderous fathers
will resonate for a Gael who must live with the historical memory of
the betrayal of a people by clan chieftains who saw profit in the
Clearances and who continue to exercise power in the land.
'Stronger than poison is the venom of selfishness' (V p. 65):

> That's why Hamlet always talks of death.
> Beyond the ruffs and doublets he saw it clear. (SP p. 150)

Crichton Smith sees it clear, too:

> This is a coming to reality.

This is the stubborn place. No metaphors swarm
around that fact, around that strangest thing,
that being that was and now no longer is. (SP p. 172)

Crichton Smith's perception of Hamlet as a figure divided
against himself illuminates his own sense of self-division in his role
as poet, guilt-stricken as he is by the fact that although he did not
learn English until the age of five when he went to school, he now
writes more in English than he does in Gaelic. In this respect,
Hamlet's unwilling involvement in systems of power provokes unsettling reverberations.

[ICS] *I really am in a very anomalous position. In 'Light to Light'*
I say:

Here in Argyllshire Scotland was begun
where the green light was nourished
by monks in their careful cells
their illuminated manuscripts. (SP p. 104)

I'm saying that this is where Gaelic first came to and yet it's
written in English. So it's a very complex relationship which goes
back, I suppose, to my childhood. I started off by knowing Gaelic
and speaking Gaelic: then I went to school and I learned English. So
I was speaking Gaelic in the house and English in the school, but
Gaelic in the playground. Then I went to the Nicolson Institute [the
secondary school serving the Island of Lewis] *and was speaking*
English in the school and coming back at night and speaking Gaelic
in the home. My first poem was in Gaelic, and I've written a fair
amount since in Gaelic. But not so much as I used to. It's by no
means a straightforward matter.

In a published paper Crichton Smith recalls that 'the very fact
that I had to learn English when I went to school was probably
registered in some obscure corner of my psyche as an indication that
English was superior to Gaelic'.[8] Referring to himself as 'a linguistic
double man',[9] he has imaged his predicament in a Gaelic poem
called 'The Fool', where a surface simplicity of utterance is disturbed and complicated by allusive gestures towards King Lear. The
translation is his own:

In the dress of the fool, the two colours that have
tormented me – English and Gaelic, black and red,
the court of injustice, the reason for my anger, and
that fine rain from the mountains and these grievous
storms from my mind streaming the two colours
together so that I will go with poor sight in the
one colour that is so odd that the King himself will
not understand my conversation. (SP p. 71)

His translation of 'Shall Gaelic Die?' explores the problematic in
different ways, drawing upon that imagery of death we have already
noticed, and adapting the image of the fool's motley:

When the Highlands loses its language, will there be a Highlands, said I, with my two coats, losing, perhaps, the two.
(SP p. 138)

The poem asks, with edgy irony, 'In what language would you say,
"Fhuair a' Ghàidhlig bas?"' The Gaelic phrase translates as 'Gaelic
is dead'.

Although they have other dimensions, recurring motifs of guilt
radiate from this aspect of Crichton Smith's development as a
writer, giving an added poignancy to lines from 'Eight Songs for a
New Ceilidh':

I will never go to France my dear, my dear, though
you are young. I am tied to the Highlands. That is
where I learned my wound. (SP p. 59)

In immediate senses, that wound is historically delivered, as a poem
like 'The Clearances' makes clear:

The thistles climb the thatch. Forever
this sharp scale in our poems,
as also the waste music of the sea.
The stars shine over Sutherland
in a cold ceilidh of their own,
as, in the morning, the silver cane
cropped among corn. We will remember this. (SP p. 34)

The more recently iterated theme of exile in his poetry can also have self-referential, as well as distinctly political dimensions:

> It is bitter
> to be an exile in one's own land,
> It is bitter
> to walk among strangers
> when the strangers are in one's own land.
> It is bitter
> to dip a pen into continuous water
> to write poems of exile
> in a verse without honour style. (SP p. 114)

But across the body of his writing Iain Crichton Smith inscribes for the English-speaking world a Highland sensibility, registering distinctive, frequently Gaelic complexities of purpose and place:

> To have fallen in love with
> stone, thistle and strath,
> to see the blood flow
> in wandering old rivers,
> this wound is not stanched
> by handkerchiefs or verse.
> This wound was after all
> love and a deep curse. (SP p. 88)

Notes

1. Iain Crichton Smith, *A Life* (Manchester, 1986), p. 9.
2. Iain Crichton Smith, *Selected Poems: 1955–1980* (Edinburgh, 1981), p. 83. Subsequent quotations will be marked SP and given parenthetically.
3. *Stand*, Winter 1988–89, p. 17.
4. Iain Crichton Smith, *The Exiles* (Manchester, 1984), p. 11.
5. Iain Crichton Smith, *The Village and Other Poems* (Manchester, 1989), p. 28. Subsequent quotations will be marked V and given parenthetically in the text.
6. Iain Crichton Smith, *Towards the Human: Selected Essays* (Edinburgh, 1986), p. 24.
7. John Dover Wilson, *What Happens in Hamlet?* (Cambridge, 1951), p. 68.
8. Iain Crichton Smith, 'The Double Man', in *The Literature of*

Region and Nation (Aberdeen, 1989), edited by R. P. Draper, p. 136.
9. Ibid. p. 137.

For Our Own and the Others

HAMISH HENDERSON

Do not regret
that we have still in history to suffer[1]

For many years, at any number of the folk festivals organised up and down the country, Hamish Henderson has helped the occasion to swing. A ceilidh has hardly seemed a ceilidh without his enthusiastic participation. His repertoire has entertained the dedicated and the curious alike. From the bawdy to the sophisticated, from lyrical to lullaby, from pensive to agitational, from ducal to proletarian, it came to seem that his memory was inexhaustible. And to it all he has brought a singular, some might say gargantuan appetite for enjoying himself which ensured that the proceedings went not with a whimper but a bang. Henderson's dedication to the preservation and promulgation of Scotland's popular culture has inspired generations of younger people, and at Edinburgh University's School of Scottish Studies he has contributed to the assembling of a unique archive of the nation's song and story. His achievement as one of our leading cultural anthropologists is exceptional, and developed from an early, clear-eyed choice as to where his intellectual, social, political and literary responsibilities lay. Temperamentally, these things began at an early age.

Born in Blairgowrie, Perthshire, in 1919, Henderson's first memories are of a cottage at the Spittal of Glenshee where there was a lot of singing, in both Gaelic and Scots. Although his mother was not a native Gaelic speaker, she had developed a love of the old

language from North Highland forbears, and had learned enough
to compete at the local Mod.

[HH] *Nowadays Perthshire is hardly thought of as a Gaelic
County, but in the twenties there were quite a number of native
speakers, even in the eastern glens. The area must have been the
extreme periphery of the Gaelic world at that time. But anyway,
both my grandmother and my mother were singers and my grandmother had a great store not only of songs but of stories and poems
too. She could recite the whole of Walter Scott's 'Glenfinlas' from
end to end: a fantastic memory for anything in metre, and up to a
point I think I've inherited that.*

What he doesn't say is that he composed a tune for 'Glenfinlas',
for he thought it needed one. But he does note that the local
mountain in Glenshee, Ben Gulbainn, meaning Curlew Mountain,
is the same as Ben Bulben in Sligo, Eire, celebrated by Yeats. In both
places, a mountain of that name is associated with the boar hunt
that led to the death of Diarmid.

[HH] *As in many cases the anglicisation in Ireland is more
distorting than we have in Scotland. When I began reading Yeats I
realised how much there was in common between the experiences of
Anglo-Ireland and the sort of semi-Gaelic world that I grew up in.*

His arrival in the School of Scottish Studies, where he was to
spend the rest of his academic life, was typically unconventional.
Expelled from Italy (where he had been translating Antonio
Gramsci) for addressing the Partisans for Peace as the Cold War
intensified, he arrived in London to find a letter from Ewan McColl
informing him that the noted American folklorist Alan Lomax was
over to make a series of recordings for the World Albums of Folk
and Primitive Music. McColl's overriding concern was that Lomax
should be kept away from the mandarins at the BBC, who had – at
that time – little regard for genuine traditional music.

[HH] *He recorded me singing a few songs and then asked would
I act as his field guide for a Scottish tour. Afterwards I suggested
that for security's sake he should deposit copies of all the tapes we
had collected with the School; which of course he did. At that time,
though it was very much being discussed, the School existed only on
paper. But Lomax and I had amassed an enormous and impressive
collection of material, and eventually I was approached to undertake my first collecting tour alone.*

In 1938 Henderson had gone up to Downing College, Cambridge, where he studied German and French as well as developing an interest in Italian first nurtured in him when he was a child. He had also engaged in clandestine anti-fascist activity in Nazi Germany just before the war.

[HH] *I was enlisted in the summer of 1939 by someone who had heard me deliver a speech against fascism in the Cambridge Union – someone who was associated with a Quaker group. I was given a list of addresses which I memorised, and what I had to do was take letters, put them in different envelopes and post them as from within Germany. I never read what was inside them, I thought it safer not to. My cover was a trip to read Hölderlin at the University library in Gottingen where I was lodged with a Jewish family, which I thought was crazy. But it was just a double-bluff; that the authorities wouldn't suspect someone staying with a Jewish family of doing this kind of thing.*

An answer to one of the questions on an interminable form for a residence permit led to a brush with the Administrative Police.

[HH] *Following my instructions, I made no secret of my anti-fascist feelings and when asked whether I had any Jewish relations or whatever, I wrote down* leider nicht *(unfortunately not). But the interview with them was not difficult, and that evening I posted my first letter. I brought back with me a little Jewish boy from the family I was staying with. This was perfectly legal, and I left Germany on August 27th, 1939.*

Rejected as a volunteer because of his poor eyesight, Henderson was drafted into the Pioneer Corps in the summer of 1940 and spent the bitterly cold winter of that year erecting tubular steel anti-tank defences along the East Sussex coast. So he jumped at the opportunity when his Company notice board announced that the Intelligence Corps was looking for people with foreign languages.

[HH] *In due course I was sent to an Intelligence Depot at Winchester, and there they really put us through it. My Jasus, the discipline and drilling was something else again! But eventually I was recommended for a commission at the end of 1941 and was sent straight out to Egypt.*

Active service took him right across North Africa as the Desert Army advanced, and on to Sicily and the invasion of the toe of Italy. He was on the Anzio beachhead in 1944 and subsequently elsewhere on the peninsular as the allies moved north.

An inveterate collector even then, Henderson found time to gather soldiers' songs which he published in 1947 as *Ballads of World War Two*.[2] Hugh MacDiarmid had originally suggested that they be published, though in the public prints in 1964 he and Henderson were hotly to contest the value of popular culture.

[HH] *I know, I know. It's not a very consistent attitude. Just after the war, of course, none of us had any idea that there was going to be such a revival of folk-song.*

But whatever else his reasons for publication may have been, for Henderson these ballads were recorded evidence of a subaltern culture voicing itself in active opposition to officially sanctioned norms, as his foreword makes clear:

> The state radio in time of war does not encourage divergence from the straight patriotic line.... For the army balladeer comes of a rebellious house. His characteristic tone is one of cynicism. The aims of his government and the military virtues of his comrades are alike target for unsparing (and usually obscene) comment. Shakespeare, who ran God close in the matter of creation, knew him well and called him Thersites. (B p. iii)

One of the more widely remembered parodies of 'Lili Marlene' is 'The Ballad of the D-Day Dodgers' which Henderson had put together.

[HH] *I had heard fragments of it sung, and I remember thinking 'Oh, we're going to make a good song out of this.' It's a genuine folk-song to the extent that it was suggested by a tune very common at the time, and different fragments had been reaching me.*

But the 'Ballad of the Big Nobs' is Henderson's own, and its last verse makes reference to military leaders of the time:

> O we had two Hielan laddies –
> Now we've got two Irish paddies.
> > Let's hope they're some fuckin' use
> > > to the Eighth Ar-mee. (B p.12)

[HH] *The Hielan laddies were the Scots Field Marshal Sir Claude Auckinleck who took over command of the Eighth Army after the fall of Tobruk, and Major-General Neil Ritchie, who immediately preceded him in that command. The Irish were Alexander and Montgomery, who were both Northern Ireland Protestants.*

Characteristically, 'Ballads' includes songs from German and Italian troops as well as French Tunisians. 'Giovinezza Tedesca', a satirical song against the Italians made by serving German soldiers, and sung to the tune of the Fascist anthem, was garnered by Henderson from two Viennese prisoners on the Anzio Beachhead.

[HH] *I was questioning prisoners because we wanted to know what the immediate plans of the Germans were. But after the interrogations were finished I often used to ask them if they had any gossip or any songs – just to enliven the proceedings.*

Constructing a rough but affectionate tribute to Stalin, another of Henderson's own compositions, the 'Ballad of the Taxi-Driver's Hat', speaks to attitudes long since demolished.

[HH] *I remember somebody saying in the desert 'I wish we had a platoon of Russians here,' and the prevalent idea at the time was that the Russians were very good troops and that eventually we would beat the Germans together. Consequently the troops felt very good about Stalin. After the Russians had withstood the tremendous initial onslaught of the Germans in 1941, the general feeling was that they were going to pull it off. And this feeling persisted. Remember that Stalingrad coincided with Alamein; two crucial battles being waged at the same time.*

Perhaps the best-known of Henderson's ballads is the 'Highland Division's Farewell to Sicily', which he began writing just after the Sicilian campaign. Its shaping of a response through domestic Scots imagery was subsequently to structure other writing:

> Then fare weel ye dives o' Sicily
> (fare ye weel ye shieling an' ha')
> And fare weel ye byres and ye bothies
> Whaur kind signorinas were cheerie.
>
> And fare weel ye dives o' Sicily
> (Fare ye weel ye shieling an' ha')
> We'll a' mind shebeens and bothies
> Whaur Jock made a date wi' his dearie. (B p. 16)

[HH] *Yes. that was the whole point of it – a kind of fusion of Scotland and Sicily in my mind. This was quite conscious and I was*

first given the idea of it by a Sergeant in the Highland Div. who
said to me, seeing an old woman there with a black shawl over her
head, 'My God, we might be in Lewis'. I took the idea and
developed it.

Over the years Henderson has developed his own ideas and skills
in the writing of song-poems, with several of his compositions now
firmly inscribed in popular consciousness. One of these, 'The John
MacLean March,' was written for a commemorative meeting held
in Glasgow to mark the twenty-fifth anniversary of MacLean's
death, while 'The Gillie Mor' also owed its conception to a particular occasion.

[HH] *I was Literature Secretary of the Scotland-USSR Society at*
the time, attending a conference at which messages from Scotland to
various USSR groups were being read out. One of them was from
the blacksmiths of Leith to the blacksmiths of Kiev, and this at once
had an almost physical impact on me. Two such marvellous names.
In many of these trades you have the idea of a superhuman indi-
vidual who is really the sum total of the work force. Gille Mór just
means big fellow in Gaelic – in clan societies he might be the chief's
armour-bearer – so strong man. I transposed it to a different
context.

Active during the anti-Polaris campaign of the 1960s, Henderson
produced what is probably his most celebrated song, 'Freedom-
Come-All-Ye'; celebrated enough, anyway, to be frequently invoked as Scotland's 'other' anthem.

[HH] *I've just written an obituary for Roy Williamson* [of 'The
Corries'] *and his song 'Flower of Scotland' is an effective alternative*
to the so-called 'national' anthem. But to be quite honest, I have
always privately opposed the idea of 'Freedom-Come-All-Ye' be-
coming an anthem because if there's one thing I don't think would
do that song any good at all would be for it to become official. The
whole idea is that it is an alternative to 'official' attitudes.

A very different 'hero' ballad is 'Rivonia,' with its activist refrain
'Free Mandela! Free Mandela!'

[HH] *Rivonia is the name of the farm in south Africa where*
African National Congress Leaders had taken refuge and where
they were captured. Their trial was usually referred to as the
Rivonia trial. I composed the song just after Nelson Mandela made
that magnificent speech from the dock in 1964.[2]

Bridging differences, whether of country, culture, class or com-

munity remains an abiding concern and when, in his Introduction
to Gramsci's *Prison Letters,* Henderson suggests parallels between
Sardinia and Scotland, he goes on to quote approvingly words of
the American Joe Gould which in turn reflect accurately upon much
of Henderson's own work:

> 'What we used to think was history – all that chitty-chat about
> Caesar, Napoleon, treaties, inventions, big battles – is only
> formal history and largely false. I'll put down the informal
> history of the shirt-sleeved multitude – what they had to say
> about their jobs, love-affairs, vittles, sprees, scrapes and sor-
> rows.'[3]

At the end of the Second World War, Henderson won the
Somerset Maugham Award for his volume of war poetry, *Elegies
for the Dead in Cyrenaica:* an early response to the literary gifts he
displayed there, recognising that a hitherto unknown Scot had
produced eloquent and moving witness to the experience of global
conflict. *Elegies* enshrines cross-cultural perceptions of radically
unusual kinds.

Wilfred Owen rose compellingly above the racial hysteria of
World War One to reach across no-man's land and image the
'melancholy army' of opposing German soldiers as clouds strung
out on the dawn of battle in 'ranks on shivering ranks of grey'.[4]
That humane gesture also lies at the heart of Henderson's poetry,
lending credibility to his claim that a 'remark of a captured German
officer ... first suggested to me the theme of these poems. He had
said: "Africa changes everything. In reality we are allies, and the
desert is our common enemy"' (p. 59). Certainly *Elegies* displays
considerable inventiveness in its various descriptions of a relentlessly hostile terrain. This 'landscape of half-wit/ stunted ill-will' is a
'dead land ... insatiate and necrophilous' (p. 17), Its 'limitless,
shabby lion-pelt' (p. 19), becomes a 'malevolent bomb-thumped
desert' (p. 20) which generates a 'sow cold wind' (p. 23). 'The
unsearchable desert's moron monotony' is an 'imbecile wasteland'
(p. 25), whipping up 'tourbillions of fine dust' (p. 27) across a
'benighted deadland' (p. 45). Imagery of the Crucifixion is transposed into the secular lot of ordinary serving soldiers. As it construes the dying thoughts of conscripts, the First Elegy alludes to the
spear in Christ's side:

                                        and their desire
              crucified itself against the unutterable shadow
                                        of someone
              whose photo was in their wallets.
              Then death made its incision.

Both the scourging and the crown of thorns appear as the military
lot of everyman in 'Opening of an Offensive':

                              The thongs of the livid
              firelight lick you
                        jagg'd splinters rend you. (p.28)

But it is the motif of the desert itself which perverts redemptive
imagery, in effect diabolising Christian tenet:

              vile three in one of the heretic desert,
              sand rock and sky. (p. 23)

    Other witnesses have testified to the desert's aesthetic appeal, but
this is nowhere evident in *Elegies*.
    [HH] *It is not. Just as Robert Burns never mentions what he
must have seen a thousand times: the mountains of Arran. But it is
because the desert meant to me at that time an enemy, though in the
Prologue there is a phrase 'a sensuous austerity' which to a certain
extent is also a reflection of the desert, and I do remember the moon
and incredible skies at night.*
    When and where had Henderson first begun to think in terms of
a related sequence of poems?
    [HH] *I first began to write the elegies in Libya, during the
Highland Division's advance, though parts of 'Seven Good Germans'* [Seventh Elegy] *were earlier still, to my recollection.*
    Towards the end of March, 1943, half-way through the Tunisian
campaign, Henderson fell ill and was in a field hospital for three
days.
    [HH] *I was lying in bed and the first part of the First Elegy more
or less came to me. 'There are many dead in the brutish desert,/ who
lie uneasy/ among the scrub.' I thought of it originally as a kind of
prose line, and then it suddenly began to become poetry. I was
looking at the landscape and could actually see the scrub.*

This opening of the sequence registers two of the most impressive themes of the volume as a whole; a recognition of the commonality of the combatants living or dead, and a transfiguring of desert war in terms of Scottish reference and experience:

> There were our own, there were the others.
> Therefore, minding the great word of Glencoe's
> son, that we should not disfigure ourselves
> with the villainy of hatred; and seeing that all
> have gone down like curs into anonymous silence,
> I will bear witness for I knew the others. (p. 18)

[HH] *It comes from a story told to me in my childhood by my grandmother, a sentimental Jacobite to whom the Jacobite Episcopalian tradition meant a great deal and for whom the Glencoe massacre had brought great shame upon Scotland. She said that when the Jacobite troops occupied Edinburgh in 1745, a son of old Glencoe, who must have been an old man himself at that time – it was either his son or grandson – asked permission of the Prince to guard the house of the Master of Stair. The Master of Stair was a kind of secretary of state for Scotland, and he was thought of as having organised the Glencoe massacre. In seeking such permission the son or grandson had said that he did not want his family to be 'stained with the villainy of hatred'. I thought what a wonderful phrase; if ever there was a heroic, magnanimous statement, here it was. And I thought it applied to us in the desert. Why should we hate this enemy? Don't misunderstand me: I went right through the war trying to be instrumental in killing as many Germans as possible. But the two feelings could co-exist.*

The Second Elegy, 'Halfaya', is dedicated to Luigi Castigliano, a cadet officer in the Italian army who deserted and joined the allies on the Anzio Beachhead.

[HH] *I used him as an interpreter and delegated to him jobs I couldn't do myself. He was a James Joyce scholar, and after the war I sent him books from the Cambridge University library, so that he could complete his thesis.*

Pursuing the relationships between the living and the dead during war, 'Halfaya' ponders sleep permanent and temporary:

> The dreamers remember
> a departure like a migration. They recall a landscape
> associated with warmth and veils and pantomime
> but never focused exactly. (p. 19)

[HH] *It's a recalling of childhood memories, I can remember in the desert having fantastic dreams in which all kinds of childhood memories surfaced.*

'Leaving the City', the Third Elegy, speaks of the obliteration of rank and hierarchy among 'the proletariat/ of levelling death':

> See our own and the opponents
> advance, meet and merge: the commingled columns
> lock, strain, disengage and join issue with the dust. (p. 22)

Seeing both sides as comrades in arms, 'Leaving the City' inserts lines from Cavafy's 'The God Leaves Anthony', a poem in which the City of Alexandria symbolises life itself. Henderson's elegy then conjures a recurrent mirror-image in which one side becomes the other. The overwhelming question here centres upon:

> these, advancing from the direction of Sollum
> swaddies in tropical kit, lifted in familiar vehicles
> are they mirage – ourselves out of a mirror?

[HH] *As I say in the preface, people captured equipment from each other so that everything, tanks, armoured vehicles, lorries, might be used coming in the opposite direction. Both sides, up to a point, were living off each other, so it was a kind of mirror-existence.*

> … this odd effect of mirage and looking-glass illusion persisted, and gradually became for me a symbol of our human civil war, in which the roles seem constantly to change and the objectives to shift and vary. (p. 59)

For such reasons, and due in part of Henderson's habitually historicised perceptions, the Fourth Elegy assumes a catholic awareness:

> Therefore reflecting
> the ice-bound paths, and now this gap in the minefields
> through which (from one side or the other) all must pass
> shall I not speak and condemn? (p. 24)

It is a catholicity which incorporates native geography, in 'Highland Jebel', as part of the sequences's philosophical concerns, uniting 'a metaphysical Scotland with a metaphysical desert' (p. 67). Lines from Hölderlin open this Sixth Elegy, in which a metaphor of migrating birds carries the flight of memory from war-torn desert to battle-scarred Scottish history. What is being suggested here is as much a sense of separation as of connection. Seeking refuge from present stress, the imagination of these Scots soldiers takes off from the surrounding sand to seek the shorelines of home. There, it:

> found the treeless machair,
> took in bay and snub headland, circled kirkyard and valley
> and described once again our love's perfect circuit
> till, flying to its own,
> it dashed itself against the unresponsive windows. (p. 25)

This distance leads to sombre historical reflection as the waiting troops hear, from beyond horizon, a more immediately threatening 'murmur of wind-borne battle'. A Scottish soldier fighting far-off wars in defence of England's imperial interest suffers particular tribulations as:

> Burning byres
> come to my mind. Distance blurs
> motive and aim. Dark moorland bleeding
> for wrong or right. (p. 25–6)

A remark in Henderson's Foreword, referring to the sleepers of the Second Elegy, is instructive both for 'Highland Jebel' and for a motif across the volume:

> It is true that such moments are intended to convey a universal predicament; yet I was thinking especially of the Highland soldiers, conscripts of a fast vanishing race, on whom the

dreadful memory of the clearances rests, and for whom there is little left to sustain them in the high places of the field but the heroic tradition of *gaisge* (valour). (p. 60)

So Henderson will include Gaelic phrases as the war triggers domestic associations in 'this highland's millennial conflict'. This process then dilates to incorporate wider associations, linking the Trojan Wars with the war-cry of the MacLeans who died in defence of their chief at Inverkeithing. Still alert to the participation of opposing troops in an allusive web tracking war and civilisation back to Greek origins, the mythic structure assembled here enables the Highland Clearances to take their place in an unfolding process towards a final assembly beyond the constraints of any single creed:

> Aye, in spite of
> the houses lying cold, and the hatred that engendered
> the vileness that you know, we'll keep our assignation
> with the Grecian Gael. (And those others). Then foregather
> in a gorge of the cloudy jebel
> older than Agamemnon. (p. 26)

Midway through the sequence comes 'Interlude', a poem called 'Opening of an Offensive'. An interlude in more than one sense, it is itself an incitement to rise and fall upon the enemy with all due ferocity, and with a famous phrase from Scottish mediaeval history, 'Mak siccar!' (Make sure!) as battle-cry. Ancestral voices prophesying war are turned to contemporary account.

[HH] *The idea is that there are moments when you have to cut the Gordian knot – rather, I should say – stick a dagger into the enemy. So I felt that a kind of ruthlessness was appropriate there. If you are engaged in war there's no point in repining. The thing has to be carried through. It just won't do to become a conscientious objector half-way through the heat of battle.*

The battle in question was El Alamein, preceded by the largest artillery barrage hitherto laid down, with 750 guns pounding the enemy on a front of five kilometres:

> Is this all they will hear, this raucous apocalypse?
> The spheres knocking in the night of heaven? (p. 28)

That discordant music is expertly inscribed as Henderson pumps his
lines with alliterative onomatopoeia, to transmit the surge of battle-
field exhilaration. Through the sound of the bagpipes local pride
orchestrates the destiny of nations:

> tell
> me that I can hear it! Now – listen!
>
>   Yes, hill and shieling
> sea-loch and island, hear it, the yell
> of your war-pipes, scaling sound's mountains
> guns' thunder drowning in their soaring swell!
> – The barrage gulfs them: they're gulfed in the
>   clumbering guns,
> gulfed in gloom, gloom. Dumb in the blunderbuss black –
> lost – gone in the anonymous cataract of noise.
> Now again! The shrill war-song: it flaunts
> aggression to the sullen desert. It mounts. Its scream
> tops the valkyrie, tops the colossal artillery. (p. 28)

[HH] *It's an astonishing thing. To this day, even in the city here,
the pipes have an electric effect on me. There are many Scots who
do respond to the pipes in this way. Imagine the effect of this, and
all that it means in Scottish history, to hear the tunes we all know so
well being played in the desert, and to know that Scottish troops
were there. In that situation it was the ideal recipe for courage.*

Returning to its central requiem for 'the dead, the innocent' (p.
18), part two of *Elegies* takes as overture the ironic pity of Sorley
MacLean's musings on a dead German youth in the desert, 'Death
Valley'. The Sixth Elegy, 'Acroma', brings a more corrosive irony to
bear upon the sterile platitudes which Staff Officers (and the
speaker too) habitually use to detach and distance themselves from
the victims of war. Perhaps casting a mordant glance at the original
version of Auden's 'Spain', 'Acroma' presents an image of the
ordered lay-out of military cemeteries. The pattern of death extends
both to the immediately opposing forces and, further back in time,
to highland experience:

> All barriers are down: in the criss-crossed enclosures
> where most lie now assembled in their aching solitude

those other lie too – who were also the sacrificed
of history's great rains, of the destructive transitions. (p. 33)

The best-remembered example of song obliterating the dividing
lines between contending armies is the German melody 'Lili
Marlene', popular with both sides during the war and since. It
becomes an echo from beyond the grave, memorialising 'Seven
Good Germans' 'as once' they were:

Seven poor bastards
            dead in African deadland
(tawny tousled hair under the
                        issue blanket)
            wie einst Lili
    dead in African deadland
                    einst Lili Marlene

The seventh of these imagined figures: 'Riding cramped in a lorry/
to death along the road which winds eastward to Halfaya,' had
'written three verses in appeal against his sentence/ which soften for
an hour the anger of Lenin' (p. 37).

[HH] *It was because verses of that kind bring ordinary basic
humanity into harsh historical necessity. Here's a young man going
to be in the desert instead of having a girlfriend, raising a family;
instead of living an ordinary life. So harsh political or military
reality interferes with his whole existence. This existential aspect is
at the heart of the matter for everyone.*

The Seventh elegy was the one which brought the sequence into
being.

[HH] *I was thinking that I'd known Germans before the war and
it struck me as most peculiar that these essentially, it seemed to me,
almost sheepish and pacific people should be such ferocious fighters
and should be the slaves of this infernal, demonic despotism. These
things were churning around in my head and I was thinking 'Who
are these people?' I had come to know some of them as prisoners I
was interrogating, and the seven characters in the poem were based
imaginatively upon those experiences and upon my pre-war
memories. The first title I had was 'The German Dead at Eleba',
and it was from that poem that the larger idea gradually developed.*

'Karnak' is the most richly allusive poem in the sequence. Its intellectual reach also makes it one of the most rewarding, with myth and irony mingling to epiphanous effect. As a connective thread weaves one civilisation to another, Ancient Egypt vying with Greece, and Greece with contemporary Germany, the poem traces German and English literary intertexts. Rival deities, and the rise and fall of imperial aspirations leave Scottish resonance to register unspoken relevance, as the poem records a visit to the Valley of the Kings.

There can be little doubt that Henderson's prolonged exposure to the brute fact of death inculcated a deep suspicion towards the longing for immortality implied in Karnak's stupendous architecture of the afterlife. Recording his first impression of the place early in 1943, Henderson remarked: 'This civilisation was filled, so great was its unshaken complacence on this earth, with a profound death-longing – it longed, dreamed, lusted, went a-whoring after death' (p. 52):

> Yes, here among the shambles of Karnak
> is Vollendung unknown to the restless Greeks.
> Here, not in Elis and Olympia
> are Edle Einfalt and Stille Grosse. (p. 38)

'Karnak' ironically transfers such notions to Egyptian architecture in the German line Henderson includes, usually translated as 'noble simplicity and serene grandeur'. In a further ironic turn, this is then transferred to the contemporary desert with: 'There is *Schwerpunkt*, not here.'

[HH] *It's a military term meaning 'point of main effort'. At Alamein the* schwerpunkt *was to the north, in a frontal attack against well-prepared, dug-in, wired and mined positions. I was bringing that military term to bear upon the notion that the central point in those Egyptians' lives was death, and the massive preparations for death.*

The lines:

>   But the envious desert
>   held at arm's length for millennia
>   had its own way at last – (p. 38)

inevitably echo Shelley's testimony to artistic survival over pride's decay. The name inscribed upon the pedestal which in Shelley's epitaph for the vanity of kings still carries 'Two vast and trunkless legs of stone', is Ozymandias, Greek for Pharaoh Ramses II whose statue may still be seen at Thebes, and who completed the great hypostyle hall at Karnak. Shelley's poem reproduces the desired epitaph for Ramses: lines which provoke Henderson's own response:

'My name is Ozymandias, king of kings;
Look on my works ye mighty and despair!'
Nothing beside remains. Round the decay
Of that colossal wreck, boundless and bare
The lone and level sands stretch far away.[5]

Henderson's poem presents a paradoxical image of permanence, punning syllabically as it denies 'die eine', and reaching towards a great nineteenth-century representation of the nation whose armies are now knocking at the city's gates:

Synthesis is implicit
in Rilke's single column, (die eine)
denying fate, the stone mask of Vollendung.

[HH] *Rilke has a poem in one of his 'Sonnets to Orpheus' where he refers do 'die eine in Karnak', the one in Karnak, the single pillar which survives to live beyond the near-eternal temples. I walked for hours all over Karnak to see if I could find a definite pillar.*

Against the backdrop of the Valley of the Kings, the poem refers to the Ancient Egyptian symbol of resurrection. Osiris, judge of the underworld, has already made an appearance; now sun god and chief deity embodies archetypal renewal:

The sun-boat travels through the hours of darkness
and Ra mounts heavenwards his chosen path. (p. 40)

In antique defiance of life's brevity, art inscribes its own continuities. The carved friezes of Karnak transform themselves into an animated tapestry of perennial human activity. For this, a shaping legacy is Keats' Grecian Urn which leaves 'not a soul to tell why thou art desolate':

What men or gods are these? What maidens loth?
What mad pursuit? What struggles to escape?
What pipes and timbrels? What wild ecstasy?[6]

Henderson's variations on Keats' Grecian theme bring ancient
civilisation through Romantic references to connect with the observer's own preoccupations in the North African desert:

Will patient labourers work the shadouf?
Is fruit on the branch: and will ripe pomegranates
be shipped to Thebes? Will rough Greeks land on Pharos?
Will prisoners of war drive the shaft for tomb? (p. 40)

Finally, the interrogative litany turns to imagine the living king on
his return to Thebes at evening after a day's hunting, blithely
unaware of:

the long ambiguous shadow
thrown on overweening temple
by the Other, the recurrent
the bearded
the killer – the rhythmical tragedy
the heir – the stranger. (p. 41)

Nor can Moslem invasion look to unchanging permanence: the
last two lines pre-scribe divisions within Islam:

Welcome O Hussein
When you enter Karbala. (p. 42)

[IIM] *This signals the origin of the Shi'ite Moslem heresy – at
least, it was a heresy for the Sunnis. Hussein was the grandson of
the prophet Mohammed, and I imagined him entering Karbala in
Iraq where he was killed and the whole Shi'ite alternative to the
more massive Sunni Moslem tradition began. Those closing lines
touch, too, upon Christ entering Jerusalem, shortly before the
crowds turn on him and crucify him. Behind that part of the poem
lies the fact that I had visited the old traditional Moslem university
at Al Azhar and saw the students rocking to and fro with the Imam
in the middle, teaching them the Koran. In some ways it put me in*

mind of the Gaelic psalm-tunes from a different, Calvinist fundamentalism up there in the Islands.

From this sweep of changing civilisations, the Tenth, and final Elegy, 'The Frontier', looks forward in time to project airline passengers 'crossing without effort the confines/ of wired-off Libya' (p. 44). The shadow cast this time is that of their aircraft, and they are as mindless of the human cost of the North African campaign as the pharaohs were of their own historical demise. Classical epic suffers the same displacement as recent desert heroism:

> Still, how should this interest the airborne travellers,
> being less real to them than the Trojan defence-works
> and touching them as little as the Achaian strategies? (p. 45)

Rejecting this unconcern, the writing fleetingly resurrects dying soldiers. A combination of German (*brennpunkt* means 'burning point' in a battle), Italian (Buonconte figures in Dante's *Inferno*) and Scottish (a coronach is a funeral lament), symbolises the alliance between the living and the dead. This is further emphasised by the reappearance here of Rilke's single pillar at Karnak as a 'solitary column' – Scots-German emblem of a mutually constructed 'cairn of patience' (p. 20):

> Run, stumble and fall in their instant of agony
> past burnt-out brennpunkt, along the hangdog dannert.
> Here gutted, or stuck through the throat like Buonconte,
> Or charred to grey ash, they are caught in one corral.
> We fly from their scorn, but they close all the passes:
> their sleep's our unrest, we lie bound in their inferno –
> this alliance must be vaunted and affirmed, lest
>   they condemn us!
> Lean seedlings of lament spring like swordsmen around us'
> the coronach scales the white aretes. Bitter keening
> of women goes up by the solitary column. (p. 45)

In a culminating intertext the apocalyptic figure who confronts Bunyan's hero metaphorically combines nightmare and reality, the living and the dead, which have been concerns of the narrative across the sequence:

Run, stumble and fall in our desert of failure,
impaled, unappeased. And inhabit that desert
of canyon and dream – till we carry to the living
blood, fire and red flambeaux of death's proletariat.
Take iron your arms! At last, spanning this history's
Apollyon chasm, proclaim them the reconciled. (p. 46)

[HH] *Apollyon appears in* The Pilgrim's Progress, *the demonic being with flames coming out of his belly, who faces Christian. It was a play on the word appalling also. After all, this is about the dead, and how are we going to reconcile the survivors with the dead except by facing up to the problems they would have faced had they been alive?*

In 1947, not yet thirty years old, Hamish Henderson went to stay with Naomi Mitchison at Carradale to put the finishing touches to his volume. 'Heroic Song for the Runners of Cyrene' reconstructs an epic context of archetypal dimensions; fitting coda for *Elegies for the Dead in Cyrenaica:*
[HH] *There was a dispute between Tripolitania and Cyrene as to where the boundary between them lay. They decided, in civilised fashion, to mark the boundary where runners from each side happened to meet. The faster the runner, the greater the amount of territory that could be claimed. When the runners met, though, those from Tripolitania accused those from Cyrene of having cheated. To settle the dispute, and to prove that they themselves had run an honourable race, the runners of Tripolitania agreed to be buried alive at the spot where they claimed the frontier should be. However, to me, Cyrene meant more in terms of civilization than its rival ever could, so I dedicated the heroic song to them.*
The notion of running to meet a fate enabled Henderson to include a metaphor which effectively bridges the opposing forces – ('And those other too') – that have structured his sequence:

                neither slower nor faster
        but as yet out of sight
                behind plateau and escarpment
        is history the doppelgänger
                running to meet them. (p. 49)

Notes

1. Hamish Henderson, *Elegies for the Dead in Cyrenaica* (London, 1948). Reprinted Edinburgh 1990, p. 22. Subsequent quotations are given parenthetically.
2. *Ballads of World War Two* (Glasgow, 1947), collected by Hamish Henderson. Subsequent quotations are marked B and given parenthetically.
3. *Gramsci's Prison Letters* (London, 1988), translated and introduced by Hamish Henderson, p. 12.
4. *Collected Poems of Wilfred Owen* (London, 1964), edited by C. Day Lewis, p. 48.
5. *The Complete Poetical Works of Percy Bysshe Shelley* (Oxford, 1965), edited by Thomas Hutchinson, p. 550.
6. *The Poetical Works of John Keats* (Oxford, 1939), edited by H. W. Garrod, p. 260.

Measuring a Needful Path

WILLIAM NEILL

Since history is the victor's compilation
whose bones had right or wrong in
altercation?[1]

Taken from his 1986 collection *Blossom, Berry, Fall,* 'On Carrick
Ground' shows William Neill in reflective mood, exploring his
present sense of relationships between life in Galloway, his poetry
and its historical and topographical locations. The robust
physicality of his writing is here incorporated but also subjected to
scrutiny, as legitimacy is sought for a specific inheritance. In the
opening stanza a roster of Gaelic poets and place-names speaks to a
poetic continuity geographically located:

> My eyes have sight that comes from other eyes
> that looked on Arran through the centuries;
> on Ailsa Craig, Creag Ealasaidh, Carraig Alasdair,
> the rocky throne where mad king Suibhne sat
> half way between Dal Araidh and Dal Riada;
> Lailocen country, ancient home of bards:
> Bluchbard and Cian, Taliesin, Burns,
> The Hielant Captain and Mac Iain Deors'.[2]

But the poem recognises that self-location within an acknowledged cultural identity is to a significant degree an act of will, a
conscious alignment of choice:

So, from the humble seed that fleshed my bones
I build a pride as high as any prince;
better this clean descent from common folk,
who lived upon this ground in bitter toil. (BBF)

By means of this constructed sense of self and its connexions, the
poet can look beyond his immediate ancestors to precursors in myth
and in legend:

The deed to their estate is my own marrow;
our eyes look to the bounds of a shared horizon. (BBF)

'On Carrick Ground', and several poems in the same volume,
achieve a calmer sense of self-definition than has always been the
case with Neill. Conflagration is often his natural temper, and a
combative spirit marks much of his work. On several occasions
during our conversation, the fire in his eye would kindle, and he
would speak with considerable animation.

Born in Prestwick, Ayrshire, in 1922, William Neill spent the years
from 1938 to 1967 in the Royal Air Force, ending up as a warrant
officer, a master navigator.

[WN] *Looking back on it now, I'd rather have done something
else with my life, but I was caught at an early age, and that was that.
I did a great deal of reading, though – when I wasn't sitting in an
aeroplane I was sitting with a book. Like every autodidact, I
suppose, much of this reading was random.*

Neill also subjected himself to diets of examinations which
would put many a younger student to different flight, before entering Edinburgh University in 1967. In 1969 he caused a considerable
stir by being one of the very few Lowlanders ever to have gained the
bardic crown at the Aviemore Mod. After graduating in Celtic
Studies in 1971 he taught for ten years in the High School, Castle
Douglas, living still in the nearby village of Crossmichael. In his
capacity as 'a patriotic polemicist'[3] he edited *Catalyst*, the organ of
the 1320 Club.

[WM] *1320, of course, was the date of the Declaration of
Arbroath. 'While a hundred of us are left alive we will never submit
to the domination of the English', says that noble document. The*

1320 Club was composed by and large of Scots of all political persuasions. MacDiarmid was a member, and he was a communist and it also had High Tories as members. The common aim was a parliament for Scotland, and the magazine was first instituted in the late sixties in furtherance of those aims. I realised that it wouldn't attract intelligent attention unless it had something more to say than just politics, though the politicians, naturally, didn't like it. I published some poets for the first time in Catalyst, *as well as established poets like George Campbell Hay and Norman MacCaig.*

But the making of Neill himself tracks back to a childhood spent in Ayr, where his family had moved when he was a five-year-old. 'Drumbarchan Mains' recalls:

> Nou there's nae horse tae be fund aboot the ferm,
> but a muckle rid tractor ahint the stable door
> syne auld-sons frae their faithers needna learn
> tae ken the fur-ahint frae the lan-afore. (WP p. 27)

('Fur-ahint' and 'lan-afore' refer to the position of horses in the yoke.)

[WN] *A great deal of my time as a youngster was spent on the farm with my stepmother's relations. After we'd moved to Ayr I spent as much time on the farm as I could. I used to go there for all my holidays, and for every weekend I could manage.*

Although a poem like 'Kailyard and After' records the distance between a childhood where broad Scots was heard, and an educated adulthood where English is the norm, 'Man, whit a contrast tae ma life-style nou...', Neill does not engage the easy warmth of sentimental nostalgia. He prefers instead to train affectionate memory onto the more realistic aspects of rural existence where, for example, a boy's inexpert milking lands him on his beam-ends, covered in cow-dung:

> an gin ye didna set in ticht eneuch
> there ye wad be, rubbin a sair hainch
> a loch o mulk aboot ye in the grup,
> the auld dug barkan and the weemin lauchan
> tae see yir breeks aa smoort wi mulk and sharn. (WP p. 19)

In similar vein though different language, 'Cart Wheels' remembers a twelve-year-old working with Clydesdale horses next to an old man who 'cursed me for a born/ fool, if I let them walk out from the edge/ or snagged the corn-divider in the hedge.'

[WN] *People didn't worry, then, about a young child working. You were another hand. If you could get someone to sit up on a reaping machine, you'd let a man free to do the hard work. The old boy who worked the tilt-board, old Jock, my step-father's half-brother, never spoke anything but broad Scots. He used tae bawl in ma lug 'keep that bluidy horse oot the corn man!'*

Was this, then, where Neill's familiar ease with the Scots tongue began? He turned naturally into it to answer.

[WN] *I learned braid Scots when I was a wee laddie sittin on the seat o the reaper listenin tae Jock Broon an aa the ithers. There's some chiels aboot think that braid Scots is deid, and that it was deean when Rab Burns was alive. That's a bleddie lee! Braid Scots was gaun fine in the fields o Ayrshire when I was a wee bit laddie. They couldnae speak English gin ye had peyed them. They couldnae hae spoken a word o Standard English gin ye had gi'en them a guinea.*

Neill's use of Scots, and the recurrent theme in his poetry of the displacement of native linguistic cultures by invading forms, made me wonder about his present feelings on the subject.

[WN] *To me Scots is the language of the heart. As a child it was the language of the people I liked most to be with. Using Scots, to me, is like sitting in an old-type Scottish farmhouse with my feet to a roaring fire and a lot of old men making dry comments in Scots: making me laugh as they did when I was a boy. It comes over to me conversationally: even if it's a sonnet, it's almost like a conversation. Robert Garioch had this effect upon me; listening to him read his poems just went straight home. MacDiarmid said we ought to lift Scots up, raise it onto some kind of pedestal – which he nobly did! But to me Scots is different, and perhaps in a sense more than that. To me it's something that I relax with. Of course at school we weren't allowed to speak it in the classroom. I remember being punished during a French lesson when someone was asked the French for dust. I didn't know, but I whispered across, 'le stour'. I wasn't beaten for making a joke. The teacher said 'where were you dragged up, using a word like that?' It was borne in upon me later, reflecting upon the incident, that here was an indication of the depths of Scottish hypocrisy – despising the language of their own king, judges, lawyers: of their own nation. A fine language that they have been brought up to despise, in favour of this chi-chi – what the Glaswegians contemptuously call 'pan-loaf' – manner of speaking.*

Neill has said that he regards Gaelic as being culturally available to all Scots. Should all Scots therefore learn Gaelic?

[WN] *I have been castigated time and time again for saying that all Scots should speak and write in Gaelic. I have never said this. I have said that anyone claiming to be expert in the field of Scottish literature should at least be able to read Gaelic in the original. This seems to me to be unexceptionable. How would we consider some-one claiming to be a Hellenic expert who did not even know the Greek alphabet?*

Did he, then, have a preference for writing in any particular language?

[WN] *That's very difficult to say because I enjoy writing in all three languages. I just sit down and write as I feel. The idea that one should write poetry in only one language is a comparatively modern phenomenon, perhaps from 1600 onwards. Before that poets would write in several languages habitually.*

So Neill's reconstruction of the past is both existential and historical. 'Map Makers' directs its scorn at 'the cold men in the city/ who circumscribe all latitude' because of the ways in which they set the seal of alteration on place-names which speak to a historical continuity thereby obliterated, and the poem puns on the Gaelic meaning of place names as it preserves their registration. 'When Irongray grew out of Earran Reidh/ the culture could not stand on level ground', and 'After Cill Osbran closed up to Closeburn/ more books were shut than Osbran's psalter' (WP p. 10). Cartographers are seen as 'slaying the history of a thousand years/ in the hour between lunch and catching the evening train.' As that final line trails out of rhythm, the poem expresses the sense of lost muscularity it has been exploring.

The strength of these feelings help to account for the lineage of poetic utterance explored in the poem whose English title is 'What Compelled You to Write in Gaelic?' Though the dramatic effect of its closing shift from Gaelic into Scots is lost in the English transla-tion, the final lines remain accurately self-referential to Neill's position as writer:

Too late now to be twisting
a rough tongue to the accents of London,
but blabbering with my Carrick lips
Gaelic and villain I must bide,
impudent in saffron back and side.[4]

What, though, was the significance of saffron here?

[WN] *It's a quote from Dunbar, and there's some dispute about
what saffron means. From my reading of Dunbar I think it's saffron
the old Gaelic cloth, which is older even than the tartan.*

So Neill's own ancestors were Gaelic speakers?

[WN] *Many of them came from Carrick and the southern district
of Kyle, so there's no doubt about that at all. Neill is one of the most
Gaelic of names. Of course it originated in Ireland, but it's been in
Ayrshire since at least the sixteenth century.*

Ayrshire recurs in Neill's work often for the sake of a poet who
also figures frequently within it. One continuous fibre is a dialogue
with Burns across many years of writing. As name, image, and
poetic progenitor, the Ayrshire poet shapes an ambience of sustaining reference. 'Mr Burns For Supper' breaks through the mystifica-
tion imposed annually upon a 'nation not merely sold but deliber-
ately retarded/ by those whose place enjoined on them to guard it',
in order to register a more bemused sense of astonishment:

The true admirer wonders how you did it....
scribbling away in the midst of the Elect,
who seeing joy would hasten to forbid it,
suspicious of all but their own miserable respect
for a stone-age merciless god of their own construct
totally without love, an idol Christ did not know,
made from a kind of prurience welded into law. (WP p. 51)

Then, 'A Knell for Mr. Burns' reflects:

Strange that the living face
should suffer so much rage,
while birth-and-burial place
grew to a pilgrimage. (WP p. 79)

[WN] *Well, I agree wholeheartedly with many of the things he* stood for. *Unfortunately they're not the things the be-kilted, be-sporraned and haggis-bespattered members of the Burns Supper Scene find attractive. He was a poet who spoke his mind at a time when it was very difficult to do so, at a time when he was being 'got at' by funny little men in Edinburgh who were telling him that he would never get on if he kept writing in Scots. He attempted to preserve things Scots when they were seriously under threat; I mean the time after the union of the two parliaments. He stood for something that is important in the psyche of any nation anywhere; the bringing of things past into the future, not because they are materially important but because they are of use spiritually. Any nation which is divorced from its past is divorced from its identity.*

There is, too, a further set of circumstances which, by a combination of choice and history connects Neill with Burns. The first of these, of course, is a fidelity to the Scots tongue:

> I share and thole the same byornar stangs
> in this auld land o deean herts and leids
> whaur the paircel o rogues hes swallt tae a haill bing;
> I'm kittled by yon maist unwycelike yeuk
> fir scrievin in the 'aulder Scottish tongue' ...
> a thenkless daurg I'm shair ye maun agree. (WP p. 115)

But the other link is the triangular pattern of movement from Ayr to Edinburgh to Dumfries:

> I hae follow't ye aboot, Maister Burns
> frae the Auld Toun o yir birth
> thro Dunedin o the Kings
> tae the Doonhamer-land o yir daith
> whase mool I micht weel share. (WP p. 114)

And 'On Carrick Ground' refers to an ancestor 'who neighboured Robert Burns'. With a twinkle in his eye, Neill expands upon this.

[WN] *I'm very proud to say that a man of my name, one Robert Neill, I think, was a neighbour of Burns's father in Alloa. My family have been in Ayrshire since people were paying for masses for the souls of dead Neills. If you go to the Kirkport in Ayr you're tripping over their tombstones. Not that I'm claiming any gran-*

deur by that; most of my ancestors sold horses or put tiles on roofs
or were joiners. But as to the actual journey from Ayr to Edinburgh
to Dumfries – yes, as it happened, I followed in the same footsteps.

There are, though, other detectable presences in Neill's work,
other affiliations and lines of relationship. The rather ambiguous
context of 'Poetry Lesson' adapts a famous phrase from
Wordsworth's Preface to the Lyrical Ballads, 'just a man speaking
to plain men' (WP p. 103), while 'Dead Poet's House' records a visit
to Wordsworth's cottage at Grasmere:

> Abandon all to find true wine, true bread,
> essence under symbol, form beneath the rock
> holding to the vision of mind beneath the mask. (WP p. 31)

'A Walk on the Hill' can find the same poet congenial company:

> Wordsworth wandered under wheeling plovers,
> boomed behind trees to frighten rural lovers. (WP p. 20)

What was the attraction?

[WN} *While trying to get away from the mundane he wanted a*
poetry which would not just be written for a few intellectuals at the
top of society, but a poetry available to ordinary people. Although
he was a pompous ass in many ways, particularly as he got older, he
did as a younger man have a kind of open honesty. He, too, walked
among the hills and the woods, and he had, if you like, a quality of
being able to smell the earth.

To harness and control his attraction towards the past, Neill has
developed a historical imagination edged with a resilient and sometimes cynical sense of realism. He has linked his awareness of
successive waves of colonisation in Scottish history to his personal
experiences in the armed services, producing a scripted continuity
of concern with imperial outposts, colonial administration, and
related themes of domination and submission. 'Colonial Service'
explores that dimension of Scottish experience which involves the
recruitment of generations of its young people for purposes of
military control elsewhere. Spoken by a serving soldier whose imperial usefulness is now spent, at its close the poem turns disconcertingly upon a barely realised sense of divided loyalties and estrangement from self:

> returning home
> with the heart heavy, loving the land we left,
> like a long-wed man of a good wife bereft.
> We set our eyes again toward spire and dome
> of that great city whence our troop had come.
> Faded the fondness for native glen and stream,
> soul-scorched for the land where my strong years had been.
>
> (WP p. 18)

With 'Looking South to the Wall', a note of local pride at the inability of the Roman Empire to extend its control successfully over Scottish territory is balanced by an awareness of the private political ambitions served by empire, and of the bloodshed entailed.

But perhaps the most succinct treatment of this theme is the title poem, 'Despatches Home', of an earlier volume:

> At last we have them all well fooled, well tamed:
> they use our baths and lard themselves with oil,
> truss up their souls and bodies in the toga

begins this serving officer in a letter to Imperial Rome from somewhere in Scotland. Cynically realistic, the seasoned soldier recognises the realities behind the submission of those who have accommodated themselves to being divided and ruled:

> Now, when our swords save them from their own kin
> and mind plays traitor, there's no need for gyves.

This sender of despatches home acknowledges a grim identity of feeling between Rome's occupying forces and continuing Scottish resistance:

> We both despise
> the Latin-lisping traitors of the town.[5]

Moments of historical recognition like this lend a sharper sense of betrayal to the closing lines of 'Viewpoint: Lambdoughty', scanning 'bare moorland with no fences,/ the rock teeth tearing at the base of the clouds':

The broken promises of history
are drowned within the silence. (WP p. 118)

Within these perceptions across time, a sustained concern is that
of giving voice to those personalities, moments and events which
shape and are shaped by Scotland's historical record. 'Envoi to the
Dean's Book' ('A Gaelic link that is not mere sentiment/... gets to
the heart of Scotland in the keenest way'), both celebrates the
collecting of the heroic poems of Gaeldom by the Dean of Lismore,
and laments a general indifference to it:

> where at the far and least illuminated edge
> all that is truly Scottish is confined
> far from what passes as the native mind. (WP p. 113)

The driving force here is more than twilit Celticism; it derives
rather from an insistence that the cultural/historical record be preserved. As Neill has remarked elsewhere, 'Celtic mistiness is an
invention of non-Celts and bad romantic novelists.'[6] A poem like
'History Lesson' reinforces the sense of his own laconic realism as it
reaches back into Scottish history for unsentimental evidence of the
manipulative arts of realpolitik:

> A king, to solve their politics and his,
> set rival gangs to fighting on the Inch:
> the Cat-men and the Kays. They clanged and battered,
> spoiled the axe-edges, locked the Islay hilts.

[WN] *One of the James's had the idea of settling clan disputes by
running them like tournaments on the Inch of Perth; like a Roman
arena – a score of men on either side fighting it out with broad-
swords. The poem refers to the legendary fight between the clan
Chattan, possibly the MacPhersons, and the Kays, possibly the
MacKays. Incorrigible enemies. On the appointed day one side was
a man short so they hired a blacksmith from the town to make up
the numbers. The slaughter proceeded nicely, until the blacksmith
dived into the Tay to save himself by swimming away.*
In the poem's metaphor, the smith is left:

swimming from a Scotland he could not understand
back to an Alba that was yet familiar.

[WN] *This is a reference to diving into the river of language to
save yourself from destruction by the establishment. The poem has
things to say about the ways in which established power sets rival
groups fighting each other.*

There is, then, added pungency in the contemporary turn of the
poem's closing lines:

It still goes on. Lolling on benches
well railed off from the clans, our rulers watch.
there is no river we can dive into. (WP p. 109)

In 'Another Letter to Lord Byron', formal imitation enables an
assessment of Neill's own impassioned determination:

I share with you, I must confess the fault,
a certain penchant for sardonic stanzas
that throw an acid literary salt
among these delicate extravaganzas
that get in print (WP p. 178)

A pronounced physicality of image in poems 'appealing to sharp-
ness of sight, hearing, touch and smell',[7] accords well with Neill's
stated preference for what he responds to in poetry written in the
Celtic tongues. 'Formal stanzas, clear images and a lack of obscurity
are the characteristics of its best exemplars... It is this "bright"
poetry which is to my own taste and I hope it has influenced my
own work.'[8] Equally clearly, it has. But that is not the whole story.
A poem like 'Inque Brevi Spatio Mutantur' raises different possibilities:

Beyond all earth and air and water and fire
the unchanging waits for all, eternal in our change. (WP p. 97)

'Sermon on Midlent Sunday' moves further into altered realms,
suggested by neo-Platonic imagery, where 'All art is a parable of
eternity' is followed by:

The singer hears within the perfect song
therefore such songs must be. (WP p. 126)

[WN] *I am attracted to that element in the Platonic scheme of
things which suggests that perfection exists somewhere, no matter
in how intangible a form, and it exists for us to strive towards.*

Related to this is a pattern of imagery which moves from the
prayer-like 'O holy island, rest again in our souls' in the poem 'Iona
Remains' (WP p. 52), to a perhaps more secular version of similar
sentiment in 'Landscapes':

over the green landscapes the heart pursues eternity
and is never satisfied, never filled (WP p. 80)

[WN] *I'm certainly not a religious poet in the sense of being a
victim of any particular type of religious orthodoxy. But I don't
think you can walk in this world, if you have eye in your head and
an ear to listen, and not be religious in those wider senses. To me it
means having an eye to the mystery of things. There is not a thought
we have that ultimately works. Even mathematics doesn't work at
the far end of infinity. I think there's a mystery behind what we call
reality that is unplumbed and unplumbable by the human senses.*

This 'religious sensibility' is explored more fully in 'Oakwood and
Gall', a poem which in some ways forms a companion piece, though
now in elegiac tones, for aspects explored in 'On Carrick Ground':

The tall trees sway over Drumnakillie
    three lifespans long for each trunk of oak
the berried rowan and the jagged holly
    stretched a long mile on the hillside's back

Shenachan's company no longer meet there
    in the high circle of the poet band;
each twig that cracks underneath your feet there
    marks out a memory of the druid ground.

Bluchbard and Cian of the Northern Gentry
    and great Aneirin gather there no more;
the fine bold singers have all left the country
    black silence reigns where there was joy before. (BBF)

Oakwoods were traditionally places sacred to the Druids, and gall suggests a bitterness now felt at their absence.

[WN] *We know very little about the Druids; they're like the Picts in that respect. Nevertheless the Druids were fought against tremendously by early Christianity which saw them as a potent and opposing force. Of course the Druids you get now are an invention of the fifteenth century. But the Gaels had Druids. They were common to all the Celtic tribes, not just the Welsh. The word goes back into early Celticism. There can be little doubt that it was a religion of high intellect; after all, there was a ten-year training period. So they were obviously men of high culture. But to me the Druids are a Green symbol: they believed in the woods and the wild places, the groves if you like, places which weren't nearly as full of blood and gore as the later Christian world would have you believe.*

There is a more generalised feeling in some of the poems in *Blossom, Berry, Fall*, of a regret, a kind of hankering memory. Not so softly focused as to be easily recognised as nostalgia, it perhaps associates more readily with the structure of feeling explored in an earlier poem, 'Hiraeth', which introduces a rather cynical emigrant back for a brief visit:

> Returned from exile he surveys the wreck
> of this old city that he left behind.

Flushed by material success and condescending in attitude, the returned native nonetheless experiences more disconcerting feelings for his birthplace:

> Scotland, he says, is strictly for the birds;
> he gives in tips more than his brother's wage,
> but finds it difficult to put in words
> an odd desire to share his brother's cage. (DH p. 27)

But perhaps such ambivalent desires are inevitable feelings for a poet so evidently fascinated by uncertainties relating to Scotland's imaginative past and political future. Perhaps, too, the strong vein of political satire running through Neill's work is necessary, for it not to slide into a more bathetic of Scotland's culture. At any rate, the tensions in his relationship to past and present are nicely caught in the final triptych of the title poem for the volume *Making Tracks*:

> Down the tanned face of the old watcher
> who knew the horses and despised the tractor
> the ruts of time give warrant to the memory.

Notes

1. William Neill, *Wild Places: Poems in Three Leids* (Ayrshire, 1985), p. 141. Subsequent quotations are marked WP and given parenthetically.
2. William Neill, *Blossom, Berry, Fall* (Galloway, 1986). No pagination. Subsequent quotations are marked BBF and given parenthetically.
3. See Neill's own dual-language presentation of the legend, *Buile Shuibhne: the madness of Sweeney* (Club Leabhar, 1974).
4. The phrase is from Alan Bold's introduction to *Wild Places*, p. 1.
5. William Neill, *Despatches Home* (Edinburgh, 1972), p. 7
6. *Wild Places*, p. 6.
7. Tom Hubbard, 'Reintegrated Scots: The Post-MacDiarmid Makars', in *The History of Scottish Literature* (Aberdeen, 1989), edited by Cairns Craig, vol. IV, p. 191.
8. *Wild Places*, p. 6.

Patch of Cosmic Pattern

TESSA RANSFORD

> Trees do not grow
> for three or four years
> after being transplanted.
> They settle their roots.[1]

Standing in a bookshop set up by the London-based Poetry Society for the 1981 Edinburgh Festival, Tessa Ransford overheard an American voice ask an attendant for the whereabouts of the Poetry Library in Scotland. No such thing existed, and that was where the idea was actively born. Three years later the Scottish Poetry Library opened its doors and Ransford has been its Director ever since. So it is intriguing that during the early seventies 'A Poem About a Concrete Poem' began:

> I shall make a concrete poem
> a place by art designed
> where the stones and sand of life
> a mould may find.
>
> I shall open it by day
> to the sunshine, and by night,
> where it will be a lighted place
> where people will find light.

> I shall fill the place with books,
> with books of poetry
> wherein the very self of things
> speaks its reality.[2]

Also in 1981, the year following publication of her Selected Poems, *Light of the Mind*, Ransford started a School of Poets.

[TR] *I had met others who felt a similar need. I had six people who had said, informally, that they would like to take part in a workshop. I wrote to magazine editors asking if they knew of anyone who might be interested, and I got six more people. I wanted to call it a School rather than a workshop because I wanted it to be for technique rather than therapy, and for people seriously writing poetry as an art-form. I'd rented a cottage in Dunsyre, and we had a residential weekend there in 1981. The School of Poets has met practically every month since then, with people attending for longer or shorter periods according to their developmental needs.*

In the tangled skein of Scotland's historic pattern of out-migration and occasional return, Tessa Ransford's arrival is something of an enigma. Her father was born in Bath in 1895. Her grandfather, a doctor there in the mineral water hospital, was the surviving child of ten born in India. Before that, her ancestors were Surgeons-General in Bengal.

[TR] *Because my father's mother was Scottish, he was sent to Fettes College in Edinburgh. She was a MacAlister. My father went into the Royal Engineers and was a sapper in the First World War. After that he went to India where he became Master of the Mint in Bombay, at that time a civilian job carried out by the Royal Engineers.*

Alistair Ransford spent twenty-five years in India and was knighted for his services in 1947. But as far as Ransford herself is concerned, 'The Dhobi's Dog' also reminds us that she has:

> lived here twenty years (Anderson forbears
> and Glasgow MacAlisters – that's baksheesh!)[3]

Who were those Andersons?

[TR] *That's the interesting bit. Jock Anderson came from Green-*

ock where, in the middle of the nineteenth century, he was press-
ganged at the age of fourteen. He became a ship's captain, and then
he part-owned a paddle-steamer on the Clyde – it was called The
Shandon. We don't know much about his first wife, but he had
three daughters, and then he married again, a girl the same age as
his daughters, and took her and her babies on The Shandon to
Australia in the 1850s. Eventually he took the boat to Singapore
where he became harbour-master. I come from the family that
stayed in Glasgow. Jessi Anderson, one of his daughters, married
William Boyd MacAlister, who was my great-grandfather.

But for Ransford's poetry it was the dialectic set up between her
experiences of India and of Scotland that was to form a continuing
leitmotif.

[TR] *I think I use them as symbols for different kinds of contrasts – using India to represent abundance and multiplicity, spon-
taneity and the sense of everything happening together. I use Scotland to symbolise dualism, either-ors, 'black-and-white', and as-
sorted rigidities.*

> As exiles cannot bear remembrance of a home
> They cannot see, yet never leave in vision,
> A continuing place, although more real,
> For clear Imagination recreates
> The daily dance of its reality ...
> So I shall ever carry my exile.[4]

The encounter with Scotland, though, continued to contrast with
childhood India. In Ransford's second volume, *While it is Yet Day*,
the poem 'With Gratitude to India' expresses just that:

> To have first found the world
> in abundant India
> is my life's greatest privilege.[5]

'Winter Sunrise in Edinburgh', on the other hand, speculates:

> On such a frosty forenoon Cockburn left
> the lawcourts,
> experienced the New Town, memorised the Old;

singing a cold cadence Fergusson
the poet
shivered down the Canongate with rhythm in his feet.

But a sense of contraries out of which Ransford must make her own
progression is best expressed in 'Ode to Edinburgh':

Much I admire uprighteousness
and your grey endurance
but it has cost me warmth.

Among the startling gorse
I am asunder
torn with endless loss;
identity is northern,
my south, my soul remedial
but unremedied forever.[6]

'My Indian Self' sparks explicit recognitions of both Northern
and Southern climes:

Let me wear the silks,
the sandals and the gold.
Let me dip my fingers
in the bowl of desire
even here in the puritan corners
of my dwelling.

Let me reclaim
myself. I cannot
be curtailed.
Extravagance is my form
not my style.
Intensity is how my pulse is rated. (DI p.96)

The shock of re-cognition that marked the beginning of her life in
Scotland was felt on Ransford's pulse in determining ways, but her
initial return was to the south of England, where she spent a year or
two with her mother, camping inside a house that had been army
property.

[TR] *I grew up in the Mint House in Bombay, a big house just beside the harbour. In contrast, the house at Burnham-on-Sea was spartan. But it had a big garden with a 400-year-old mulberry tree held up by crowbars. I was quite lonely, with my brother at boarding school and my father back in India, and I spent hours sitting in the mulberry tree reading, writing and teaching my dolls.*

After the partition of India, her father came back and in 1948 became bursar at Loretto school in Musselburgh. It was with Ransford's arrival in Scotland that traumatic experience began in earnest.

[TR] *My father's elder sister was a headmistress, and she suggested that I be sent to Saint Leonard's, a girl's boarding school in St Andrews. For me it was a disaster because it was crushing. To begin with, I was separated from my parents, and all my life had been centred around them since I'd never really had a 'home-base'. In a sense I'd been spoiled; in India there had been servants, and when I'd lived alone with my mother I'd always been treated as a companion. And then into this institution run as if it were a combination between a nunnery and a school for delinquents. I'd never been treated like that. ... I actually left at sixteen with anorexia, though they didn't have a name for it then.*

In the school library Ransford found Rabindranath Tagore's *Gitanjali* and read it avidly.

[TR] *When I found Tagore I must have known unconsciously that I couldn't go on in that school. Anyway, I determined that if I went to university at all it would be Edinburgh and I would live at home. That's what I did.*

A prize-winning undergraduate, Ransford studied German, with courses in philosophy, English literature and geology.

[TR] *We had to do a science subject, and I hadn't done any at school. I chose geology, and in those days we didn't do evolution at school either. I knew nothing about dinosaurs or anything like that, so I had this wonderful revelation about the earth and the ages of things, and everything continually in transformation. I wanted to carry on the subject, but didn't have enough science to continue. What I could do instead was a year of archaeology.*

After marrying a Church of Scotland minister who was about to go abroad as a missionary, Ransford went to Pakistan for eight years.

[TR] *To be truthful, I liked the idea of going to Pakistan. Over there, though I never believed in 'the Blood of the Lamb', 'Saved by Christ' and so on, what the missionaries were actually doing in the Punjab – schools, hospitals, welfare centres – seemed to be pretty good. I could make myself useful. But I also came to realise that my own survival was entirely dependent upon the Pakistani women who made my life possible for the first five years. For the last three years we were in Karachi, which was a very different existence. We had to live and work amongst both the Western and the Pakistani communities and also be a bridge between them. It meant that we spoke Urdu and Punjabi fluently.*

In a life marked by tensions geographical, existential and onto-logical, Ransford produces a poetry instinct with religious feelings. In the sense that a central project of Romanticism was to determine the ego in a knowable space and time; she might be read as a latter-day Romantic. A phrase like 'the soul of the land and people' (DI p. 30), enters her lexicon in unassuming ways, and when her verse conjures the space where 'God in us and we in God may enter' (DI p. 56), the notion of an 'Oversoul' immanent in the universe further establishes those nineteenth-century affiliations. 'Poetry of Persons' utters the desired identifications:

> We complete each other constantly
> but grow to a new whole;
> we form a part of all that is,
> and all that is forms us a soul. (LM p. 49)

The gods and more prevalently goddesses who inhabit her writ-ing express her religious inclinations. Some of this aspect of her work is traced to the French theologian and palaeontologist Teilhard de Chardin, whom she first discovered during the fifties while still at university.

[TR] *He suggested ways in which evolution and religion could kaleidoscope. He talked about what he called Christo-Genesis, the whole universe becoming Christ. He was also a dialectical thinker with a theory of creative evolution occurring when contraries come together to create a new whole. That spoke to my experience too. I felt that the Indian and the Scottish in me had to come together to be creative:*

Lines from 'Epistle' suggest that part of the attraction de Chardin held sprang from his conception of Mind as:

> an upward fall
> towards spirit and communion of mankind
> in sea and earth and universe we find;
> all diversities answer their milieu
> Christ – within, without, alpha and omega. (DI p. 56)

While working in the publicity department at the London offices of the Oxford University Press in 1958, Ransford started going to Quaker meetings.

[TR] *I took one of their courses on religion and politics and found it very interesting. So I thought, well, if I can agree with the Quakers I can call myself a Christian.*

In 'Epistle', a poem which in some ways shapes a credo, the philosopher John MacMurray, who had taught Ransford during her time at Edinburgh University, is praised 'for his lucid word:/ two people are a person when related'. (DI p. 55).

[TR] *MacMurray was also sympathetic to the Quakers, and the title of his Gifford lectures says something about his philosophy. There were two volumes – the first was* The Self as Agent *and the second was* Persons in Relation. *He considered that we are a balance of faith and fear, and we need the balance on the side of faith. If the balance moves onto the side of fear we're either too aggressive or too timid. He also thought that you are only a whole human being in relation to other human beings; that the human unit is itself dual, a composition of self and other. Another early book of MacMurray's,* Reason and Emotions, *was also liberative in that it helped me to see the validity of emotion, and that it needs to be educated as much as does the intellect.*

To trace Ransford's development of a fit speech for these concerns, a glance at some of the titles of her 1984 collection *Fools and Angels* is instructive enough. 'Love's Baptism', 'The Cost', 'Reflections on Waking: Easter Day', 'Love's Reasoning', 'Epilogue: The Gardener' – each of these suggests reflections upon and filiations with a seventeenth-century discursive mode where an often religious wit linked logic with passion and mingled the erotic and the divine with the quotidian. Certainly a reasoning rhythm is required, as 'Mind's Love' concludes, to acknowledge that a function of writerly precision:

... is to penetrate the exactitude
of how you feel and what you mean to say;
and to respond with the appropriate note
of assurance, acceptance
of separate identity,
and merged, yet heightened, humanity. (DI p. 68)

At any rate, John Donne in particular was used as a model for technique, with Ransford as a student honing her own skill by writing imitations of his work.

[TR] *He had this rigorous thinking going on with all that passion. But it was fused. And he had these wonderful ideas in him like 'the amorousnesse of an harmonious soule'.*

In turn, Ransford articulates a desire to harmonise divergences in a variety of ways. While 'The Balance of the Brain' celebrates 'the Yin and Yang of our fine microcosm' (LM p. 12), a 'Recumbent Buddha' is seen:

> dancing in a whirl of energies
> conflict caught in secret harmonies
> movement in rock, solidity in sky
> renunciation locked with liberty. (LM p. 16)

Within a Christian emphasis, 'The Ecstasy of St Teresa (Bernini)' prays for her achievement of:

> the resting-point
> where spear becomes space,
> pain becomes peace,
> with flames a circling halo, (F&A p. 20)

The final poem in *Fools and Angels* conjures a visionary Eden where:

> gods and humans come and go as they will –
> precarious spirits are balanced in every atom –
> world without end. (F&A p. 56)

But precarious this striving will always be, as 'Moderation' admits:

> I'll look for balance and the golden mean,
> but such restraint itself may generate
> its own unspoken postulates. (DI p. 75)

A central harmony in Ransford's work is the congruence between her apprehensions of Scotland's Celtic culture and her experience of India. She sees in Celtic art configurations of fluidity,
interaction and change. These cross-cultural identifications serve a
significant function as the self she inscribes in her writing is gradually adumbrated:

> We must make believe:
> we must make up our minds
> and our minds compose us. (DI p. 79)

An early poem, appropriately called 'Incantation', weaves a spell of
memory from 'this sinking of the sun/ in livid clouds/ at Arisaig',
and from 'the darkly-gentian sea/ and eagle-headed/ Sgurr of Eigg'.
But these climatic and topographical impressions are enchantments
for the senses only, from which the poem turns inwardly 'toward/
people through the centuries here' and 'the legends of their tragedy':

> Now as the sun suffuses all
> in golden blood
> and swords of light
> I pledge my feeble watching love
> to those whose lives
> are here by right. (LM p. 22)

The opening poem of Ransford's first volume *Poetry of Persons*,
suggests traditional ambiguities in western inscription from the
beginning:

> These vicious circles
> Herakles knots
> snake-heads traced with tails entwined,
> tangled persons
> knit together
> by knots that strangle, knots that bind.

That was soon to change, as the closing poem of *Light of the Mind*, 'Spirals', demonstrates. In a later poem, an ambiguous reference to 'Eve with her serpent locked in coils of prophecy' (DI p. 36), suggests a deepening complexity of response, and by the time of 'In Praise of the World, the Flesh and the Devil', not only is the serpent rejoined to notions of Christian rebirth, but Indian values are simultaneously re-inscribed in Western mythic perceptions:

> Order of the snake: on the silver chalice
> Twines a tree as handle, with climbing serpent.
> This my christening present, my Indian birthright,
> Sacred religion. (DI p. 83)

Given the imagery of serpentine spirituality in her poetry, frequently in conjunction with goddess figures, was there a sense in which Ransford was going back to paganism to resurrect those elements useful to her design?

[TR] *Resurrect maybe, but not going back. Of course, as a symbol of feminine wisdom the serpent has a long history. If you go to Crete you'll see it; the goddess with serpents entwined all around her. The serpent is the healer, the wise one. It was taken over to stand for healing by Asculepius. Then it was made evil by the Old Testament writers, because they had to crush this fertility religion with its feminine emphasis. So it was made into the sign of evil. But as far as the connecting world of pagany is concerned, which it represented to itself by a multiplicity of interrelated gods and goddesses, I want to bring that forward, I hope, if not into the future then at least into the present.*

Not until her 'Medusa Dozen'[7] sequence, though, were some of these attributes and identifications more fully worked out.

[TR] *Although the 'Medusa Dozen' poems grew out of a particular relationship I was having at the time, the shape it took owed something to other sources. I was given a wonderful book called* The Encyclopaedia of Women's Myths and Secrets. *Medusa, you remember, had this head of snakes, and was so magnificent that you couldn't look at her. She was tremendously powerful. It was re-written that she was terrible and turned men to stone, and Perseus was sent to slay her by cutting off her head while looking at her mirror-image on his shield. Women who have effective power are perceived as a threat, and they actually petrify men, hence the turning to stone. This was the theme I felt was coming to me. The first poem I wrote was the one which became 'Medusa Five' and writing that, I think, gave me the idea of a Medusa sequence.*

> The man I love has turned to stone,
> He may have seen the snakes in my head.
> Now he cannot look at me
> or touch. He finds my serpents
> dangerous, their true imagining.

The poem internalises traditional perceptions of the goddess to convey the anguish, represented as a kind of Medusan migraine, which results from such an emotional/intellectual impasse:

> Blood-vessels in my brain have turned
> to writhing snakes. Tensed, then dilated,
> they throb and twist and stretch and hiss.
> They are killed by hammering
> with clubs, until I retch and cannot move. (MD p. 46)

[TR] *It's almost as if woman's intelligence is in her body, that women don't actually have a mind separate from body; it's all one. Wordsworth claims that poetry is emotion recollected in tranquillity – well, it isn't like that for women. We don't separate the hemispheres of the brain in the same way; we don't have to stop feeling in order to think or thinking in order to feel*

Varying its moods from the angry to the interrogative to the transcendent, the sequence meditates upon modes of male domination, of female otherness, and upon the mystifications and confrontations these can generate: mysteries which prompt the question as to why this 'Dozen' comprises thirteen poems.

[TR] *Thirteen is unlucky in the Christian era because it was sacred to women and to women's mysteries. There are thirteen moons in the year, so it's also a fertility symbol.*

A Dancing Innocence, also published in 1988, includes a shorter series of poems, 'Icons', which bring together ideas about art and divinity. Although the immediate stimulus came from reading a book on the subject, some of the ideas had been maturing for some time.

[TR] *I'd always known that icon meant image, and I'd known, too, that Russian icons are not just a picture of the sacred: they are the sacred because they embody the elements of the universe. They're made of wood – vegetable; the paint dyes are mineral; the egg-white they use is animal, and they represent pictorially the spiritual in human form. So each icon is like a piece of the cosmos. The book I was reading was called* The Search for Icons in Russia, *and its theme was the recovery of icons lost or hidden because of communist destruction of village churches. Sometimes the icons were hidden by the faithful; sometimes inadvertently made into horse-troughs or crates or doors. When they were found the art-collector could search for the original icon because they may have been painted over, often many times. The newest ones weren't always the best and you could, sometimes, get back to a twelfth- or thirteenth-century one. So there was this idea of going down into the innermost layer, which is, of course, a symbol of the spiritual journey.*

The first poem, 'Resurrection', connects the pictorial representation of Christ before the gates of hell to precisely that process of restoration which brings back to life the original art-work. The second, 'Horses', constructs its syllabic music to record another such retrieval, and the third, 'Rescue', ponders the effort required to save a sacred object once believed to possess its own miraculous 'saving' powers. 'Protector and Prophet' then considers the fate that has overtaken a painting of Russian patron St Nicholas and Old Testament prophet Elijah (type of Apollo, sun-god in his chariot): 'and now?/ An old sick man keeps the disused key' (DI p. 91).

In compressed diction the fifth poem, 'Truth', excavates wider significance for iconic representation and resurrection:

> Broken church, startled dragon,
> slaughtered again they do
> not die. Layer by layer we simplify,
> seek our own origin,
> experience destruction –
> for truth, an image we rely on. (DI p.92)

The next poem, 'Martyrs', explores further some of the relationships between the fate of icons and human life and death, and includes an italicised line which carries echoes both literary and from the New Testament, 'They should go by water' (DI p. 92).

[TR] *Oh that's fascinating. When an icon was finished, either not worth restoring or the wood had rotted or whatever, you weren't allowed to burn or otherwise destroy it. What you'd to do was float it down a river with the picture facing upwards; so it was like restoring it to nature, to the cosmos, 'returned to the source whence they derived'* [DI p. 92].

Of *Shadows from the Greater Hill* (1987), Alan Riach noted that the area of this volume 'is local beyond a particular landscape.... It is broadened with delicate strokes.[8]

> Turner's water-colours
> are not exposed to view
> except in Scotland's January,
> month of darkness
> when no strong light destroys them. (SGH p. 41)

What we notice, too are unobtrusive possibilities of integration for:

> my wispy, slender, Scottish
> Asian, aching, striding,
> enduring, joyous, anxious, hopeful
> woman-shape. (SGH p. 20)

And taking its cue from the actual contours of Arthur's Seat, the entry for 'February 14th' re-ignites Edinburgh's extinct volcano as it plies cross-cultural reference to Indian mythology:

> Or shall I paint the mountain
> as an elephant-god
> fat, sleek, pregnant,
> feet turned up
> navel protruding
> and wide, flat ears?
> He is detached from predicaments
> of weather or winter;
> laughingly knows of desire's flame
> never quenched to nirvana,
> but lit anew in rock and sinew
> year by year. (SGH p. 46)

[TR] *I decided, after I separated from my husband and was living with my daughter, that I must be less emotional in my poetry, more 'objective', and must look more outside instead of inside. From my flat I had a beautiful view over Arthur's Seat, so I thought that I would look at this each day and write as objectively as I could. I started on March 9th, 1985, went to Canada in October and showed what I had done so far to Fred Cogswell* [Canadian poet and founder and former editor of *The Fiddlehead* literary journal]. *He was encouraging. On my return, I continued with the work, finishing on March 9th and spending the summer of 1986 revising and reordering. I had jotted down lots of 'entries' in a desk-diary: not every day, but most days, and worked them up from there. Except for the first and last, which I wrote separately, they're all in free verse. The only one in rhyme was also written separately, for New Year's Eve.*

The last poem in Ransford's first volume had already recognised an identification which becomes a stabilising metaphor in *Shadow*. The second stanza of 'Trees' reads:

> I trace the grooves of growth encircling me.
> They mark me as I was when I became,
> define me as I am
> and as I will be when I have become.

The trees that feature in *Shadows* were planted in February of the year Ransford began making her diary entries. The planting triggered the series. The opening poem, 'Holyrood Park at Night', derives emotional signification from winter trees with their:

> Hardened branches blurred by the pallid light;
>   Nearly home I find beneath them
>   Circles of softness where earth is warmer.

Earlier perceptions of warmth vying with cold, what Ransford has referred to as her Indian and Scottish 'force-fields', are here brought into tentative conjunction.

The first entry proper, 'March 9th', develops resonance from growth, as 'sorrow took root/ and grew a spindly tree', to end on a note of affirmation:

Today
it was transplanted
into deep soil.
Its narrow shadow lies
in the oval grove. (SGH p. 1)

This organic metaphor recurs throughout the volume, on the way incorporating concerns registered earlier in Ransford's writing. To the idea of young trees surviving winter – 'an ordeal undergone and to their credit' – and taking nourishment from sunlight which causes 'separate snow melting at their base/ and running to their roots', the poem responds:

I call in vigil
on whatever god or goddess
can take hold of serpents
and win their beneficence. (SGH p. 4)

'Now I know', a later poem says of trees, 'why we worship them':

we see in them
our own toughness
and our weak extremities,
our own endurance and ephemera. (SGH p. 13)

As it unfolds, the sequence delivers symbolic expression for a rooted sensibility and its sense of a tremulously achieved identity:

As if from a tree-top I accept the scene
given each morning
calm, grey light.

I want no sudden sun,
no burst of rain or wind.
This peace, this unemphatic,
non-expectant, poised
detachment
I have worked for. (SGH p. 27)

Notes

1. Tessa Ransford, *Shadows from the Greater Hill* (Edinburgh, 1987), p. 9. Subsequent references to this volume will be marked SGH and given parenthetically in the text.

2. Tessa Stiven, *While it is Yet Day* (London, 1977), pages unnumbered.

3. Tessa Ransford, *A Dancing Innocence* (Edinburgh, 1988), p. 28. Subsequent references will be marked DI and given parenthetically in the text.

4. Tessa Ransford, *Fools & Angels* (Edinburgh, 1984), p. 31. Subsequent references will be marked F & A and given parenthetically in the text

5. Tessa Stiven, *Poetry of Persons* (London, 1976), pages unnumbered.

6. Tessa Ransford, *Light of the Mind* (Edinburgh, 1980), p. 21. Subsequent references will be marked LM and given parenthetically in the text.

7. Tessa Ransford, 'Medusa Dozen', *The Fiddlehead*, Summer 1988, No. 156, pp. 43–54.

8. Alan Riach, 'Beyond Landscape', *Cencrastus*, Summer 1988, No. 20, p. 51.

Dimensions of the Sentient

DOUGLAS DUNN

> I won't disfigure loveliness I see
> With an avoidance of its politics[1]

From its opening line, the subtle comedy of 'Lovemaking by Candlelight' involves a recurrent and self-conscious inclination to connect present intensities with the past: 'Skin looked like this two hundred years ago' (N p. 3). Since even erotic intimacy is invaded by 'echoes of Florentine/ Intrigue', it becomes evident that the Muse of History is one aspect of the woman being described, and Clio is a figure with whom Dunn has developed a productive relationship. In the same volume, 'Memory and Imagination' consider poetry's ability to incorporate the past, transfigure fact, and inscribe dream within an expanded sense of present possibilities:

> Where here
> Meets there
> And now meets then,
> That hard frontier
> Where pencil, paint, wood, stone
> And numbered rhyme
> Converse with music on the edge of time (N p. 69)

Dunn describes this poem as a consideration of art from a position he calls neo-classical.

[DD] *I think that neo-classical has come to mean a state of mind*

which practises the present through an exercise of the past; espe-
cially a past that takes into account the values of Greece and Rome,
which are the foundations of European culture. A civic or civil
element is a part of this. It's only in the twentieth century that we
get private concepts of art which introduce all sorts of horror, and
frightfulness, self-indulgence, obscurity and incoherence. I think
that the world we live in is so vulnerable that to indulge in obscurity
and incoherence is a sin against your neighbours. Never mind the
Holy Ghost [laughs], *it's a sin against your neighbours. The attempt*
must be made to reach some sort of clarity and candour; and to bear
witness clearly. But by temperament I'm a quasi-mystical nature
poet. I like nothing better than walking through the woods down by
the shore thinking magical thoughts; yet here I am writing pam-
phlets about the poll-tax, political verses and all the rest of it. You
get a bit impatient with yourself: it feels like a kind of trahison des
clercs, *compromising the literary values to which you'd otherwise*
devote your life.

An uneasy dialectic, then, pervades Dunn's poetry, with a lyrical
self in tension with public utterance. He has said that in spite of his
desire to celebrate, the way he ends up writing some poems 'is by
the *via negativa*, which to me seems the only appropriate way of
dramatising my testimony. To do it from purely lyric motives, in
confrontation with various phenomena, natural or otherwise, is to
be dishonest, and evasive, when I have other things on my mind
which I'm condemned to remember.[2]

[DD] *What I'm trying to get at is that I know what a pure lyrical*
impulse means, but I think it is honest to be distracted by impure
social actualities. If a poet takes on social and political issues, he can
only do it in the ways in which poetry can do it. The first person
singular in a political poem is the same first person singular as you'll
get in a lyric love poem. It's just that you're negotiating with a more
public subject than your own moods.

Born in Renfrewshire in 1942 and brought up in Inchinnan, Dunn
remembers a childhood environment where the urban and the
agricultural co-existed.

[DD] *At that time Inchinnann was the first countryside west of*
Glasgow – farms, a village a Western SMT bus garage and the India
Tyre factory where my father worked. The Clyde shipyards were

visible, and much other industry on the north bank. It was a busy
river in those days. And there were woods, defunct quarries,
streams, ponds, lanes, reed beds by the river and hulks on inshore
sandbanks. I picked up quite a bit of botanical and creaturely lore
as well as a feeling for the agricultural year. Parallel to that, because
it was in sight of heavy industry and close to Glasgow, I sensed the
vulnerability of the place – time past, time present, and time to
come. I don't think it functions in my poetry so much as pervades it.

'The Competition' recalls a bus journey to Hamilton at the age of
ten, and an early encounter with the kind of prejudice and social
exclusion which Dunn has so effectively thematised. Nothing
daunted by the expensive uniform worn by another boy, young
Dunn is thrilled by the fact that they both possess the same toy
airplane, and tells him, so:

> His mother pulled him to her, he sat sullen
> As if I'd spoiled his game. I spoke again,
> And he called me a poor boy, who should shut up.
> I'd never thought of it like that.[3]

It returns as a galling memory, though, as the poem insinuates,
quietly contextualising the encounter excrementally. But the lesson
in social proprieties based upon income turns to a different kind of
insight into social relations. Years later, running in a race and
determined to win even though barefoot, having worn out his
spikes training, Dunn took the lead, but mistook his 'best com-
petitor', and: 'on the last lap, inches from the tape, was beaten/ By
someone from Shotts Miners' Welfare Harriers club' (SP p. 80).
These are indicative ironies, with both race and poem reflecting
on truer relationships within a community. And a companion
poem, 'Boys with Coats' instructs a ten year-old Dunn in the plight
of those lower down the social scale than himself, as it conjures
memories of left-wing ambience and prevalent assumptions in the
immediate post-war years. We watch a matured voice in the
making.

Refusing to go to John Neilson School in Paisley, or to Paisley
Grammar School, which he describes as his first political decision,
Dunn attended Camphill Senior Secondary and then worked in
local libraries, and took advantage of the time to read, before
qualifying as a librarian. In 1966, after a couple of other jobs,

including one in the U.S.A., Dunn went to Hull University where he took a first in English Literature.

[DD] *I couldn't get a place at a Scottish University. The Attestation of Fitness (as it was called) demanded subjects I wasn't prepared to waste time studying when their only purpose was an entrance requirement. I don't feel bitter, although I did at the time.*

While at Hull, Dunn met Philip Larkin, and although it would be difficult to imagine two writers further apart on the political spectrum, in a published lecture Dunn has paid handsome tribute to the older poet in ways which shed light on his own practice. 'What influenced me heavily', he writes, 'was the up-to-dateness of observation in Larkin's verse.'[4] He goes on to remark: 'As for the breaking of barriers, the primary hurdle to be overcome is the inhibition surrounding the first person singular. From inside the imagination and the psyche, the poet must unfasten and set loose private concerns and their rhythms' (UI p. 4). Among the qualities Dunn responds to in Larkin, and again it has relevance to his own very differently oriented perceptions, is 'an effort to return poetry to its social lucidity on one hand, a deserved mystery and lyricism on another, and, more intimately, to insist on the lucidity and truth of himself and by himself' (UI p. 4).

[DD] *I can see Larkin touches here and there in* Terry Street. *Overall, the difference between us then was that he had seen such houses and people, while I lived in one and the people were my neighbours. For some, Hull is a name from the music-hall jokes, so a poem like Larkin's 'Here' could give you confidence. As soon as I got to know Larkin better his influence on me stopped. Negative influences might not be discussed enough – and it doesn't need to be dismissive; it can be as affectionate as any other influence. Knowing what you don't want to do might not sound very helpful to a writer, but it's a start. Some of Larkin's attitudes, for example, were reprehensible, and he knew that I thought so. On the other hand, some of his purely literary convictions struck me and still strike me as admirable – his concern for scrupulous honesty, for artistry, for not faking it. In more intimate matters, his profound loathing of selfishness and envy are qualities in his life and poetry that I try to abide by. It isn't often that a novice in his twenties is befriended by a poet acknowledged as 'major', and I'm grateful for the privilege. Having said that, I might add that we argued a lot.*

The poems in *Terry Street* bring a discomfited light to bear upon

its denizens and their quality of life. It was an irony of circumstances that took a poet temperamentally disposed to celebrate life's
possibilities to an area where economic and cultural deprivation
were relentlessly apparent. He has already said that 'an explanation
of why I wrote about Terry Street, and a way of understanding the
moods of these poems, is that I felt myself a stranger in the street
and town where I lived.'[5] He has also referred to 'the quite self-
conscious sense of decency which people of my father's generation
upheld and which as the years went by they noticed were being
eroded. My father once came out with a phrase about 'the death of
decency',[6] and Dunn's experience of the working-class community
in which he grew up could only exacerbate the sense of emotional
conflict he felt as he looked out at Terry Street.

Although it has a natural justification – Dunn has poor eyesight
and likes to work by daylight – the window which frames several of
these poems is a mark of his separation, as an alienated sympathy
inscribes unsettled and unsettling responses. A fierce loyalty to the
truth of his own perceptions is antagonised by:

> A street of oilstains and parked motorbikes,
> Wet confectionary papers becoming paste,
> Things doing nothing, ending, rejected. (SP p. 11)

A sense of distance complicated by erotic undertones – 'They look
strong, white-legged creatures' – permeates a poem like 'Young
Women in Rollers': 'I want to be touched by them, know their lives,/
Dance in my own style, learn something new' (SP p. 16). But while
that element of desire is present, the poem is also exposing levels of
dislocation, with Dunn enjoying high culture, and the young women
mocking from a world away. Feeling distant from his own origins
adds a further dimension as the watcher becomes the watched:

> This time they see me at my window, among books,
> A specimen under glass, being protected,
> And laugh at me watching them.
> The minuet to Mozart playing loudly
> On the afternoon Third. They mock me thus,
> They mime my culture. A landlord stares.
> All he has worked for is being destroyed.
> The slum rent-masters are at one with Pop.

Was Dunn not guilty, as one reader charges, of voyeuristically appropriating the poor as objects?[7]

[DD] *God forbid! I lived there. I saw them. We were neighbours, though we hardly spoke very much. Terry Street was a dispiriting place: it depressed me. I distrusted how it rested on TV and record-player culture and not much else. I suspected what I thought were the differences between me and my neighbours. I felt estranged; and I grew to share their downtroddenness. And of course I was torn with remorse for having inflicted this upon my wife – my first wife studied at Hull College of Art. But I lived there and I was compelled to write. I gave in to the muse. I agree with Sartre – I don't want to, but I do. Poetry is very largely about defeat and failure. There's an element of fighting back, of course, of contesting the inevitability of defeat and failure. But I don't share the Left's cheap faith in the indomitable character of the urban working-class. Most of my neighbours seemed to vote Tory.*

Towards the end of *Terry Street*, 'Landscape with One Figure', written before the *Terry Street* sequence, returns to the Clyde and gestures towards a possible future direction for Dunn's writing. But it is as yet a suspicious and uncomfortable sense of relationship with a particular location:

> If I could sleep standing, I would wait here
> For ever, become a landmark, something fixed
> For tug crews or sea bound passengers to point at,
> An example of being a part of a place. (SP p. 28)

In several respects, *The Happier Life* (1972) continues to focus upon social deprivation, but deepens a stylistic concern with the eye of the beholder, with the structuring of perception as a mode of self-revelation. 'Midweek Matinee' examines the observer as much as the observed – the embarrassment of the comfortable as much as the plight of social derelicts. Again commercial transaction gives an edge to the response.

> I don't want you here on my page, pink faces
> Under spit and stubble, as fools and martyrs.
> You are not new, you have nothing to sell ...
>
> You claim the right to be miserable

And I can't stand what you bring out into the open. (SP p. 46)

'The Hunched' turns to 'sullen magnates' at the other end of the social scale to open with a complaint that it is social polarisation itself which demands care and concentration: 'They will not leave me, the lives of other people./ I wear them near my eyes like spectacles' (SP p. 47).

[DD] *Both poems dramatise a personal witness to the dynamics of observation or perception itself and the extent to which it's possible to be possessed by who and what you see.*

While 'Under the Stone' sees a similar discomfiture in the washed and the sober, caused by drunks and beggars, in part because 'these men remind them of the back of their minds' (SP p. 53), by describing them as 'splendid barbarians' it also looks forward to a different, though related pattern of development.

[DD] *I've been mesmerised by social contrasts from a very young age, usually in such a way that the question 'Why?' has begged me to try and answer it. I don't know the answer to large-scale social injustice, but I know the question, and I know it can be asked of everywhere.*

The appearance of *Love or Nothing* in 1974 showed Dunn making greater use of the world of childhood feelings in the shaping of a poetic identity, as well as reconsidering his relationship with Scottish perspectives. He continues, too, to probe the processes of perception. 'Renfrewshire Traveller' has little that is comforting to record about a return to Scotland. Feelings of estrangement mingle with attitudes of rejection complicated by suspicions of corrupted perception:

> Johnny Walker blinked
> imperfectly; history
> Is whisky, lacrimae rerum.
>
> Have I come back?
> I am Scots, a tartan tin box
> Of shortbread in a delicatessen of cheddars
>
> And southern specialities.
> I am full of poison. (SP p. 73)

[DD] *The poem evokes a visit. In those days the train I caught at Leeds went up through Kilmarnock to Glasgow Central. Johnny Walker's marching geriatric was my sign that I was home. Soon after that came Glasgow – a city about which my feelings have always been ambivalent to say the least. There were always people on that train who looked as if they were experiencing the same euphoric misery, wondering who they were, holding off sentimental junk about 'exile' but unwilling to think of themselves as visitors. I remember speaking to someone who seemed to be suffering from a particularly bad case of return-itis. He was full of sentimentality and undeserved pride, with the result that I wrote the poem. The repeated 'Not this' is, if I remember, a Buddhist formula for dispelling the awful, for driving away what you don't want.*

In 'I am a Cameraman' both the framing of a subject and the gap between framer and framed are focalised. 'They suffer, and I catch only the surface./ The rest is impossible, beyond/ What can be recorded. You can't be them' (SP p. 87). The problem of identifying with the Other while remaining true to the dimensions of his own identity is a continuing problematic as 'I am a Cameraman' concerns itself with the ability or otherwise of public pronouncements to represent suffering with any fidelity. 'Politics softens everything./ Truth is known only to its victims' (SP p. 87).

[DD] *By the early seventies it was becoming clearer to me, mainly from conversation, and newspapers, that film was rated the authentic art of the times. I didn't believe it then, and I still don't. Up to that point, though, much of my work had been 'photographic', at least to an extent. So the persona was meant to be part cameraman, part poet. Both aspects of the persona are disenchanted. They speak up for truth, mystery, the possibilities of art. We've all seen film of the concentration camps and their emaciated survivors. Horrified as we might be, what do we really know about being a victim in that extreme of humiliation and agony? In the end, poetry is about testing your honesty to its limits in the hope of reaching the truth. Any poet has to break a reticence barrier. He or she has to have the courage of melancholy and delight, and live and work without embarrassment at what poetry does.*

These can be extremely awkward boundaries: 'I walk home./ A suitably ashamed/ Observer of the poor' (SP p. 172), but Dunn remains faithful to his choice of speaking feelingly about human relationships in known communities.

In such circumstances, to speak to and for alternative modes of connexion and identification might itself be construed a political act. As a check upon his own directions, Dunn habitually scrutinises the process of observation. The registration of his own feelings might thereby serve the circumstances within his poetry. The price of appraising public sensitivities is the inventive revelation of his own sensibility.

For a Scot there are additional complications in this kind of venture, in which a background of Presbyterianism shapes a central difficulty. 'The kind of mentality', Dunn has noticed, 'which you inherit from the religiosity to which you were exposed as a child is – in my case, because it was Presbyterian – a state of mind which induces the ability to be sentimental as well as the hard-headedness which fights against sentimentality.'[8]

[DD] *That dichotomy or antithesis is very strong in the Scottish psyche. It's a part, I suppose, of the Scottish antisyzygy. I think of Gregory Smith's remark about the Scottish psyche, particularly in poetry, being such that it can accommodate a saint kneeling beside a grinning gargoyle. I find it enthralling that the Scottish psyche can go from the most abject sentimentality to the most hard-headed intellectual rigour and sternness. I'm glad I possess elements of it because it's through conflict like that that creativity emerges; in an attempt, always hopeless, to achieve some kind of reconciliation between opposed poles. They can never be resolved, but the work is to bring them out, expose them, and attempt a reconciliation.*

In one direction, the neo-classical impulse in Dunn's writing resurrects an eighteenth-century concern with sensibility as a reaction against the theories advanced by Hobbes and others that humankind is motivated almost exclusively by self-interest. In Scotland, a similar reaction took place against the rigours of a Calvinism which saw humankind as essentially depraved. At that earlier time, writers felt able to indulge a conscious effort to induce emotion, together with an optimistic over-emphasis on the goodness of humanity. The scrupulousness to which Dunn is committed, to say nothing of his own hard-headed realism, makes his a more fraught project.

There was a five year gap between *Love or Nothing* and Dunn's next collection, but when *Barbarians* appeared in 1979 it became clear that senses of political commitment, and a stylistic apparatus appropriate to them, had considerably advanced.

[DD] *The delay was due to my doubts about style and the role of political and social feeling in poetry. My links with my 'background' were far from severed in reality, but in writing I found it much more difficult to establish the kind of relationship I wanted – more truthfully, I didn't know what the relationship could be so I had to find it. I'd worked hard, and technically speaking I think I may have been more self-confident, less willing at any rate to cloud a poem with imagery, and less willing to subdue the iambic pulse or muffle rhymes....*

Political poetry always runs the risk of eliciting partisan interpretation which is not always as responsive as it could be to the structures of particular poems.

[DD] *If you are engaged in social and political subjects, then people are likely to react to a poem in much the same way as they react to political ideas; they are likely to reject it because they respond to the political significance of the piece of writing rather than to the piece of writing per se. So getting involved in these subjects means putting yourself pretty much on the line. Personally I don't much like being on that line. That's one of the reasons why I talk about being 'shackled' with that kind of subject.[9] But involvement with social and political subjects in poetry often means that people think you are involved in politics, which I am not, in any practical way. I don't carry a brief, nor do I have the right to speak for any political party.*

As far as the politics of style is concerned, *Barbarians*, written largely in metre, has a calculated design, with Dunn hoping that the book would 'portray a gesture of affront to readers who might be expected to approve a metrical way of writing, while finding the meaning of Barbarians disagreeable.[10] Bringing his own linguistic skills to bear upon the ways in which language itself shapes attitudes, the Graeco-Roman definition of barbarian forms a base-line upon which Dunn develops contemporary resonances. 'Just as the Goths especially sought not to dismantle or destroy Roman institutions, but to take them over and use them for their own ends, clean them up and reform them, revitalise them', Dunn sees a working-class movement in politics seeking 'not to destroy British institutions, or Scottish or English institutions or whatever, but to reform them and revivify them. So barbarians are people who contest the Establishment and the degeneration of the state'.[11] At the same time, Dunn spoke of the process of writing as a discovery of form, in terms which connect with his remarks about political reformation. 'I find that in using a set form, which I often reach half way through the draft, and then, obviously, go back and start rewriting in the stanza or whatever metrical line I've discovered as true to the poem – I find the challenge of that makes my imagination work, simply because it's harder to write than free verse.'[12] But was there not a danger that such an approach to form might constrict?

[DD] *There certainly is an element in metre, rhyme, stanza – there's certainly some truth in how, if you lower your guard formally you can indulge in what some critics have called an archaising mode. That's always a possibility. I was tremendously aware of that when I was translating* Andromache.[13] *Rhyming couplets is one style that instantaneously can turn into the eighteenth century. If you stop smiling at the form, it winds its way back in time. But you can use formal verse in a way that is sufficiently self-aware to be guying the style at the same as you are using it sincerely.*

These conjunctions of literary and political territory figure in the opening poem of *Barbarians*, 'The Come-on', with its acknowledgement that 'seepage from "background"' can take over and displace whatever 'intellect/ Was nursed by school or books'. Naming the material from which gowns were made for barristers, the clergy and university dons, gives costumed definition to a social order experienced as alien:

> Men dressed in prunella
> Utter credentials and their culture rules us,
>   A culture of connivance
> Of 'authority', arts of bland recoveries. (SP p. 99)

Class prejudice is a rancorous emotion, and the hostility it generates extends to the linguistic terms with which it chooses to identify itself. Property-based social exclusion and the signifying systems it generates are in alliance. No alteration is countenanced, and there is no admission to the excluded:

> Unless we enter through a narrow gate
>   In a wall they have built
> To join them in the 'disinterested tradition'. (SP p. 100)

The Biblical eye of the needle, a gateway in the walls of Jerusalem, is unobtrusively echoed to point up the hypocrisy of wealth in the culture it generates.

[DD] *After* Love or Nothing *I felt that I was going up a dead end. I'd been infatuated by some French poets and I think the influence of that is quite clear. I decided I needed something more robust, more public – but public in a way that didn't debar the possibility of subtlety or irony. I went through a phase of reading a great many books about politics, almost self-consciously politicising my mind; a dangerous thing for a writer to do. I wanted a style to accommodate my reading as well as a style that would express what I felt about my origins, about society, about various psychologies current socially at the time.*

'In the Grounds' continues the property metaphor to turn a more experiential screw upon a bourgeois culture uncaring of the hurt it gives. Visitors to a country house, encountering a spinsterish hostility and suspicion, are embarrassed, and would prefer:

> A noise less military and more kind
> than our boots make across her wide parterre.
>
> (SP p. 101)

At its close, the poem reflects upon:

> Their surly nephews lounging at each gate,
> Afraid we'll steal their family's treasured things,
> Then hawk them – pictures, furniture plate –
> Round the encampments of our saddle-kings. (SP p. 102)

[DD] *The poem began with a trip to Nunappleton House near York, where Andrew Marvell had been a tutor to General Lord Fairfax's daughter. I went there with some of my students in May, 1975, when I was writer-in-residence at the University of Hull. One of the number was planning a film about Marvell. We were granted a sniffy reception. Our every move was shadowed. We visited the local parson after he'd seen us in his church in Bilborough. He was a delight, and brought us home for tea – in retrospect I wish I'd managed to get him into the poem. Nunappleton, though, was the sort of experience that cripples the mind.*

The continuing cross-weave between literary culture and oppressive social hierarchies becomes a subject for historical excavation in

'The Student of Renfrewshire, 1820' for whom self-education, with all its attendant hardships, was the only option. 'I study Tacitus. It takes all night/ At this rough country table which I scrub/ Before I sit at it, by candlelight'. Political conflagration and opposing senses of literary responsibilities create a general conflict. The refrain ending each stanza suggests that contending with authoritarian repression and mastering intellectual thought are related processes:

> In Paisley when they read the Riot Act
> We faced the horsemen of the 10th hussars.
> Men's bones were broken, angry heads were cracked –
> Provosts, sheriffs, guns and iron bars.
> We thrashed the poet William Motherwell,
> That depute-sheriff and the law's law-minstrel.
> *Difficult Latin sticks in my throat*
> *And the scarecrow wears my coat.* (SP p. 107)

[DD] *My English teacher, the late Thomas McCrossan, digressed for an hour or so on the riots in Paisley in 1820 – aftermath of Peterloo. He had a few contemporary pamphlets to show us. He was an inspired teacher. Years later, in 1970, I reviewed Ellis's and Mac a Ghobhainn's* The Scottish Insurrection of 1820 *in the* New Statesman. *I'd been there before, and I was glad to go back. 'The Student' began with me in 1970, but it was more than half-a-decade later when I finished it, and even then I found myself revising it after publication. It's about the insult of high culture and the effort by a self-taught man to domesticate the Classics for his own ends. The re-possession of Classicism was one of my objectives at the time.*

Dunn historicises his own sensibility. His 'barbarian pastorals' constitute a textual 'country in which to reconstruct a self'. (N p. 26). That, too, is a continuing process, and he now thinks that some of the poems included in *St. Kilda's Parliament* (1981) could rightly take their place in *Barbarians*. One of these is 'Green Breeks', which takes its inspiration from an episode in Walter Scott's life when some Edinburgh middle-class youths beat 'The ragged street-boys from the tenements'. Playing upon the Christian injunction to turn the other cheek, the poem looks directly at the violence of social prejudice: the boy called Green Breeks, '"The very picture of a youthful Goth"', suffered a 'sword-cracked skull'. But signifying systems, and the coercive history they entail, are very much the

subject of a narrative which centres upon a fight over 'a handsome
set of colours' given to Scott by:

> that Highland bitch
> Who'd later clear her kinsmen from her land,
> That Duchess-Countess named for Sutherland. (SP p. 180)

Dunn's self-awareness inhibits any easy conscription of attitudes,
though in its self-referential musings the poem's loyalties are clear:

> Peasant baroque, like this, its nuts screwed tight
> In praise of rabbles and those sans-culotte,
> > Won't change a thing. It whets an appetite,
> > Unfankling truths inwoven like a knot.
> It gestures like a ghost towards a ghost,
> And, bringing Green Breeks back, or trying to,
> > It reckons with desire, the human cost
> > In losing what was old, and fierce, and true. (SP p. 180)

And in a metaphoric development, Green Breeks refuses money
offered in compensation – 'He would not sell/ His wound: let them
remember it.'

Also connected with this thread in Dunn's development is
'Tannahill', a poem in which he is able to identify with a fraternity
oppressed by the prejudice of social convention.

'Tannahill' turns to a history of different class structure for
stabilising, and inspiring, definition and self-definition:

> By singing you, I understood
> That poetry's lax brotherhood
> Lived in my town; and it was good –
> > Aye, Tannahill –
> To learn that verse did not exclude
> > A local skill. (SP p. 182)

Later, the poem affectionately asks:

> As you could weave, teach me to scan
> > And turn a rhyme,

> Fraternally, like Caliban
>   His low sublime. (SP p. 184)

[DD] *Robert Tannahill is often referred to as 'the Paisley poet.'*
Some of his songs survive and are still sung. His 'Epistle to Alexan-
der Borland' contains the lines:

> Though fate forbade the gifts of schoolmen mine,
> With classic art to weave the polished line,
> Yet miners oft must gather earth with gold,
> And truth may strike, though e'er so roughly told.

I think these are good lines. Again, my teacher at Camphill
Senior Secondary, Thomas McCrossan, introduced his class to
Tannahill. He showed me the culvert where Tannahill drowned
himself, depressed by his publisher's refusal of a new edition of his
poems.

The title-poem of *St. Kilda's Parliament* brings to fruition another aspect of Dunn's attentions. Subtitled 'The photographer
revisits his picture', it constructs a historical image of viewer and
viewed. The cameraman 'who took/ This photograph in a year of
many events –/ The Zulu massacres, Tchaikovsky opera –', makes
dubious discriminations. The persona ends by wondering whether
the expressions he has recorded, and/or the manner of their recording, is benevolent or malign. 'But who,/ At this late stage, could tell,
or think it worth it?/ for I was there, and am, and I forget.' (SP p.
145) along the way, though, the poem does tell: that the photograph
was taken 'Fifty years before depopulation–/ Before the boats came
at their own request/ To ease them from their dying babies'; that
marginalisation has extreme embodiments and effects. As an image
of Gaelic community, the poem probes structures of feeling from an
earlier age. Then, towards its close, 'St Kilda's Parliament' presents
an opposite image of the endless interplay between observer and
observed:

> Outside a parliament, looking at them,
> As they, too, must always look at me
> Looking through my apparatus at them
> Looking. (SP p. 145)

But what kind of parliament had it been?

[DD] *The men of St. Kilda would meet two or three times a week to discuss what they were going to do. They'd a very hard life, and the only way to survive was by pulling together – they would decide whether they were going to collect eggs today, or go to fish. It was a kind of survival democracy, achieved by speaking together.*

Although it could not be arranged until 1984, Dunn had wanted to return to Scotland for some years. 'The Apple Tree' speaks of his relationship with a Scottish people and place, and registers, too, Dunn's sense of the religious. 'My religious feelings', he has recorded, 'are unorthodox and multiple, so terms like "salvation", "covenant", "faith", "missionary", and "gods", lean towards paganism instead of replicating a Presbyterian vocabulary'.[14] And, 'An Address on the Destitution of Scotland' acknowledges senses of fidelity to 'this undeclared Republic':

> Permit me, then, to join your circle around your fire
> In this midden of warm faces and freezing backs.
> Sing me your songs in the speech of timber and horse.
>
> (SP. p. 150)

But fidelity to the truths of his own emotions is always and everywhere a primary concern, and after the death of his first wife, Dunn produced, with his widely celebrated *Elegies* (1985), a volume where private grief and love found responsive form. His commitment to a strict and scrupulous honesty faced a difficult challenge, and the problems in such intimate self-revelation are openly confronted. In the words of 'The Clear Day', 'I shall sieve through our twenty years, until/ I almost reach the sob in the intellect'. That sob is stylistically present at the moment of death, in 'Sandra's Mobile':

> She did not wake again. To prove our love
> Each gull, each gull, each gull, turned into dove. (SP. p. 239)

[DD] *The disclosure of feeling is what poetry does. But in the twentieth century so many poets have been afraid of it, mainly through the example of T. S. Eliot and his notion of impersonality which is bound up in a great deal of modernism. Yet in the poetry that we all know and love – 'How shall I love thee, let me count the*

*ways' – the poet's first person singular is right up there, naked and
quivering. The self is on the line. Elegies is the kind of area which is
taboo, or whatever you like to call it; but to be any kind of a writer,
perhaps particularly a poet, you have to break what I've called a
reticence barrier, and you've to touch your own candour. Elegies
was a subject I simply had to address myself to. It was very simply a
question of surrendering to the words that the experience gave me.
If I had turned my back on the experience, that would have been to
repudiate the muse, or however you want to put it. I don't know
how to be clear about it. If I had denied that experience its life in my
own work, then I would have compounded a death with another
death.*

In 'Winter Graveyard', Dunn memorialises a generation whose
male children:

> Young in 1914 –
> Are not buried here
> But died abroad defending an Empire's
> Affectionate stability
> And an industry of lies. (SP p. 62)

As he articulates emotional responses across a range of subjects, a
historical subjectivity, his own included, is habitually foregrounded.
As he 'writes' his life, the writing of lives is exposed. In this respect,
'Green Breeks' makes due acknowledgement. 'Though vanquished
from the subtly written book/ That's history, the street-boys often
won.' (SP p. 178). And 'John Wilson in Greenock, 1786', whose
own writing was subjected to censorious litigation, sets Robert
Burns against social oppression:

> The alphabet
> They cannot thole to hear as melody
> Will do them down as sure as they downed me
> Unless they learn a way of blotting truth
> And shut his mouth, and shut his singing mouth
> As they imprisoned mine and dispossess
> His art with purchased righteousness. (SP p. 190)

Few have been better placed than Dunn to trace the operations of cultural dispossession. In 'Here and There' the wit he brings to his own defence against the metropolitan literati for whom living in Tayport is cultural suicide makes a persuasive poetic testament. But across his writing, the intersections of art and power inscribe a compelling sub-text . As part of his concern with the construction of social perceptions, he considers, in 'In the 1950s', the coming of television, setting promise against actuality. Here, processes of metropolitan domination are brought to the surface;

> And half the time his mouth hung open on
> A wonder or resentment as he prowled
> The screen, his eyes on all fours, watching, fooled
> And frightened by those toffs 'in town tonight'.
> Names that he couldn't talk to were his masters.
> 'Some day,' he said, 'I'll take us both to London.(N p. 48)

Interactions between possession and perception, ownership and attitude, are graphically registered by the persona of 'Gardeners' addressing the Lord of the Manor and reflecting upon the 'hills, moors and meadows which your named eyes own' (SP p. 105):

> Our eyes are nameless, generally turned
> Towards the earth our fingers sift all day –
> Your day, your earth, your eyes, wearing away
> Not earth, eyes, days, but scouring, forcing down
> What lives in us and which you cannot own. (SP p. 106)

'At Falkland Palace', gives contemporary definition to the construction of historically conditioned perception:

> In a country like this
> Our ghosts outnumber us:
> A ruined artifice
> Empty and sonorous,
>   Malevolent
> In how its past force-feeds with filth
> Anachronism's commonwealth
>   and history bemoans
>   What history postpones,
>   The true event. (N p. 2)

What we encounter here are forms of alienation not dissimilar to 'The Silences' of *Terry Street* whose inhabitants no longer see the truth of their condition. 'They have looked at it so long, with such disregard,/ It is baked now over their eyes like a crust' (SP p. 17). Transforming these perceptions is a sustaining project in Dunn's life of writing.

[DD] If my 'life of writing' has a meaning, then I think it pertains to something that Trotsky said. I hold no brief for Trotskyism, but he is still a hero of mine, no matter what's been happening in recent times. In one of the pieces collected in Art and Revolution, *he was having to contend with some kind of proletarian organisation of writers, and was drawn to reprimand them for becoming too self-consciously proletarian and neglecting what the Russian revolution had originally been about, the achievement of a genuine, human culture. I don't find anything wrong in that: in fact the very opposite. I think it is as true today as it was then. Tendencies in modern societies might be leading us away from that kind of aspiration, but if* glasnost *and* perestroika *mean what I think they mean, then it is an attempt to get back to that germinating, fructifying, dynamic ideal that was represented in some of those early hopes. It is still a source of inspiration.*

Notes

1. Douglas Dunn, *Northlight* (London, 1988), p. 25. Subsequent quotations are marked N and given parenthetically.
2. John Haffenden, *Viewpoints: Poets in Conversation* (London, 1981), p. 23.
3. Douglas Dunn, *Selected Poems 1964–1983* (London, 1986), p. 80. Subsequent quotations are marked SP and given parenthetically.
4. *Under the Influence: Douglas Dunn on Philip Larkin* (Edinburgh, 1987), p. 3. Subsequent citations will be marked UI and given parenthetically.
5. P. R. King, *Nine Contemporary Poets: A Critical Introduction* (London, 1979), p. 221.
6. Robert Crawford, 'Douglas Dunn, an Interview', *Verse* (1985), no. 4, p. 26.
7. Alan Robinson, *Instabilities in Contemporary British Poetry* (London, 1988), p. 87.
8. John Haffenden, p. 18.
9. Ibid. p. 29
10. P. R. King, p. 225.
11. Robert Crawford, pp. 27–8.

12. Ibid., p. 29
13. Jean Racine, *Andromache*, translated by Douglas Dunn (London, 1990).
14. *The Best of Scottish Poetry* (Edinburgh, 1989), edited by Robin Bell, p. 36.

Knucklebones of Irony

LIZ LOCHHEAD

> It's chockablock with life
> and lives we can make for.[1]

The knowing Naiad who speaks 'What the Pool Said, On Midsummer's Day', opening poem of *Dreaming Frankenstein* (1984), is alive with sexual magnetism; and it is to the male's fearful insecurity that she addresses her attentions. Her control is beyond question and her honesty uncompromising:

> my wet weeds against your thighs, it
> could turn nasty.
> I could have you
> gulping fistfuls fighting yourself
> back from me. (p. 9)

The consummation of the poem turns narrative upon itself, leaving male tension vying with the text's completion:

> I watch. You clench,
> clench and come into me.

This unlikely combination of narrative registers is characteristic of Liz Lochhead's work. Colloquial idiom takes the place of classical formulae as readily as canonical text is transformed into the lively writing of the street. Conventions of readerly poise are abolished.

Her poetry constitutes a vigorous reorientation in favour of every-day speech, often in West of Scotland cadence, and the liberated womanhood to which it gives voice is as frequently disrespectful of feminist response as it is to male presumption.

[LL] *I'm very ambivalent about women: they're people with problems too. I get at them because I am one. I'm allowed to. Although I am a feminist, I don't want to give my writing back only to women, I don't want to become a feminist separatist, nor do I want to 'solve the world' solely for women because I find that position too bleak. I don't have a lot of faith in much of the male culture that's around in Scotland, but I think of its recent macho flowering as a last bastion, a mask. I don't like the splitting apart of the male and female that we have. What I would ideally like to do is give the male halves of themselves back to women, and the female halves of themselves back to men. We are divided within ourselves and the real task is the completion of selves. Tom Leonard speaks for lots of us in that line of his, 'ahmaz goodis thi lota yiz so ah um'.*[2]

Combatively forging intertexts out of contending discourses, Lochhead jeopardises conventional securities to reconstruct the reader by rendering traditional literary hierarchies popularly accountable.

Several of the poems in Lochhead's first volume, *Memo for Spring* (1972), were written purely for herself and with no thought of publication. Looking back on them, she already feels the distance of time.

[LL] *They seem to me to have been written by somebody else – it's nearly twenty years ago, and I was only around twenty at the time. I think, now, that I was recording a place I was actually about to leave, which I probably knew at the time of writing. Now some of the poems seem rather folksy: I could quite understand people saying that all they have is a kind of naive charm.*

While there may be some truth in that, other aspects of this early work are recognisable as elements that would subsequently shape a distinctive vivacity of rhythm. Lochhead has made it her business to attend to the otherwise unremarkable circumstances and concerns that give definition to countless lives. Focusing upon the everyday, including the predictability of a hitherto constricting range of phrase and saying, she delivers crystalline expression in which the commonplace comes newly edged. As an apparently exhausted

demotic finds invigoration, we look again at what might otherwise
be passed by. 'Homilies From Hospital' is a case in point:

> There was a bit of an upset
> one afternoon. Well, waking
> from an after-dinner nap (you get so tired) I
> heard sounds, moans I suppose you would call them,
> small cries, a kind of whimpering. (p. 153)

Phrases which follow show ailing powers of expression struggling
to achieve articulation: 'But on the whole here'; 'to tell the truth';
'this is only natural'; 'to be honest'; 'But for the most part'; 'we all
agree operations fairly take it out of you' (pp. 154–5). An ear for
common parlance is already being registered and part of the challenge is, precisely, *not* to pass by on the other side.

   The place that Lochhead was about to leave – 'such a town/ I feel
at home to be at odds with' (p. 128) – was Motherwell in Lanark-
shire where she was born in 1947:

> We lived, my mother, my father and I, in a single upstairs
> room in my grandparents' house. My father's side. Roughcast,
> Pebbledash. Six in the block. In the shadow of all the steel-
> works, Colvilles, Anderson Boyes, the Lanarkshire – number
> thirteen, the Broadway, Craigneuk, Wishaw. Whenever I
> heard on the radio the Lullaby of Broadway I thought they
> were singing about us.[3]

[LL] *My parents hadn't a home of their own after the war, so
they lived first with one set of my grandparents then with another,
which I think was important in several ways. I lived with lots of
grown-ups, since both my mother and father were the oldest members of their respective families with their younger brothers and
sisters getting married and leaving home. Later we got a new
council house at Newarthill about four miles from Motherwell
town centre.*

   'For my Grandmother Knitting' constructs an affectionate
memory of age and frailty unable to cast off a life-time of habitual
work. Almost obsessively, 'as if your hands/ were once again those
sure and skilful hands/ of the fishgirl' (p. 137), the old lady, incapa-
ble of translating former scarcity into present sufficiency, produces

garment after garment, as the poem pays witness to a life of toil and
of caring:

> Once the hands of the miner's wife
> who scrubbed his back
> in a tin bath by the coal fire
> once the hands of the mother
> of six who made do and mended
> scraped and slaved slapped sometimes
> when necessary. (p. 138)

But even as she writes these remembered beginnings into the shape
of her developing craft, Lochhead was also trying out other elements in the language with which she was subsequently to make a
wider impression. Her attraction to puns, and to ways of making
conventional diction resonate in a kind of 'double-take' for the
reader is already in evidence. 'On Midsummer Common', when we
hear 'football rowdies/ all going over the score', we are exposed to
Lochhead's typical ploys. Similarly with 'The palais and troc and
choc-full/ of gaudy girls dressed in parrot-fashion', where the pun
on colourful uniformity is conveyed by means of a dead metaphor
describing repetition. The poem ends with knowing *brio*:

> Oh it's nice here, but
> slagheaps and steelworks
> hem my horizons
> and something compels
> me forge my ironies from a steel town. (p. 128)

In this first volume, an awareness that her own linguistic vitality
confronts lives of often frustrated possibility can produce chasten-
ing results. The enforced auctioning of domestic possessions to pay
creditors leads, in 'After a Warrant Sale', to registration of the brute
civility displayed by sheriff's officers who have come to the house of
a socially inadequate next-door neighbour:

> impersonally
> to rip her home apart –
> to tear her life along the dotted line
> officially. (p. 130)

[LL] *I wanted no allusion in my writing at that time.* Memo for Spring *contains poems which make stories out of working-class life using real people: my grannie, the girl next door.*

As part of this design, problems large and trivial, tragic and humorous, attendant upon male-female relationships fascinate Lochhead, and are subsequently to create some of her finest textual effect. These, too, find appropriate prefiguring in her early work, with emotion often masked by small ritual or the object-dominance of everyday utility and consumption. 'Morning After' charts dawning senses of separation through 'Sunday papers/ held like screens before us':

> Me, the Mirror
> reflecting only on your closed profile
> You, the Observer
> encompassing larger, Other issues. (p. 134)

'Inventory' traces female loneliness in things left at the end of an affair, and the woman's loneliness figured in 'a/ you-shaped/ depression on my pillow' (p. 135). A character who is to recur variously in later writing focalises the remembered conversation of 'three thirty-fiveish women' in 'Overheard by a Young Waitress':

> All agreed love made
> excessive demands on them,
> wondered how long it must be missing
> before it could be
> presumed dead. (p. 140)

And talk in 'Cloakroom' registers the urgent complicity of young women in the eternal dance of the sexes as it recognises:

> the all too easily faked closeness
> of close-mouth kisses
> which always
> leave a lot to be desired. (p. 151)

[LL] *Even at that state, I used to work at the language; it didn't simply come naturally, I always used to play around. Always with puns, puns and clichés. That was obviously what started me off. I remember my mentor at that time was Louis MacNeice. I loved him*

*because he did pictures, and he always had a very colloquial flavour. I
know Auden is supposed to be better at this kind of thing, but I just
happened to like MacNeice. I copied some of his techniques, but it
came out so differently that nobody noticed.*

One poem in *Memo for Spring* is noticeable for other reasons.
'Revelation' tells the story of a young girl's visit to a farm for eggs
and milk. The dark immensity of the black bull she was shown there,
'at the threshold of his outhouse', terrifies her. 'I had always half-
known he existed – / this antidote and Anti-Christ his anarchy/ threatening the eggs' (p. 124). Lochhead recalls how the poem was made.

[LL] *The bull poem was an important one for me to write, and I
remember working on it over a weekend when I was coming to the
end of my second year as a student at Glasgow College of Art.
Stephen Mulrine ran a writers' group there and I had a feeling,
writing 'Revelation', that this was closer to what a poem should feel
like. When I showed it to Stephen he was terrific, terribly academic
and precise which was exactly what I needed. We cut it by over a
half, down to thirty lines. When I wrote it, 'Revelation' was definitely about darkness and light for me; but it wasn't about male and
female at all, I knew that the symbols were powerful to me: I knew
that it was about chaos; and creation, contained creation. It was
about small versus large, human versus animal: but it wasn't about
male versus female, not consciously anyway.*

Fear of the bull's massiveness, 'threatening the eggs, well-rounded,
self-contained', starts an image that is to recur in Lochhead's writing.

[LL] *I remember seeing a programme about Graham Sutherland's big tapestry in Coventry Cathedral, and he was talking about
the egg being a self-contained act of creation. At the foot of his
Christ is a huge egg shape and that of course is a potent symbol. So
I was aware that in my poem eggs and milk and gentleness were in
contrast to the bull; though even then I knew that you didn't write
symbolically, that you wrote about real things and let those other
elements take care of themselves.*

Painting and the visual arts are important for Lochhead, both as
a general imaginative stimulus and for the construction of particular images. How had she made that early transition from one
medium to another?

[LL] *What happened is very clear to me. I didn't do any writing
at school for fun. I did what was asked for and sometimes I enjoyed
it, but none of it was for me. When I took up art at about the age of*

fifteen, I would paint and draw for fun: not just things I was supposed to do, but other things as well. and I drew a great deal through my second year at art school. My drawings are clumsy; I'm not good technically, but I still feel that some of them have a nice feeling. And then, just exactly at the point that writing came back through for me, painting became the 'school work' that I did, and all the pleasure went into writing. It's stayed there ever since.

When *Dreaming Frankenstein & Collected Poems* was first published in 1984, its second poem, 'An Abortion', concerned the 'Guernica of distress' endured by a cow labouring to deliver something malformed and already dead. With hindsight it reads, perhaps inevitably, as a companion piece to 'Revelation'.

[LL] *It is; though it was written sixteen years later, and I never had the earlier poem at all in mind when I wrote 'An Abortion'. It was only afterwards that I became aware of it. I remember thinking 'Well, it's taken you sixteen years to come some sort of full circle and realise that a cow is a very powerful creature.' By that time, of course, I was far more aware of gender issues.*

Other lines referring directly to the bull in 'Revelation' speak uncannily to areas of concern which were to occupy Lochhead over the coming years:

> They called him Bob – as though perhaps
> you could reduce a monster
> with the charm of a friendly name. (p. 124)

[LL] *In a strange way it does link up with some of the material I worked on more recently; the Draculas and the Frankensteins. That work was very much concerned with a part of the monster we carry inside us, though I'm not really in the business of reducing them. I'm trying to explain them, to make people take responsibility for them, as Prospero does when he says of Caliban 'This thing of darkness I acknowledge mine'.*

Though her first volume contained poems recording experiences in the United States and in Canada, *Islands* (1978) marks something of a new departure in that it strikes different notes of introspection. Arising from a six-week visit to Skye, the poems touch upon a Gaelic culture to which Lochhead acknowledges that she is a stranger. The first of the 'Outer' poems registers both this strangeness and also more private feelings:

Another life
each spare rib croft
each staggered drystane wall
that makes slicing up bare land
look next to natural. (p. 106)

In the sequence, her incomer's eye preserves the difference of 'another world entirely' (p. 106) as it traces the intrusive paraphernalia of a modernising economy upon young islanders:

At Woolworth's beauty counter
one smears across the back of her hand
the colour of her next kiss.
The other nets in her wiremesh basket
Sea Witch.
Harvest Gold. (p. 111)

The first 'Inner' poem deploys a painterly eye to probe sameness and difference, and again the encounter with 'another language ... on Lewis' is tinged with inner reference. In the second poem a crow:

bashed his great horny beak twice hard
against the glass

as if he were in an egg
big hoody was determined to smash

[LL] *What happened to make me write these poems was that someone had loaned us a cottage on Skye, and I had gone with a boy-friend. It poured with rain; we weren't getting on well, and I wrote a series about insides and outsides. They are unlike anything else I've written, and I'm not sure that they are so connected to the body of my work. A lot of things were emotionally painful for me at the time, and these were love-poems of a sort, in response to that. They were the first poems that I'd written not to do aloud. It was a deliberate attempt at a quieter voice, things that were not dramatic statements. I think maybe they were the start of the splitting apart of the dramatic and the more meditative or private aspect of my work.*
    Though still a love-poem, 'The Bargain' returns to that more familiar territory of public places and faces; this time Glasgow's

street market known as the Barrows, and the transforming dislocation of dead metaphor is again in evidence: 'So what if every other
tenement/ wears its heart on its gable end' (p. 117). Idiomatic
expectations are disrupted with a deceptive facility: 'drunks/ you
could easily take to the cleaners', and 'believe me/ this boy really
knows his radios' (p. 118). Typical, too, is the interior turn at the
poem's close: 'I wish we could either mend things/ or learn to throw
them away' (p. 120).

'In the Francis Bacon Room at the Tate' reads a celebrated
portrait of Van Gogh as colour correlations of dark portent:

> a figure in a landscape that bleeds
> on all sides from the picture's edge,
> flows from him all ways,
> harshened under cruel sun
> to acid scarlet and poison green. (p. 121)

In different tenor, these modes of perception feed into
Lochhead's demythologising of bloodier archetypes in tales by the
Brothers Grimm. In *The Grimm Sisters* (1981), she reconstructs
fairy tale and romance towards contemporary and feminist applica-
tions. Lochhead's faultless ear for dialogue brings archetypal narrative into domestic immediacy.

[LL] *I was interested very much at the time not only in the
Grimms' fairy tales and Greek legends, but also very much in the
Border Ballads which were among the only poems I had liked at
secondary school. As I think about it, I suppose I have always liked
the macabre. Even as a very young child I remember being read to,
and it was things like Nathaniel Hawthorne's* Tanglewood Tales,
Europa and the bull – *things like that. I remember reading*
Wuthering Heights *when I was seven or so, and although I really
loved it, it wasn't any 'better' to me than* Good Wives, *or* Little
Women.

Lochhead's first step is to cast the 'Storyteller' as a woman
spinning yarns while daily domestic labour continues:

> for as the tongue clacked
> five or forty fingers stitched
> corn was grated from the husk
> patchwork was pieced or the darning done. (p. 70)

The protagonist of 'The Father' is initially characterised as 'loving and bungling' in a poem which mingles the figure who offended 'the evil fairy by forgetting/ her invitation to the Christening' of his daughter *Sleeping Beauty*, with the father of the maiden in *Beauty and the Beast*, 'tricked into bartering his beloved daughter/ in exchange for the rose he only took to please her.' Symbolically, incest might be disfiguring the seeming innocence of the narrative here, while at the surface, Sleeping Beauty's father compounds his initial wrong by 'over-protectiveness and suppression/ (banning/ spinning wheels indeed/ when the sensible thing would have been/ to familiarise her from the cradle/ and explain their power to hurt her)' (p. 71). It is, anyway, sexual awakening in some of the original tales, and the sometimes violent repressions they buttress and endorse, which focus Lochhead's rhythms. When the experienced daughter returns 'wide-eyed and aware' with her lover, it is the parent who suffers:

> Stirring, forgiven, full of love and terror,
> her father hears her footstep on the stair. (p. 71)

Suppressed erotic sub-texts in several of the Grimm stories are not the only sources for Lochhead's novel interventions.

[LL] *I found myself taking on these myths, and some of the poems are jokes in a vein of feminist reductionism, But the book as a whole was an attempt to find the muse. If you are a female looking for the white goddess, where can you find it but within yourself? The search was for an internal, as opposed to an external or male muse.*

The original tales involve social, often marital and familial, relationships which are as observable, *mutatis mutandis*, elsewhere in Lochhead's writing. They propose stances and circumstances which Lochhead's satiric wit would always mould to her own intentions. Given the recurrence not only of wicked stepmothers and evil queens but also, as in *Hansel and Gretel*, a mother who schemes for the deliberate abandonment of her own children, it is appropriate that 'The Mother' should turn archetypal account to disturbing contemporaneity, again incorporating elements from different tales, before concluding with comic incredulity:

> Tell me
> what kind of prudent parent

would send a little child on a foolish errand in the forest
with a basket jammed with goodies
and wolf-bait? Don't trust her an inch. (p. 72)

Bringing these conjunctions into autobiographical narrative. 'The
Grimm Sisters' proposes the continuity of fanciful mythologies in
schoolgirl memories of the 1950s where ritual and orality find
debased but widespread echo in brand-names and pop-radio: 'Lux-
embourg announced Amami night', while preparations for a social
occasion proceed:

Wasp waist and cone breast, I see them yet.
I hope, I hope
there's been a change of more than silhouette. (p. 74)

A constant concern in *The Grimm Sisters* is with a satiric sub-
version of the female stereotype, moulded according to priorities
imposed from elsewhere, and interpreted according to dominant
preferences. We watch Lochhead expropriating linguistic territory
hitherto in male possession, as she satirises and parodies male
assumptions about the social construction of reality.

'Harridan' is the first of three 'Furies' poems which draw upon
those Greek mythic figures who were the avengers of crime, especially crimes against kinship. The poem's immediate inspiration is
Breughel's portrait, executed in the manner of Hieronymus Bosch,
of Dulle Griet moving in her derangement across a demented landscape. Armed with kitchen utensils and a long sword, Mad Meg
makes as if to attack the devil in his stronghold. She is followed by a
group of housewives also fighting devils. The poem is concerned
that academic approaches to such visions of hell serve to keep them
at arm's length, preserving distance and inhibiting emotional open-
ness. In these ways the history of art is alienated from histories of
experiencing subjectivity, a process to which the persona has been
exposed: 'I chose it for my ... essay, took pains/ to enumerate the
monsters, reduce it all to picture planes' (p. 74). Incorporating the
details of Mad Meg's appearance in Breughel's painting, 'Harridan'
substitutes for scholarly distance a fiercely direct identification. 'I
know Meg from the inside out' (p. 75).

'Spinster' also conjures the aphoristic rules used to disguise
desolate womanhood while 'Bawd' dons a different mask, that of

libertine and temptress, which conceals emotional emptiness beneath public artifice: 'I've hauled my heart in off my sleeve' ... 'I'll
be frankly fake.' But sexual bravado echoes disconsolately in the
closing lines: 'No one will guess it's not my style' (p. 76).

Resistant veneers both inhibit and express antagonism when a
potential mother-in-law is visited by her son's partner in 'My
Rival's House': 'she glosses over him and me./ I am all edges, a
surface, a shell/ and yet my rival thinks she means me well.'

Lochhead is weaving her own tapestry, the weft of past narratives intersecting the warp of the present, and the first of 'Three
Twists', 'Rapunziltskin', reconstructs two folk tales in a medium of
flip jargon. Rapunzel's rescuing prince, with 'his tendency to talk in
strung-together cliché', becomes a predatory male content to ex-
ploit a trapped woman's helplessness. Her realisation of her plight
brings no release but instead an image of the gruesome death
suffered by the original Rumpelstiltskin.

The disruption of traditional narratives and of their role-playing
protagonists, dislocates a poem called 'Beauty and The' with echoes
from *Rapunzel* and from *Little Snow White*. Emphasising rampant
male sexuality and oppressed female endurance complicit with it,
the phrase 'so you (anything for a quiet/ life) embrace the beast,
endure', leads to reflections upon the likely fate of the erstwhile
victim:

> Yes, Sweet Beauty, you'll
> match him
> Horror for horror. (p. 80)

Alternatively, the growing attractions of sexual adventures for a
queen absconding with her lover, in 'After Leaving the Castle',
challenges the promise of blissful fidelity favoured by traditional
fairy-tale closure: 'When they passed him on the road/ on the fifth
day,/ she began to make eyes at the merchant' (p. 81).

The Grimm Brothers corresponded with Walter Scott on the
subject of Scottish balladry, and Lochhead opens 'Tam Lin's Lady'
with the first stanza of Scott's 'The Young Tamlane.' She produces a
street-wise but not unsympathetic response to 'Janet's' tale of preg-
nancy by Tam Lin from the fairy world. Parodying the repressive
stereotypes in Scott's version, her ballad becomes a lens through
which surviving illusions of romantic attraction and devotion are

focused. A glib and condescending voice speaks modern tones of acceptance to answer the original tale:

> – have it your own way.
> Picking apart your personal
> dream landscape of court and castle and greenwood
> isn't really up to me.
> So call it magical. A fair country.
> Anyway you were warned. (p. 82)

In this context, the intrusion of modern equivalences strikes a sceptical note:

> You're not the first to fall for it,
> good green girdle and all –
> with your schooltie rolled up in your pocket
> trying to look eighteen. I know.
> All perfectly forgivable.
> Relax. (p. 82)

The present becomes a lens through which past narrative expectations are refracted. In Scott's version, Janet's rescue of her lover from the fairy-world can only be accomplished by her clinging on to him as he undergoes a series of frightening metamorphoses; and she does. In Lochhead's response, this symbolic test of commitment is perceived as far less enchanting: 'As usual the plain unmythical truth was worse' (p. 83), and the mocking realism of the poem's closing question speaks to the destruction of romantic fantasy which the passage of time and changing circumstances might be expected to expedite: 'How do you think Tam Lin will take/ all the changes you go through?' (p. 84).

Clichés ironised; comic but confounding gaps exposed between the observer and the observed – these are the linguistic contours re-shaped in Lochhead's writing. Metamorphosis in classic Shakespearian text is re-located in 'Midsummer Night': 'was that a donkey braying in my dream?', where the union of poetic and cliché'd diction produces its own contradictions. 'Nothing tonight could decide / what form to take./ We are good and strange to one another and no mistake' (p. 90).

Bringing irony into play, Lochhead casts platitude ('petit-gout

mouthfuls of reported speech' (p. 94) in different lights to expose
the complacency which unthinkingly adopted phrases preserve.

[LL] *I tend to have my cake and eat it in that irony is my
characteristic mode, and irony is victim-talk.*

But while irony has long been used as a device for avoiding
commitment, it also enables the underdog to triumph by effectively
demolishing dominating attitudes and perceptions.

[LL] *That is what it attempts to do, to subvert from within. It
relates to my attractions to cliché, which you cannot use without
acknowledging it to be a cliché. You enter into a relationship with
the reader whereby you have the reader join in the game with you,
to complete the acknowledgement. So cardboard cut-out things,
like women's magazine phrases, I like to treat as more archetypal.
Of course they are stereotypes, but they are more than simply that.
They contain kinds of truths.*

True to its title, the last section of *The Grimm Sisters*, 'Hags and
Maidens', presents female figures in a variety of ways, some of them
sharply critical. In a characteristic collision between classical narrative and the idiom of contemporary situations, 'The Ariadne Version' buckles mythic symbolism to modern equivalent to re-focus an
episode from the story of Theseus:

> Of course Ariadne was in it
> right up to here
> the family labyrinth – lush
> palatial and stained with sacrifice. (p. 96)

Acting in betrayal of her father, King Minos of Crete, Ariadne
originally gave Theseus a thread by which he was able to enter the
labyrinth, find the Minotaur, slay the monster and come out again.
But Lochhead's version emphasises Ariadne's pampered and purpose-
less existence, 'sizzling on the beach all day/ with school out'. Since
Daedelus had first designed the maze, he figures here in the parental
construction of Ariadne's repressive bemusement: 'tricked out chintz-
ily/ to her mother's fond idea of some subteen dream –/ all those
Daedelus dolls dangling for godsake!' (p. 96) Minos' infidelity is
matched by his wife's sexual liberality – 'some labyrinth. It fitted
them like a glove' (p. 97) – and Ariadne looks forward to her own
elopement with Theseus. But this cross-weave of familial deception
brings its own retribution signalled by the poem's closing lines:

Over the horizon
appeared a black sail...

In Greek myth, Theseus forgot that he had arranged with his father
to signal the success of his mission by hoisting white sails for his
return. When Theseus approached Athens under black sails, Aegeus
his father, believing his son to be dead, drowned himself.

Plying back and forth from the mythic to the modern in this way,
Lochhead's synthesizing techniques dramatise a conviction that any
story-telling activity carries significance beyond the intention of its
maker, that story itself functions as a vehicle for meanings which
relate to inner and recurrent elements in human experience. Varying
the theme, a longer poem, 'Legendary', excavates mythicising processes in the lives of two people whose relationship is characterised
more by subconscious antagonism than by spoken rivalry. But the
rivalry is corrosive and spills over into a contest for possession of
language and song. Beginning and ending in guilt, and involving the
woman's death and the man's compromised survival, the poem
juxtaposes fairy-tale symbol and the trappings of Romance with
separating senses of frustration. These characters self-consciously
partake of myth, despite the domestic vernacular which presents
them. Now medieval huntsman, now father buying Clark's shoes
for his children, the husband is figured in imagery which mingles the
symbolic and the mundane, since 'nothing is too menial –/ at any
rate in fairy tales':

When she scrambled the eggs he'd so carefully collected
purely to contemplate the Creation Myths
he had to swallow it, say nothing. (p. 63)

Given their entanglement in mythic self-projection, an inability to
discriminate the metaphoric from the actual contributes to their
tragedy. Line-spacing indicates distance:

My wife is a handsome woman.
I can never love her again.

I have no idea what goes on inside her head.

One week later she was dead. (p. 64)

[LL] *'Legendary' marks the end of a phase in my writing, and it should have been included in* The Grimm Sisters *but for various reasons wasn't. I had read Sylvia Plath's letters and found them heartbreaking. Compelled to tell herself that she was important, she mythologised herself to herself. Consequently some of her early poems are just clever. It's as if they're embroidered; and then the real hell came through. What happened was that I mythologised Ted Hughes and Sylvia Plath – people who had mythologised themselves, or had been mythologised. Although I enjoyed writing it at the time, I think that perhaps it is a mask, a trick. I was telling a real story as though it were already a famous myth. When I became conscious of it, it became a method, with everything written as if it were something else.*

But the construction of myth and the nature of writing continue to fascinate, and the three poems which comprise 'Dreaming Frankenstein' focus attention upon a figure well-known to popular consciousness.

[LL] *The three poems were written at different times, but each one was a wee present to myself after I'd finished a draft of the play, which I'd write over and over and over again.*

In turn, Mary Shelley becomes for Lochhead a way of exploring the creative process:

She said she
woke up with him in
her head, in her bed.
Her mother-tongue clung to her mouth's roof
in terror, dumbing her, and he came with a name
that was none of her making. (p. 11)

[LL] *Mary Shelley was herself uncertain, When she wrote about the competition which was organised to get her to write the story she says – 'I did not sleep, nor could I be said to dream, just by my side stood that pale student of unhallowed arts, looking down at me with yellow, pale and watery eyes.' And in that sentence she has already become the monster.*

In some way it is to do with her own creativity being monstrous to her. Maybe the confusion which so many people still share, about who is Frankenstein and who the monster, is a sharing of that reality because it concerns a split psyche. And what books of this kind have in common is that sense of not sleeping or dreaming but being compelled to write. So 'Dreaming Frankenstein' concerns having a male muse, which is a part of yourself. This aspect became more interesting to me, and Mary Shelley's disgust at her own creativity, her self-disgust, comes out strongly in the way that Frankenstein is the villain of the book, and the monster very quickly becomes the hero.

Accordingly, 'What the Creature Said' registers his sentimental identification with a fellow outcast, 'bent/ above the hot soup, supping/ his solitude from a bone spoon' (p. 13). Then, in very different vein, a camp and jocular eroticism marks the parodic treatment of 'Smirnoff for Karloff', while allowing for the recurrence of an identifiable image:

> Ain't going to let nothing come between
> My monster and me. (p. 15)

In 'The People's Poet' Lochhead pays tribute to Edwin Morgan, whose repertoire of monologues recaptured Scottish discursive space for the elaboration of personality through voice. From the beginning, Lochhead's poetic practice has looked to performance for its effects, and Morgan identifies the last poem in *Dreaming Frankenstein*, 'Mirror's Song', as key. His Foreword pays tribute, in turn, to Lochhead's elaboration of a woman's point of view and to its anchoring in concrete detail of place, voice, object or colour remembered or imagined. 'The tone varies from the rueful to something very forceful and deck-clearing indeed. Darker undercurrents [are] suggested by the book's title [and] accompany an emerging theme of self-exploring and self-defining' (p. 5).

Several poems in *Dreaming Frankenstein* record experiences in the United States and in Canada, and give vent to a returning desire to shape love-relationships in a variety of moods. But inserted in these explorations of response and reaction in unfamiliar surroundings is a home-coming poem which suggests in brief compass the extreme alienation of womanhood in a male culture. 'Inter-city' begins:

> Hammered like a bolt
> diagonally through Scotland (my
> own dark country) this
> train's a
> swaying caveful of half

> seas over oil-men (fuck
> this fuck that fuck
> everything) bound for Aberdeen and
> North Sea Crude

and ends:

> The artsyfartsy magazine I'm
> not even pretending to read
> wide open
> at a photograph called Portrait of Absence. (pp. 33–4)

Not surprisingly, one of the American-set poems, 'In The Cutting Room' reflects upon Lochhead's preferred practice: 'Under the light of the/ anglepoise I am/ (beauty and the beast) at my business/ of putting new twists/ to old stories.'

Lochhead's dedication to the sometimes mute and often socially inglorious can involve a reductionism that may not always best suit her satiric purposes. 'The Dollhouse Convention' is as introspective as it is social:

> Is it for the mere satisfaction of seeing
> into every room at once, even
> the ones as children we were locked out of,
> that we reduce
> what we most deeply fear might be trivial
> to what we can be sure
> is perfectly cute? (p. 57)

But the seriousness of her frequently comic presentations, and her commitment to the trick of speech, sharpen techniques for tracing the social construction of experience. If writing in Scotland is problematic for a woman, the repressive formation of others less articulate remains an abiding concern. 'Don't/ let history frame you/ in a pretty lie' (p. 21) might stand as epigraph for much of Lochhead's work, and the role of education in the conversion of social norms into moral aspirations is the subject of the four poems which follow 'The Dollhouse Convention'.

As she plays with the phrases of common parlance, Lochhead achieves what might be the most pervasive structure of feeling in her work. There is a Brechtian effect lurking just beneath the surface of much of her writing; and its success depends upon the reader recognising different contexts where its meanings can be applied. Parody distorts the work it imitates, often producing cathartic laughter but also re-shaping responses as it ridicules its original.

Lochhead's satiric and sometimes affectionate disguises dramatise a longing for eloquence , and an indignation against popularly absorbed colloquialisms. Even bathos is subjected to a dead-pan reversal which deflects attention to social realities within and beyond the poem. As her linguistic exuberance re-figures ready-made expression, both are initially projected as comfortably assimilable. In these contexts dead metaphor generates lively disturbance.

A developing attraction for live performance, evidenced in the raps and monologues which comprise *True Confessions and New Clichés* (1985),[4] brought some of these issues into sharper relief.

[LL] *If an actress performs a poem like 'The Other Woman'* [p. 92], *she has to decide which of what might be equal ambiguities to emphasise. The other will then become a sub-text. But a poetry-reading delivers the same poem in a slightly flatter voice, giving a different signal to the audience; that you're not going to help them as to which of the ambiguities is surface- or sub-text.*

In some ways, Lochhead builds upon and develops traditions of popular entertainment, which suggests that she is attracted to the idea of resurrecting music-hall.

[LL] *I am. The subversive laughter of the music hall appeals to me a great deal. The trouble is that the folksy in this culture can become cosy and self-congratulatory: hand-knitted instead of subversive. At some point I'd like to do something about the male impersonators of an earlier era, like Vesta Tilley and her 'Burlington Bertie' routine. I'm not sure how much they understood of what they were doing, but they always subverted the class thing. It was working-class women dressing up not just as men, but as the toffs.*

For some years she has been deepening her contemporary sense of possibilities for the dramatic monologue: now in *True Confessions*, she calls some of her pieces 'raps'.

[LL] *The attraction of the dramatic monologue for me is that often the speakers are people with masks, telling the audience one story. But mostly they don't see through themselves: they're unselfconscious people without much sense of humour, and that is what makes them funny. The dramatic conflict upon which good theatre depends should happen in the heads of the audience, seeing the difference between what this character thinks she is telling you, and what in fact is being communicated. That is entirely true of Browning's 'My Last Duchess'. Raps are different: they are vehicles for me to do cheeky-faced bits, like the last poem in* True Confessions ['Man Talk', (TC p. 134)].

The verse that Lochhead developed for her translation of Molière's *Tartuffe*[5] brought dramatic sense differently into Scottish rhythms, and far from seeing it simply as an earlier flowering of bourgeois culture, it was the play's connections with Scottish attribute and precedent that formed part of the attraction.

[LL] *Well, Burns is such a huge presence throughout the West of Scotland, and working-class people are always quoting him. In* Tartuffe *there is a great deal of the hypocrisy that 'Holy Willie's Prayer' captures so brilliantly, a wonderful dramatic monologue in poetic form, that, full of the kinds of irony in which Molière delighted. I see a lot of relationship between Holy Willie and Tartuffe the hypocrite. Then Molière's language seems so gutsy and splintery and rather like Scots-English. I didn't originally know I was going to do it that way, but I wanted the actors to have a text that suited the Scots tongue. I wanted to catch some of the warmth and also some of the music-hall qualities that are in* True Confessions.

She felt naturally at home with the overlap between Molière satirising a French bourgeoisie and herself doing the same for a contemporary Scottish equivalent.

[LL] *If Molière is writing about a bourgeoisie, then so am I, but about a Scottish bourgeoisie; the so-called respectable people who put on airs and graces – but they're still Scots. Not all of the characters are bourgeois, of course. The maid in* Tartuffe *is a great character who pulls all the strings and runs everybody. I like these characters whose play it isn't, like Caliban, like Puck, the people who are sent around doing the work and making things happen. I'm interested in them because they have a special relationship with the audience, and that, too, is quite like the dramatic monologue.*

So Liz Lochhead writing dialogue for a seventeeth-century French character whose world is falling apart is more than a prospect to wonder at. Molière provides her with a text through which she can examine her own society and her relationship as writer to it.

[LL] *I still have more of that Scottishness to explore, perhaps because until recently I've felt that my country was woman. I feel that my country is Scotland as well. At the moment I know that I don't like this macho Scottish culture, but I also know that I want to stay here and negotiate it. This place of darkness I acknowledge mine; this small dark country. I can't whinge about it if I don't talk back to it, if I don't have a go.*

Notes

1. Liz Lochhead, *Dreaming Frankenstein: & Collected Poems* (Edinburgh, 1985), p. 8. This edition prints the poems in reverse order of their dates of publication. Subsequent quotations are given parenthetically.
2. Tom Leonard, *Intimate Voices: Poems 1965–1983* (Newcastle upon Tyne, 1984), p. 14.
3. *Jock Tamson's Bairns* (London, 1977), edited by Trevor Royle, p. 112.
4. Liz Lochhead, *True Confessions & New Clichés* (Edinburgh, 1985).
5. Liz Lochhead, *Tartuffe* (Edinburgh, 1985).

Widdershins This Life O Mine

RON BUTLIN

And now, what burning inside me?
what light trapped in a clenched
sky?[1]

Since an autobiographical myth informs and extends his range of reference from first to last, it might be useful to approach Butlin's writing through the group of poems which closes *Ragtime in Unfamiliar Bars*. This would be justified by the fact that three of them, 'The Colour of My Mother's Eyes', 'Poem for my Father', and 'My Grandfather Dreams Twice of Flanders' are incorporated from his first volume *Creatures Tamed By Cruelty*.[2] But three other poems which form a natural sequence, though they were not written together, allow us direct access to the body of his writing to date: 'Inheritance', 'Claiming my Inheritance', and *Ragtime*'s final poem, 'My Inheritance'.

In the first of these, an older self muses to his younger counterpart concerning an irredeemable sense of loss associated with the childhood crushing of birds' eggs.

[RB] *Yes. he knows that the fall is about to come, that it's inevitable because he can't remain a child, and he offers a kind of reassurance. What he's saying, I hope, is 'this is going to be terrible, but I can't tell you that. It is going to be terrible, but you have to go through with it; trust me'. It is done in different voices, but really it is confirmatory.*

The last line, with the child's fist clenched 'on fragments of an unfamiliar tense', show us the child's entry into time.

[RB] *'Inheritance' took a long time to write, and at one stage he simply broke the eggs and ran home, perhaps unable to accept his inheritance. That is why 'Claiming My Inheritance' contains the lines: 'I could not explain/ what made me run home faster than/ I ever ran before.' The idea was that he was trying to catch up with himself as he might have been if he hadn't broken the eggs. But instead I stopped it, to suggest that by the breaking he had entered time. It's one of the few poems that is directly autobiographical; I actually did break the eggs. And although it all felt wrong to me at the time, it was not until much later that I began to understand more fully just how and why it felt so wrong.*

Extending this theme, when 'Claiming My Inheritance' ends, the sense of unease, 'As if the present tense were happening too soon', is sharpened:

> The older I become the more
> I am aware of exile, of longing for –
> I clench my fist on nothing and hold on. (RUB p. 45)

[RB] *It is, I suppose, more difficult, more desperate. As you get older, there is nothing to hold on to. But then that's the way it is.*

> Instead
> the emptiness that stained
> the empty sky above mc blue
> gave definition to
> my isolation.
> Only this completed world remained. (RUB p. 45)

It is not until the secure structure of the final poem, 'My Inheritance', that 'every tense/ becomes a plaything we can share'. And while the speaker is still left at one point to 'cling even to my despair', that point is now two-thirds of the way through the poem. By the time of its figurative return to an opening moment, significant developments have been registered in the speaker. The tenth anniversary of his father's death leads to the reflection that Odysseus was away at the Trojan wars for the same length of time, leaving his son Telemachus doing nothing, and his wife Penelope weaving and unweaving her tapestry. In this way, a

mythic structure develops for the speaker to situate, distance and
so explore more deeply his sense of his own development. Now he
feels:

> Like Penelope,
> forced to stay behind, I weave each hated thread
> into its rightful place then tear the tapestry
> apart, dreaming I cancel out my grief. (RUB p. 51)

[RB] *Perhaps the most personal of the poems in this volume, it is
one of the most playful. But it's also deeply serious. For me it's some
kind of an attempt to find my centre; a statement of a theme which
I find preoccupies me:*

> In time the ghosts
> and demons we create as though from nothing, to share
> our loneliness, become our overlords. These hosts
> of our invisibility demand our blood
> to let them speak. (RUB p. 45)

[RB] *Even though my father is dead, I am, like Telemachus as it
were, waiting for Odysseus to come back. I'm saying that whatever
I may wish to do seems scarcely mine. It's as if I'm scared that he's
going to come back and claim not only everything that he's left
behind, but also any improvements I might have made; in other
words what I may have done with my life. Figures from the dead
world come into the ascendant, and it's like a battle. You have to
fight to get your inheritance. You've got to fight within yourself for
the right to be yourself.*

In such ways a mythically conceived autobiography lends structure
to Butlin's writing, and his life thereby becomes available for interpretation in a variety of ways. His three volumes of poems, and his
collection of short stories. *The Tilting Room,*[3] show him precari-
ously, but insistently, coming to terms with a poetic self's corrup-
tion and debasement. Seen one way, his writing has been sweated
out of a personal experience which can leave only a dark and
painful iconography of loss, anomie, and of restless psychological
turmoil; a record of unrelieved anguish with little to offer in the way

of consolation. In this reading, the sestet from Robert Lowell's 'Night Sweat' offers suitably sombre epigraph:

> One life, one writing! But the downward glide
> and bias of existing wrings us dry –
> always inside me is the child who died,
> always inside me is his will to die –
> one universe, one body ... in this urn
> the animal night-sweats of the spirit burn.[4]

But while feelings of this order have relevance to Butlin's writing, they might suggest that the Scottish poet was unable to escape the confines of his angst-ridden world. And to suggest that would be to read him in the wrong light: he is also a love poet of unaffected felicity. The success of his writing might be more profitably construed as art snatching a grace beyond the reach of life.

Though born in Edinburgh, Butlin moved to the tiny village of Hightae before his first year was out, living there until he was eleven years old. Situated on the coastal fringes of the Southern Uplands of Scotland, where the river Annan winds into the Solway Firth, Hightae survives on the dairy farming which the Annandale valley supports. Butlin's memories of the place are still 'very, very strong', and he willingly grants that 'my soul, if you like, has been fashioned by that curve in the river near the village.' The move away from Hightae, first to the town of Dumfries, then, at the age of sixteen leaving home and plunging south into London to make his way in a variety of jobs, is an itinerary of classic transition from the country to the city – with all the tensions of separation, disinheritance, exile and alienation which that entails. Strange and disturbing for a teenager to cope with.

[RB] *In fact, it really was 'from the country to the city'. Within a week of arriving in London I was living in an old-fashioned kind of agency with about half a dozen others, footmen and butlers, and the chap in charge hired us out to all kinds of people. I'd been taught the necessary things that a valet would do, and eventually I graduated to being a butler, going to cocktail parties and such things. It was a bizarre life, from the country to all of this. One of the first places I went to belonged to a famous actress, with champagne-filled baths and so on. In some ways, even, I regard my life as a kind of metaphor for the Fall.*

If that is so, and the poetry suggests that it is, then the life of writing is very much a paradigm of regeneration, for Butlin's work is characterised as much by the private stress of its feelings as by its expression of sensuous pleasure beyond the realm of pain. His first book takes its title, *Creatures Tamed by Cruelty*, from a poem called 'I shall Show you Glittering Stones', and the counterpoint is as typical as the opposition of light and darkness in his work.

>   I shall tell you that the sky
>   is the underbelly of a crouched animal,
>   I shall tell you that it tunnelled once
>   upon a time into the daylight,
>   and that it stayed there
>   tense and afraid:
>   – then we will become whatever our embrace
>   can liken to ourselves
>
>   and to that creature as it turns upon us. (CTC, p. 30)

Animal warmth and feral wariness figure the struggle of experience outwards and upwards into expression, and thereby shape an uneasy poise; a precarious achievement which threatens the making even in the process of being made. Revelation is also exposure and as the poem moves towards resolution it postpones closure in favour of a vulnerability which extends into the possibilities of a still jeopardising present.

'I haunt myself since childhood', claims 'Poem for my Father', and later: 'Time and again his dead hand reaches for mine'. The poem 'Strangers' develops the theme:

>   I am being lived in:
>   strangers enter and depart, the rest perishes
>   ...
>   Lest they depart forever
>   I fashion them day by day to resemble me. (CTC p. 17)

'Two Landscapes: Father and Son' approaches from another direction:

>   My father becomes a forest without birdsong
>   Where sometimes the keen wind blows in high branches:

but down here where I am
it is sunless and silent
until he dies. (CTC p. 19)

Clearly, a compulsive thread in this design concerns a father-figure of various symbolic attributes who haunts a life of writing, and who deprives the producing subject of any stable sense of self. The reconstruction of that self in verbal artefact leads to some of Butlin's most recognisable effects. In the precise image of evanescence, sunlight playing to its own reflection through a phantasm of mist, the second part of 'Two Landscapes' conjures exactly the processual chimaera of solution/dissolution/resolution which is at the core of many of Butlin's poems; an insubstantiality endlessly caught and released in the moment of its configuration:

where colour coming from the sun
resolves endlessly towards an image
that rises from the water
to become other than what's here
between my shadow and the sun,
resolving whatever accident I am. (CTC p. 19)

The sheer insistence of a father-figure's presence in Butlin's verse proposes a biographical symmetry. This is at first intimated in the numbered 'Fictions':

There comes a dead man walking upon water
where the sun has never set finally.

[RB] *They weren't written together at all, but probably the third and fourth were written together, because they are concerned with the relationships between generations. My relationship with my parents bordered on the horrendous, and these poems are to do with that.*
So the figure of the father, then, refers also to a real father?
[RB] *In answer to that I would probably say that I never had a father in any real sense. I mean, he was there in body, a rather threatening body, though not physically threatening; but not there in spirit. Or rather, he was only threateningly there, too; felt as a spiritual threat and not as a comfort. And I think over the last few*

*years this has very strongly been coming to the surface in me.
Things like 'Poem for my Father' and 'Fictions' are either a longing
for what might have been, or a recognition of what my attitudes to
him actually were. Never stated directly, they are, rather, betrayed;
the literature betrays me, and I'm actually trying to deal with the
problem now. That happens quite a lot, and in my stories too.*

Under these pressures of denial, guilt and abnegation, re-forging
a viable self assumes urgent priority, and in the early work 'becoming' is perhaps the most exploited term.

[RB] *I like the idea of becoming in that Aristotelian sense of
entelechy, gradually becoming a whole in a qualitative as well as a
spatial sense. I am fascinated by that concept: every moment I am
becoming the person that I am: I am the meaning of my own history
at every moment.*

It has meant a continuing reorientation of his own life's possibilities, and a sustained effort at drawing together whatever might be of
use to him in his often painful process of discovery. History and
personality continually interact in his text as this written reconstruction proceeds. And against the ruin which threatens his stable
voice, he shores fragments from wherever they might be excavated:
a fraught dream of possible love in his translation of Paul Valéry's
'Footsteps', or the grimmer, but still resilient vision of a Glasgow
graveyard in Luis Cernuda's 'The City Cemetery':

> The writing on the tombstones is unreadable,
> and anyway
> for the last two hundred years they have been
> burying not men
> but corpses without friends even to forget them,
> dead secrets. (CTC p. 62)

At a period which forms a watershed in his work, Butlin returned
to a native strain in his upbringing and inaugurated a more radical
re-location.

[RB] *I wasn't sure where I was going. I was brought up in the
village, I moved to the town, I went to live in London, strayed
myself all over Europe. I was living in a huge emotional turmoil. I
always had been. And then suddenly I go right back to the beginning. In the sudden discovery, or re-discovery of the whole sound-
world of the Scots language I had known and felt as a child, I was*

able to draw on an emotional life and point of view that I recog-
nised as mine. It was a sound-world that I couldn't sustain for long,
but it released in me what appeared to be a sense of humour, a lack
of self-consciousness. Something gave way at that point, some
resistance I'd overcome. It just dissolved. I began, in fact, to pull at
least one strand tense enough to start getting sound out of it. It
wasn't, finally, appropriate for my writing purposes, but it was a
very necessary thing to go through. I think I've always had to forge
an identity, to think of how to recover an identity. When one is
writing, one is continually creating a new listening. It's a continu-
ous process. I think that the Scots language put me in touch with
parts of myself that English couldn't reach. And, Scots having
opened them out, then English can get to them. Oddly enough, the
first Scots poem that I wrote was about Milton.

But not perhaps so odd when we consider the displacements that
are implicated in such a choice. Milton looms sometimes uncom-
fortably large in many a literary consciousness. As Puritan moralist
he is perhaps the mythic father-figure we are all glad we never had
to endure. As colossus of English republicanism, he might elicit
complicated responses from a contemporary Scot. As epic architect
in iambic pentameter of the Fall from Paradise in Christian iconography, his rhythms held English prosody in thrall for generations.
He might well assume giant, daunting proportions for a young poet
from Annandale seeking a viable self and a sustainable voice.

In *The Wunnerful Warld O John Milton*,[5] Butlin's strategy is to
mock with a jester's irreverence, and to goad with the provocations
of an Elizabethan fool. In these tactics, autobiographical pressures
and literary-historical precedence coincide. Milton becomes the
father to be circumscribed, the voice to be dumbfounded. Native
accents speak their irreducible difference: a Scots volubility mouths
its dissent and utters its now mischievous, now philosophical opposition. The poem 'Ootlins', in its explicit identification with the
outcasts of Eden, already prepares us for a radically alternative
moral promise:

> as ootlins o paradise we're yin
> wi aa the craturs o hell
> forbye that we micht love sae weel
> anither saul's keethin. (CTC p. 45)

In these tensions, distinctive voice makes its presence felt:
I canna conceive Milton's view o things withoot distress,
fer ony man become a prince o his ain darkness
wad blindly mak a Paradise just fer hissel
an mak each warld Milton's Hell. (CTC 52)

And we can also track this tremulous emergence in a poem like 'A Bit Sonnet' ('Whae scrieves nou in this auld-fanglit style'), which, disconcertingly, consists only of the octet.

Butlin's deployment of writing as the self's reconstruction comes, too, in his collection of poems from the Chinese, *The Exquisite Instrument*.[6] Here a selection of eighth-century poems, and also poems from the work of Wen-I-to (1899–1946), enable him to examine a world of loss and separation through the frame of an adopted empire of feeling. Freed from the encumbrance of immediacy, a clarity of utterance creates painful or desolate images in a sympathetic medium. In these ways the frontiers of personality are extended as is the sense of a shared history:

> This stretch of deadwater is dead ditchwater
> Where the weakest go under and the rest go to
> seed.
> The corrupt and the sickly are each playing
> seducer
> – let's leave them and see what they breed. (EI p. 16)

From these perspectives, it is perhaps inevitable that a poem which ends: 'Yet sometimes my thoughts seem like blow-flies/ crawling where garbage lies' (EI p. 10), or final lines like: ' – Lastly, crying out China's name/ I stand and vomit out the heart/ that's tearing mine apart' (EI p. 22), must involve ironic echoes of more localised, and self-referential kinds. These three examples are all translations from the same person, and Butlin is concerned to preserve the relevance of their original provenance.

[RB] *Wen-I-to was a political revolutionary, but he was also a poet, and I think he had difficulty in reconciling the two ideas. Wen-I-to actually rhymes, and what I tried to do as I translated was to write poems that were in that milieu, with rhyme and careful scansion; and they are in fact quite close. The other ones are much freer poems.*

In some cases, Chinese originals simply provided stimulus for the development and strengthening of Butlin's text. 'This Embroidery', for example, is entirely his own, with Yuan Chen providing only the situation of an elegiac setting; the man laying out the clothes of the dead woman. Similarly with 'Nocturne', where the very beginning comes from Wen-I-to, while the rest of the poem is Butlin's invention. But perhaps the most instructive example of intertextual adventure across time and space occurs with 'An Address to Li Shang Yin'. Butlin's own account makes both the process and the relationship clear.

[RB] *Li Shang Yin I read so much of, I became very aware of his personality, his spirit. Here was a poet, a Zen master, a civil servant, who wrote a poem where he said he was writing a letter, and he looked up and there was the woman to whom he was writing. This letter took the form of a poem to his muse. So I was able to take that a stage further: I could translate the poem. And then I felt as if his spirit was in the room. Then I made a further contrast, by making the first part of the poem his, while the second half concerned me: what it felt like being me translating his poem, and how the world looked to me, using the present tense to contrast with his past tense. And it was a remarkable experience; he felt very tangible to me. I like to think the poem is a mixture of both of us.*

The kind of intersection inscribed in 'An Address to Li Shang Yin', is identified in lines from 'The Drummer', which usefully bring together two images frequently and variously manipulated in Butlin's writing:

> Silence gives leave
> for a song without words: one harmonious phrase
> of sudden and subtle perfection to weave
> our two lives together. (EI p. 27)

Music, as theme and figure, permeates his text, and is always and everywhere the analogy which springs to his lips when he talks about his work.

[RB] *To me a poem is a kind of counterpoint. That overall counterpoint is what you're aiming at; it's not the meaning in itself. To paraphrase something which Mendelssohn once said: someone asked him what his songs without words mean, and he said that he couldn't tell them, not because words are too precise and would tie*

*down the music, but because the music's too precise to be tied down
by words. My poems, too, are composed in that way. Meaning is
only one strand in the counterpoint.*

'The Exquisite Instrument' further suggests a kind of direct and
unmediated equation between music and life. This prevents a too
easy incorporation of Butlin's poetry into that prevalent reading of
contemporary texts as merely self-referential. Butlin senses such
readings as life-denying, and resists them.

[RB] *I would not want to be thought of as merely writing about
writing. I am being quite definite: a man's a man and a butt's a butt,
and everything is as it is about us. I don't demand a particular
reading, but I do try to get the right sound, and I hope that other
people will hear it, if they bring their whole history to it in the way
that I did. I celebrate the joy of discovery through poetry and
sound. This is really what I am concerned with.*

> Quite by chance this cithern has a string
> for each year in my life, making
> fifty in all. It is an exquisite instrument:
> there is such joy in tuning it
> and in turning each peg tight. (EI p. 12)

In Butlin's work, desire and its loss co-exist so intimately that it
comes to seem as if, simultaneously, 'everything is ruined and
precious' (RUB p. 23). And the verse continually represents these
opposing states, whether as 'deftly ravelling years and days and
hours together' (CTC p. 22), or as the elegiac:

> only a mess of coloured thread
> remains to fold away:
> this embroidery you said was part-dream
> and part imaginary; (RUB p. 13)

or when, combining the elements of parting in order to join, 'A
Gentle Demolition' deconstructs its own litigation conceit:

>   let's tear
> this court-house down – a gentle demolition;
> then leave as friends and lawyers might –
> together (RUB p. 32)

'The Embroideress' weaves together the figure of the poet, the process of dream transference in an exchange of selves, and the sense of an arrested moment of release which may paradoxically already have eluded the speaker:

> For too long I have been struggling with this dream
> of endless stitching and endless mutilation:
> everything depends upon the moment of awakening
> – a moment that may have already passed. (RUB p. 36)

Butlin's discovery that 'The Gods That I know Best', who cause such anguish when they 'wrench these depths and distances apart to pierce/ me through', could also be themselves dissected in his prose, gave him the opportunity of extending his writing techniques. The title of his short story collection *The Tilting Room* is an image which occurs in his writing before its publication and since. In 'My Grandfather Dreams Twice of Flander' (RUB p. 47), 'the ceiling tilting crazily' is one such moment, to which a much earlier discovery that: 'the crack in the ceiling/ hides the crack in the sky/ that is no smaller than a star' (CTC p. 33), seems related. In the story 'The Cousins', we read: 'at the same time he could sense the angles in the room coming apart: the floors and walls were buckling' (TR p. 109).

Each instant points to an opening out, or else a freezing and then a violent adjustment of the moment; a dislocation in the frame of things which might then facilitate vision, heighten perception, or generate an increase in understanding. It is, anyway, an appealing figure for Butlin.

[RB] *Yes, I think it's the slight wavering one gets in the notion of 'objective reality' – I don't accept that there is such a thing as objective reality in any plain sense. But an awful lot of us, and maybe me in particular, exist on that tilting level, just at that balance, and I think that sometimes it just tilts a bit far, and that's really when we begin to be able to see. Now I'm beginning to think that all moments are potentially epiphanous; that it's up to us, our imagination can do so much with every moment. The first sentence of the novella I'm working on goes: 'everything that has ever happened to you is still happening.'[7] We could, then, almost go on to say that anything that is happening anywhere is happening to you.*

That kind of unexpected connexion between a self or selves and a world either unseen or shunned is an attribute of the unpredictable and nightmarish neighbourhood of *The Tilting Room*. The writing glides with seductive fluency across areas of public and private horror, merging aspects of history with those of the psyche, and then dividing again, often to strange effect. An overall result is a blurring at the edges of what is real and what is not; a disturbing play on the frontiers of what may and may not be. 'Scenes From an Opera', for example, figures a technical fascination with the uneasy coexistence of high art and a bloody, uncertain violence.

[RB] *I'm not at all of the kind of school that sees a beauty in cruelty. But I do feel that the world we're living in has developed a really astonishing expression of the basic cruelty of people – expressed in a very high-tech, highly polished, consumer-orientated world. I think that there is a kind of pollution that goes on with the raising of the level of fear in the world, because no matter how 'good' you are, that fear is taken into you. So there is no 'objective' world; the objective world is inside you, and that is already, if you like, the clear waters being polluted: the same waters that give you life. And that is the world we know.*

So a reading which tracks a long journey out of the self in the transforming struggle between self and world seems viable. Butlin's writing develops an incantation and a ritual of exorcism together with repeated intimations of the possibility of love. Then, a persistent weaving together of images of disjunction voices a deeply felt desire to express a separate self in a world of its own making. Butlin's poetry articulates an urge towards individuality within a world of connexions. The sometimes conflicting pressures foreground an acute tension between a sense of shaping and of being shaped, of producing and of being produced: as though the discourse might be writing the self as much as the self creating the discourse. The self which emerges is de-centred; a self that is apparently stable, but which is actually the product of those patterns of meaning imposed upon it – to which it sometimes consents. Necessarily, these are uneasy relationships. They suggest an unease with self-containment, and thus potentially with the self-containing environment of poetry. Hence, perhaps, that tendency already noted towards techniques which suspend or postpone closure in favour of continuing possibility – however fraught and uncertain that process may be.

[RB] *I'm probably thinking that if we do retreat from the threat without, we won't be able to make music; we won't be able to love. We have to negotiate on all levels or none. We can't be half alive. Poetry is life as much as anything else is. It is a powerful expression, a powerful exorcism, and indeed often is a powerful action. My unease might be that I would discover the action in the poetry but then not realise it in other spheres. Love without action would be merely sentiment, and life without action might be merely poetry. Similarly, too much suffering would mean a withdrawal from the art; entry into a kind of neurosis. And I think art makes life bearable.*

> But when this exquisite instrument is tuned,
> then I shall play howsoever I please
> upon its fifty strings. (RUB p. 13)

Notes

1. Ron Butlin, *Ragtime in Unfamiliar Bars* (London, 1985), p. 17. Subsequent citations are marked RUB and given parenthetically.
2. Ron Butlin, *Creatures Tamed by Cruelty* (Edinburgh, 1979). Subsequent citations are marked CTC and given parenthetically.
3. Ron Butlin, *The Tilting Room* (Edinburgh, 1983).
4. Robert Lowell, *Notebook* (London, 1970), pp. 1 75–6.
5. Ron Butlin, *The Wunnerful Warld O John Milton* (Edinburgh, 1974).
6. Ron Butlin, *The Exquisite Instrument* (Edinburgh, 1982). Subsequent citations are marked EI and given parenthetically.
7. Ron Butlin, *The Sound of My Voice* (Edinburgh,).

A Kind of Logic

IAN ABBOT 1944–1989

Born in Perth, the son of a housepainter, Ian Abbot recalled his tenement upbringing as a fairly bleak one. No internal water supply meant a daily ritual of washing in the communal sink at the stairhead, shared between the people across the landing and his own family.

[IA] *You'd to queue up there in the mornings; break the ice off in the winter-time.*

His secondary schooling at Perth Academy came to an end when he was fifteen and for a time he became active in left-wing politics. Working in the Tay Salmon Fisheries led to further political effort, and he subsequently remained concerned.

[IA] *I think you owe it to yourself to undermine as far as possible the things that people are trying to make you think, trying to make you feel; things you're expected to think and feel simply because you're in a certain level of society or belong to a particular stratum.*

During the early sixties Abbot attended Dundee Commercial College to try for the Highers he had left school without.

[IA] *This was a significant time for me since among others I met William Montgomerie there, who was lecturing in English at the time. He took an interest in my poetry and it was his advice and encouragement which made me decide that I had something reasonable to contribute to the field.*

After various jobs, including a stint as psychiatric nurse in the Royal Edinburgh Hospital, and working in a geriatric ward, which might account for the rigorously unsentimental attitude towards death which his writing exhibits, Abbot entered Edinburgh Univer-

sity's Medical Faculty. He transferred to a psychology degree at
Stirling before realising that academic study was not for him.

[IA] *Studying medicine I had at least a basic scientific training; it
gives you another set of terms you can apply to the creative process,
another set of connexions you can make when you're writing.*

During the years which followed, one of the things which Abbot
undertook was learning the techniques of a silversmith, before
moving in 1974 to Whitebridge just outside Inverness. His attempt
to set up a silversmith jewellery shop failed and for several years he
earned a living doing casual farm labour, including fencing.

[IA] *A march fence might go for ten miles into the Monadhliath.
It takes you five or six weeks; you go out there and live in a tent.
You carry the materials out, on your back more or less. Most of the
time you work alone, most of the jobs you can do alone. If it's a
high fence, a deer fence, you need somebody to hold the posts. But it
gets easier the better you get at it.*

Abbot's poetry can sometimes seem relentless in its resilient awareness of death's annihilation but the resilience is often the point.
Though it is raised by being communicated in controlled rhythms,
there is a sombre, lonely feeling in many of his lines, like these
from 'The Astologer', a pervading sense of the skull beneath the
skin:

> But now observe this globe I offer you.
> A globe of dirtied bone, that bears
> across its dome
> a web of intricate sutures that will speak to you
> as all the choiring voices of the planets never could.[1]

'The Knight' (p. 25) looms like a Doré cartoon, but the figure of
Death speaks the poem, producing a neo-gothic imagery to contain
and subordinate human aggression. A functional use of archaism
to address a disturbed and disturbing present is a favoured technique. It is perhaps Abbot's pieced and plotted syntax, and the
sense of driving urgency it conveys, which acts as a constraint
upon his necessary fictions. But his seriousness springs from other
sources, too. There is an expressive violence in his single collection
which can sometimes bring to mind the Ted Hughes of the
nineteen-sixties. Abbot's verbal energies, though, are different. He

lived in a different country and while his writing moves beyond the
local, to Cortez and Montezuma, to an oriental archer and to
poems taking their inspiration from Holbein woodcuts, Abbot
became conscious of an increasingly Scottish feel to his work,
though he preferred to think of it as distinctively Highland.

[IA] *There's a very strong sense of historical deprivation there in
the Highlands. You can see it every day, using your eyes, working;
the way the culture has evolved and been beaten down over the
years. And so I find I need, I suppose, to do something about this.
To record it at least, to try and capture that smell of it; and to try
and influence people's minds and feelings. Because the culture's
quite unique, you know, and there are enough remnants of that
culture there in the Highlands to make it worth recording.*

The poetry's compromising expression of mood and feeling
seems to speak directly to and for a spirit of place caught in natural
imagery. 'One Place in the Highlands' initiates a characteristic
response to an initially communicative environment:

> This is a land familiar with destruction.
> The low hills, brows beaten down,
> and the stubborn, ravaged crags
> speak of it, each in its own inimitable voice. (p. 28)

'Before the Flood' addresses itself to a Highland river in spate to
catch historical resonance differently:

> ... while carcases
> of sheep and men
> will swim in all your exultation,
> yawing on your face like dirty clouds, (p. 22)

and 'Ewe Against the Fence' turns its laconic attention to the life-
cycle of the Highland Cheviot:

> do not think you are alone
> in giving up your bones, your flesh,
>
> your blood or destiny to those
> who might supplant you with the turning of a coin. (p. 20)

There is, too, a perhaps related structure of feeling in imagery which associates predatory violence with Christianity in a poem like 'The Bestiary of Cortes' and its continuing effects in the dangerous attractions of 'Ga-Cridhe'

The phrase 'landscape of the mind' occurs in 'Fishing Through a Hole', and reading Abbot's work leaves the impression that often the landscape shapes his emotions, making him feel what it feels so that when he speaks back to it the landscape seems directly to control his terms of reference. A persuasive fusion of language and image results.

[IA] *I'm urban by upbringing, come from the city: the country I never knew terribly well until I went there in my late twenties. I'd never seen landscape like this; and not just never seen it, never lived in it. That poem 'Landscape for a Highland Gentleman', for instance; people really are shaped in that way. It's hard, it's difficult, it's solid and the people in Whitebridge grow out of it, you know, directly. Pretensions disappear; they're straightforward. Everybody up there responds to it. I just happen to respond in a way which produces poems. It's become such a part of my life that I don't even know when I'm doing it. And sometimes I only realise it's winter when I've written a poem that has that feeling in it.*

Such climatic 'feeling' functions in different ways in Abbot's verse. 'Love in February' shapes human sensation in seasonal terms and 'Marriage', too, explores emotional congruence in terms of wintry images. 'Blizzard Conditions', which dramatises emotional conflict as harsh weather conditions, is in turn traceable to contours of personal experience.

[IA] *In the wintertime you get a lot of snow; you really are forced in on each other and the flaws, if any, in your relationship are laid bare. Memories and other sorts of things which you bring up under such conditions start to grate: they put more of a pressure on your relationship, which gradually gets buried under the weight of snow like branches which start to break, and then things begin to fall apart.*

Many of Abbot's poems speak of identity and relationship and perhaps 'Hephaestus Preaching' combines memories of his own attempts at silversmithing with earlier political experiences, roaring 'seditious sermons in the street'. Processes of self-definition and self-awareness are problematised in 'Wax Resist', a poem which grew out of an error.

[IA] *I made a blunder about it which Norman MacCaig once corrected. I thought it was trout that have these thumbmarks on their bodies, you know, the little whorls you see. He said no, it was something else – I forget what sort of fish it was now. These marks look like wax-resist imprints or paintings and I thought how almost invisible they are, though you can see them if you look for them. Then I thought that this is the way that people leave traces of themselves on others they meet. The poem is about my inability to leave these traces on the people I meet. There's a Borges story, too, about a man whose character is only revealed through its effects on the actions of others. It concerns someone searching for this man, trying to track him down through the influence he has on other people, and he feels all the time that he's moving closer to this fellow at the centre of the ripples. The poem is about that, too.*

In *Avoiding The Gods* Abbot's constructed voice enables representative identifications of connected kinds. 'Ariel' in this volume is freed to 'work in ... dreams and air' only at someone else's 'dark sharp/ whispered word', returning each morning:

> To feel your collar fixed about my neck
> and my soul fastened to the iron in the earth. (p. 14)

What Caliban hoards and treasures and seeks to share is his real inheritance', his 'language/ glittering the coins beneath the watered sun'. (p. 19). And this is Abbot's saving grace too, a sensuous delight in the language of communicated feeling.

Insofar as his writing represents a search for and expression of origins and contexts for his own self and being, 'A Memoir From the Mind-Camp' constructs metaphoric case-history. Abbot's grandmother was a Jewish immigrant of the nineteen-twenties and although she never talked about it, he picked up various implications from what she did say concerning people she'd written to who had never replied, photographs of people who had disappeared during Hitler's regime.

[IA] *This was my speaking to roots that I'm not aware of having but that I know are there. I don't feel Jewish at all, but I wanted to feel I could tap into something. Maybe I wrote it as something for her, though it's curious I felt terribly ambivalent about her when she was alive; but it was important to me to write it. At the same time I didn't want to be too literal, to set it all down.*

Ian Abbot did not think of himself at all as a nature poet in any of the more transparent senses of the phrase, one reason being that local flora and fauna came to seem inseparable from the poetic process itself in much of his work:

> My language is a deer dismembered under pines,
> bloody and netted with shadows.
> An intricate labyrinth of entrails,
> lit from within
> and patiently transfigured by the lightning grin of bones.

A recurring theme is that of poetry as the subject of the poem; its refining discipline is frequently at the centre of Abbot's concerns. 'Ferns Like Poems' makes the appropriate opening invitation:

> ... I warn you
> to approach them with respect.
> Carelessly fingered, every cowering stem
> will strip you to the bone (p. 7)

The move to Whitebridge, then, amounted almost to learning a new language, acquiring, in his words, 'the voices of the various kinds of landscape'.

[IA] *Sometimes the landscape suggests a word or phrase to you; not necessarily a specific word but rather the tone you get from having a certain number of words set next to one another.*

The house he lived in is situated at around 700-800 feet above sea-level, and from 800 to perhaps 1000 feet on the Monadhliath mountains the country is fairly rolling. Then it gradually gets more and more severe, until on the high tops it resembles a lunar region.

[IA] *And it has different voices: each level of it speaks in a different way, or suggests a different way of speaking. At least there's a kind of logic in being able to see it in terms of speech, of language.*

So it seems appropriate that many of Abbot's poems take pleasure in relating their own unfolding processes to an imagined world. The image perceived becomes its written embodiment in ways which comment upon their inseparability, as if the act of writing surprises the act of seeing into formal statement. 'Finishing the Picture' and 'Crossing Carn Donnachaidhe' are such poems, while others explore very different sources and effects for seeing and saying. Violent imagery in 'Raptor' compares its own inception to the hawk which swoops:

> Then rises and soars away. Leaving the mind
> among a carnage of phrases, smeared
> with words and the colours of words.
> And the poem torn into being.

In contrast, 'Digging For Victory' sets the mind's ploughshare furrowing and sees smooth poems 'furling out behind it', before the gap between finished form and messy process is reinstated – an arch example of the poem interrogating the sheen of its final appearance:

> Turning
> from the window I prepared
> the clumsy, long-familiar tools
>
> and set again to hacking at reluctant roots. (p.31)

This sometimes harsh, always uncompromising intensity of relationship between a natural world imagined and poem shaped on the page might be most usefully illustrated by 'Scott's First Voyage'. The poem developed out of an incident when Abbot, who was out putting up a fence several miles long, misjudged the onset of snow and found himself stranded in his tent on the mountainside. For the day and night that he was trapped he spent much of the time scribbling by the light of his small gas-lamp.

[IA] *Eventually I had to cut up the tent, turn it into snow-shoes and walk out. I put webbing over the poles and tied them on my feet. It was hard going.*

Sitting in the tent the notion came to him that this perhaps was what it might have been like for Scott; that from its beginnings his whole life had been influenced by snow and ice and cold.

[IA] *I was thinking that this was how I, too, was going to finish, and cast back in my mind to see what I could remember, as Scott did perhaps, from my past life which might account for this ending. I've always had this strong sensation of white, cold, and an image of childhood hospitalisation came to me and I thought, it was just a fancy, that maybe for someone like Scott such things might have influenced however the rest of his life went. And so the poem came out of it, like the first voyage into the world, into this whiteness, this coldness; and maybe that's what obsessed him. It seemed a connection at the time, when I was sitting in this tent, very cold and a bit worried about how things were going to go.*

It was as much a flaw in his language as anything else, Abbot later felt, which led to him being trapped on the hill.

[IA] *I hadn't communicated properly with it. It was trying to tell me all the time 'you're going to get stuck out here'; but I hadn't listened to it enough.*

Listening to the muscular cadences of his own writing serves in turn as a kind of release for us, one which brings the pleasures of literary communication into careful focus. Given Ian Abbot's untimely death, the closing lines of his title poem might serve as a reminder of the continuing strengths of human self-sufficiency to which his volume speaks:

> And let us look for our salvation
> in the language we have come to teach ourselves.

Notes

1. Ian Abbot, *Avoiding the Gods* (Edinburgh, 1988), p. 28. Page references for subsequent quotations are given parenthetically in the text.

Index